# HUMAN
## JUDGMENT
### and DECISION
#### PROCESSES

# HUMAN JUDGMENT and DECISION PROCESSES

*Edited By*

## Martin F. Kaplan

Department of Psychology
Northern Illinois University
DeKalb, Illinois

## Steven Schwartz

Department of Psychiatry
University of Texas Medical Branch
Galveston, Texas

Academic Press, Inc.  New York  San Francisco  London  1975

A Subsidiary of Harcourt Brace Jovanovich, Publishers

*Academic Press Rapid Manuscript Reproduction*

ACADEMIC PRESS, INC.
111 Fifth Avenue, New York, New York 10003

*United Kingdom Edition published by*
ACADEMIC PRESS, INC. (LONDON) LTD.
24/28 Oval Road, London NW1

Library of Congress Cataloging in Publication Data
Main entry under title:

Human judgment and decision processes.

    (Series in cognition and perception)
    Expanded versions of papers delivered at a 3 day
conference held at Northern Illinois University in
Oct. 1974.
    Includes bibliographies and indexes.
    1.   Decision–making--Congresses.    2.   Judgment
--Congresses.    I.   Kaplan, Martin F.    II.   Schwartz,
Steven.    [DNLM:    1.   Decision making--Congresses.
2.   Judgment--Congresses.    BF441 H918 1974]
BF441.H815        153.4'6        75-29491
ISBN 0–12–397250–7

PRINTED IN THE UNITED STATES OF AMERICA

# CONTENTS

*Contributors* ix

*Preface* xi

*Acknowledgments* xiii

**1. Public Values: Multiattribute-Utility Measurement for Social**
**Decision Making** 1
  Peter C. Gardiner and Ward Edwards

  Introduction 2
  The State of the Art in Land-Use Regulation 3
  An Overview of Decision Analysis as It Applies to
     Planning and Evaluation 8
  Outcome Evaluation Using Multiattribute-Utility Measurement 12
  A Simple Multiattribute-Rating Technique (SMART) 14
  The Case Study 24
  A Public Technology for Land-Use Management 33
  References 36

**2. Decision Processes in Recognition Memory** 39
  Steven Schwartz

  Decision and Memory: A Hypothetical Mechanism for the
     Influence of Semantic Memory on Episodic Recognition-
     Memory Tasks 41
  The Decision Model: Evidence from Experiments on the
     Recognition of Words and Names 47
  The Decision Model: Evidence from Experiments on the
     Recognition of Word Strings and Sentences 51
  Relationships between the Decision Model and Other
     Views of Memory 56
  Conclusions 58
  References 59

**3. Portfolio Theory and the Measurement of Risk** 63
  Clyde H. Coombs

  Introduction 64
  A Theory of Risk Preference 69
  The Measurement of Risk 74
  Discussion and Interpretation 79
  Appendix 80
  References 83

*4. Formal Models of Dilemmas in Social Decision Making*          87
   Robyn M. Dawes

   Introduction                                          88
   Social Dilemma: A Formal Definition                   89
   The Commons Dilemma                                   97
   References                                            106


*5. An Information-Integration Analysis of Risky Decision Making*   109
   James Shanteau

   Introduction                                          110
   Information-Integration Theory                        110
   Multiplying Model                                     112
   Adding Model                                          124
   Discussion                                            130
   References                                            134

*6. Information Integration in Social Judgment: Interaction*
*of Judge and Informational Components*                           139
   Martin F. Kaplan

   Introduction                                          140
   The Basic Model                                       140
   The Judge in Social Judgment                          144
   Interaction of Judge and Informational Variables      156
   Concluding Comments                                   162
   References                                            164


*7. Integrating Verbal Information: The Referential-Communication*
*Paradigm*
   Melvin Manis and Marjorie B. Platt                    173

   Introduction                                          174
   Related Work                                          175
   Redundancy and Communication                          177
   Ensemble Size and Communication                       189
   Concluding Remarks                                    197
   References                                            197


*8. Judgment and Decision Processes in the Formation and Change*
*of Social Attitudes*                                             201
   Harry S. Upshaw
   Introduction                                          202
   An Overview of the System                             204
   Phase 1: Processing Information about Alternative

Positions on an Issue 207
Phase 2: Choosing among Alternative Positions 214
Phase 3: Describing Oneself on Attitude-Related Variables 219
Phase 4: Attitude Change and Judgmental Change 224
Conclusion 225
References 225

9. *The Role of Probabilistic and Syllogistic Reasoning in Cognitive Organization and Social Inference* 229
 Robert S. Wyer, Jr.

Introduction 230
The Nature of Cognitions 233
Tests of Subjective-Probability Models of Social
 Inference 236
Implications of a Syllogistic Model of Cognitive
 Functioning 246
The Contribution of Nonlogical Factors to Inference
 Phenomena 255
Concluding Remarks 266
References 267

10. *Social-Judgment Theory* 271
 Kenneth R. Hammond, Thomas R. Stewart, Berndt Brehmer,
 and Derick O. Steinmann

Why Is Judgment Required? 272
Basic Concepts 272
Quantitative Method 277
Discussion of Unique Contributions in Four Cases 291
Summary 305
References 307

*Author Index* 313
*Subject Index* 321

# CONTRIBUTORS

*Numbers in parentheses indicate the pages on which the authors' contributions begin.*

**Berndt Brehmer** (271), Department of Psychology, University of Umeå, Umeå, Sweden

**Clyde H. Coombs** (63), Department of Psychology, The University of Michigan, Ann Arbor, Michigan 48104

**Robyn M. Dawes** (87), Oregon Research Institute and Department of Psychology, University of Oregon, Eugene, Oregon, 97403

**Ward Edwards** (1), Social Science Research Institute, University of Southern California, Los Angeles, California 90007

**Peter C. Gardiner** (1), Social Science Research Institute, University of Southern California, Los Angeles, California 90007

**Kenneth R. Hammond** (271), Institute of Behavioral Science, University of Colorado, Boulder, Colorado 80302

**Martin F. Kaplan** (139), Department of Psychology, Northern Illinois University, DeKalb, Illinois 60115

**Melvin Manis** (173), Department of Psychology, The University of Michigan, Ann Arbor, Michigan 48104

**Marjorie B. Platt** (173), Department of Psychology, The University of Michigan, Ann Arbor, Michigan 48104

**Steven Schwartz** (39), Department of Psychiatry, Division of Child Psychiatry, University of Texas Medical Branch, Galveston, Texas 77550

**James Shanteau** (109), Department of Psychology, Kansas State University, Manhattan, Kansas 66502

**Derick O. Steinmann** (271), Department of Personnel Research, Metropolitan Life Insurance Company, New York, New York 10010

**Thomas R. Stewart** (271), Institute of Behavioral Science, University of Colorado, Boulder, Colorado 80302

**Harry S. Upshaw** (201), Department of Psychology, University of Illinois, Chicago Circle, Chicago, Illinois 60680

**Robert S. Wyer, Jr.** (229), Department of Psychology, University of Illinois, Urbana-Champaign, Urbana, Illinois 61801

# *PREFACE*

Man's interaction with his environment, whether as an initiator or in response to environmental events, is preceded by the judgments and decisions he makes concerning potential actions and their effects. In this sense, human judgments and decision making are fundamental to the study of behavior. During the past four decades, experimental psychologists have devoted increasing amounts of attention to the ways in which man uses information in order to make judgments about his world. Their work has gone well beyond strict behavioristic approaches, which view such behaviors as residues of prior conditioning and changes in affective states. The vast majority of work today is an attempt to understand judgment and decisions in terms of the cognitive operations performed on beliefs and expectations about the state of the world. Increasingly, these cognitive processes are being represented in mathematical form.

That judgment formation is described today as an essentially cognitive process does not imply that such behavior is entirely rational or that it requires the awareness of the decision maker. Certainly the decision maker need not make public his cognitive processes for them to be inferred, nor need his reasoning agree with that of others, nor his outcomes optimize "goodness" of choice.

This volume attempts to present the breadth and variety of theoretical approaches to judgment and decision making. It grew out of a 3 day conference held at Northern Illinois University in October 1974. The conference was sponsored by the Graduate Student–Faculty Committee under the auspices of the Department of Psychology. The book contains expanded versions of the papers delivered by the speakers, together with two additional chapters prepared expressly for this book.

The 10 chapters can be grouped into two substantive parts. The first five chapters are concerned with recent developments in the laboratory study of decision making by normal human adults. These chapters have in common a focus on mathematical models of decision making but are applied to different experimental questions. Theoretical focuses differ as well. Among the research problems included are dilemmas in social decision making, decisions under risk, and recognition-memory processes. The theoretical orientations represented include information-integration theory, signal-detection theory, multiattribute-utility theory, and portfolio theory. Chapters 6 through 10 focus on judgmental processes, particularly those involving interpersonal situations. The reader will note, in fact, that the bulk of the substantive areas discussed in this volume revolve around social behavior. This emphasis, we feel, accurately reflects the trend of current work in the field toward socially relevant problems. As with the first five chapters, the second five derive from basic theoretical positions, with ramifications for the study of person perceptions, attitude measurement and change, social judgment, and probabilistic social inference.

The contributors to his volume are among the leading figures in contemporary behavioral science. They contribute a wide range of theoretical orientations and substantive issues. Hopefully, this volume will serve the dual purpose of reviewing the field of judgment and decision making, while raising new questions to stimulate readers to pursue this very important psychological domain. Judgment is too central an area to human behavior to be left to psychologists alone; it is hoped that other behavioral scientists (economists, political scientists, sociologists, educators) will find the book stimulating.

We wish to acknowledge the assistance we received from Academic Press in all phases of the preparation of this volume. In addition, the help of Carol Lacina in indexing and the competent typing services of Rosemary Hattoon are gratefully acknowledged.

# ACKNOWLEDGMENTS

The editors wish to express their appreciation to the various publishers who permitted the reprinting of copyrighted materials. Figure 2, Chapter 2, Figures 1, 2, 9, 10, and 11 and Table 1 in Chapter 5 were reprinted from the *Journal of Experimental Psychology*. Figures 2, 3, and 4, Chapter 6 and Figures 3 and 4, Chapter 9 originally appeared in the *Journal of Personality and Social Psychology*. This material appears in the present volume with the permission of the American Psychological Association. Figure 4, Chapter 2 was reprinted from the *Bulletin of the Psychonomic Society* with their permission. Figure 4, Chapter 10 originally appeared in the *Journal of Cross-Cultural Psychology* and is reprinted with the permission of Sage Publications, Inc. Figures 1 and 2, Chapter 7 are reprinted from *Contemporary Issues in Cognitive Psychology: The Loyola Symposium* edited by R. L. Solso with the permission of the Hemisphere Publishing Company. Finally, thanks go to Academic Press for permission to reprint Figure 1, Chapter 6 which originally appeared in *Journal of Experimental Research in Personality*.

# 1. PUBLIC VALUES: MULTIATTRIBUTE-UTILITY MEASUREMENT FOR SOCIAL DECISION MAKING

*Peter C. Gardiner and Ward Edwards*
University of Southern California

| | |
|---|---|
| Introduction | 2 |
| The State of the Art in Land Use Regulation | 3 |
| Folkway 1: Passionate Advocacy | 4 |
| Folkway 2: Distinctions among Stages of Evaluation | 4 |
| Folkway 3: The Environmental-Impact Report (EIR) | 5 |
| Folkway 4: The Mushroom Approach to Evaluation | 7 |
| Folkway 5: Agendamanship | 7 |
| An Overview of Decision Analysis as It Applies to Planning and Evaluation | 8 |
| Outcome Evaluation Using Multiattribute-Utility Measurement | 12 |
| A Simple Multiattribute-Rating Technique (SMART) | 14 |
| Flexibilities of the Method | 20 |
| Independence Properties | 20 |
| Interpersonal and Intergroup Disagreements | 22 |
| The Case Study | 24 |
| A Public Technology for Land-Use Management | 33 |
| References | 36 |

INTRODUCTION

This paper defines the problem of public values and summarizes some of what we consider to be the difficulties of
present approaches to its solution. Then it presents a technology, based on ideas drawn from contemporary decision theory,
for amelioration of some of these problems, together with a
study illustrating and applying that technology. Although
the technology is quite general, our discussion, for specificity, focuses on problems of social decision making about land-
use management, and in particular about coastal-zone management. Ideas presented here are intimately related to those
contained in Edwards (1971), Edwards and Guttentag (in preparation, 1975), and Edwards, Guttentag, and Snapper (in preparation, 1975), and conceptually, these discussions overlap.
However, the area of application, the empirical evidence, and
the focal issue differ here from what can be found in those
papers. In this paper the central issue is that of social
conflict over values, and the central idea is that multiattribute-utility measurement can be expected both to reduce the
extent of such conflicts of values and to provide a mechanism
for their resolution. Explicit value measures can greatly
reduce the enormous cost of case-by-case decision procedures.

Our focus is on planning. We do not understand the differences among evaluations of plans, evaluations of ongoing projects, and evaluations of completed projects; all seem to us
to be instances of essentially the same kind of intellectual
activity. Our technology is equally applicable to all three.
But our example comes from land-use planning, and so our arguments are mostly addressed to that topic.

To complete this introduction, let us state our fundamental
idea in one paragraph. Arguments over public policy typically
turn out to hinge on disagreements about values. Such disagreements are usually about degree, not kind; in a coastal-
development fight, both sides usually agree that economic
development and ecological balance are important and worthwhile but differ about relative importance. Normally, such
disagreements are fought out in the context of specific
decisions, and so are fought out over and over and over again,
at enormous social cost each time another decision must be
made. Technology exists that can spell out explicitly what
each participant's values are and show how and how much they
differ--and in the process can frequently reduce the extent
of such differences. The exploitation of this technology
permits regulatory agencies to shift their attention from the
specific actions being regulated to the values these actions
serve and the decision-making mechanisms that implement these
values. By explicitly negotiating about, agreeing on, and

2

publicizing a set of values, a regulatory agency can in effect inform those it regulates about the ground rules, thus removing the uncertainty inherent in planning and the need for costly, time-consuming, case-by-case adversary proceedings (except in borderline cases). Thus, explicit social policies can be defined and implemented with a maximum of efficiency and a minimum of ambiguity. Moreover, such policies can be easily changed in response to new circumstances or changing value systems, and information about such changes can be easily, efficiently, and explicitly disseminated, greatly easing the task of implementing policy change.

## THE STATE OF THE ART IN LAND-USE REGULATION

In land-use regulation, as in other kinds of public decision making, decision makers are ordinarily some kind of regulatory body, such as a commission or council. Members may be appointed or elected, knowledgeable or ignorant, concerned with the problem or with their political futures or both, adequately supported by competent staff or not. Most such bodies have one characteristic in common: broad diversity of values among members. This reflects the diversity of the values held by the constituencies to which the regulatory body is ultimately responsible.

In such bodies, decisions are normally made case by case. Each case can, and many do, turn into a value-oriented dogfight. Ardent proponents of strong points of view testify pro and con. Serious conflicts among members of the regulatory body may (or may not) be thinly masked by the courtesies of debate. And finally decisions, often compromises, are made, reflecting in part the merits of the case and in part the political realities to which the regulators must respond.

The cost of this procedure is enormous. Usually, the regulatory agency has a long backlog; the lag from proposal to decision can range from months to years. Framers of proposals cannot know how they will fare, so much effort goes into preparing proposals that fail or that must be modified. The zealous guardians of each major value must be ever alert, informed, ready to do battle.

Yet, for the observer or the thoughtful regulatory-body member, the whole contentious process is deadly dull. The same issues arise day after day. The same speeches are made again and again, with only minor variations to fit them to the current decision problem. Most votes and voters are highly predictable; most compromises are obvious from the start. New conditions or new people introduce variety--but these too quickly become stereotyped. The reflective observer

3

cannot help feeling that the enormous cost of case-by-case regulation is mostly waste. The cause of the waste is obvious enough: The same values are in fact relevant to many different decisions, and so any case-by-case decision mechanism must, in one way or another, examine how they bear on this particular case. And our tools for performing that task are unbearably clumsy and inefficient.

We have some alternative tools to propose. Before doing so, however, we wish to focus our criticisms by examining what might be called folkways of land-use regulation.

## FOLKWAY 1:  PASSIONATE ADVOCACY

The builders, in the limit, want to build and develop everywhere; the environmentalists, in the limit, oppose any building and development anywhere. In a coastal-zone context, advocates of these views arrive before the public decision makers, at least some of whom are also advocates of these views, and the efforts at persuasion, administrative infighting, marshalling of biased facts, and dubious, overstated arguments all begin. Such advocacy, of course, leads to polarization of points of view; it enhances rather than reduces social conflict. Perhaps worse, it leads to the confounding of planning and the accumulation of impact information, values, and decisions rather than to an orderly progression from facts to their linkages to values, to an aggregation process, to a decision. The decision, when it finally comes, is usually a compromise, but often not a wise compromise. And worst of all, it takes inordinately long, and is in other ways inordinately costly.

## FOLKWAY 2:  DISTINCTIONS AMONG STAGES OF EVALUATION

Evaluation researchers often distinguish among different kinds of evaluation, depending on when they occur. Typical language distinguishes prior evaluation, concurrent evaluation, and retrospective evaluation. Arguments can be found in the evaluation-research literature that different methods are appropriate at these different stages; in particular, those who think of social-program evaluation as similar to laboratory experimentation have difficulty saying how evaluation should be done before the program has been in progress for some time (see Edwards & Guttentag, in preparation, 1975). As a plan becomes implemented, at least four kinds of changes occur. First, the values of both those in the community served by the plan and the planners change in response to experience with the plan in operation and in response to other, external causes. Second, the plan evolves and changes

4

shape and character. Third, the external societal circumstances, to which the program is a response, change. And
fourth, knowledge of plan events and consequences accumulates.
All four of these kinds of changes affect the answer to the
decision problem--and all four are continuous.

In our view, evaluation techniques should and can be
equally continuous. They should assess plan merit continuous-
ly, taking into account all four kinds of changes, and should
permit exploration of the merits of alternative programs that
could be had by changing this one, whether the changes are
great or small.

*FOLKWAY 3: THE ENVIRONMENTAL-IMPACT REPORT (EIR)*

The EIR approach is an example of a very common, and in
many ways very sensible, approach to evaluating current plans
and proposals for building and development. In principle, it
is little more than a question-answering mechanism--a method
for assembling the information relevant to a decision into
coherent, retrievable, easily understood form.

To the extent that this ideal is realized, the EIR is, for
planning purposes, an instance of what Edwards and Guttentag
(in preparation, 1975) have called the baseball statistician's
approach to program evaluation. They chose the name because
the baseball statistician in fact assembles all the information he can about box scores, earned run averages, batting
averages, and the like; calculation of means or percentages
is about as sophisticated as this kind of information processing ordinarily gets. Yet it is widely used, in baseball
and elsewhere, simply because it is widely useful.

This approach provides a public decision maker with detailed information, which can be very timely, about what is
expected to be going on as the result of his plan. It provides decision makers with a set of numbers of which at least
some must be relevant to their interests and the proposed
plan's purpose. And it provides interested parties with
evaluation reports that are thick enough to be thorough--and
detailed enough to be thoroughly unread. As owners of the
Kinsey reports, or even of an almanac, will agree, a massive
and unreadable book with an indexing system that permits
retrieval of an occasional stimulating statistic can be a
useful and appealing product.

Nowhere is the overwhelmingness of statistics more appreciated than in an advocacy situation. Environmentalists
frequently use the EIR as a basis for substituting more staff
study for action and for delaying public decisions. Builders
and developers also use EIRs for furthering their goals. They
have enormous momentum, a full-size staff capable of devoting

full time to EIR preparation (in contrast to the meager staff
resources often available to environmentalists), and strong
economic incentives to seek favorable decisions. What content
an EIR is required to have is often unclear. So the builder-
developer is naturally tempted to say as little as possible,
to slant what he does say so that it strengthens his case, and
to encase the result in a massive, semirelevant or irrelevant
shell of obfuscatory statistics in three-color glossies.
Moreover, he is likely to feel strongly about growth, progress,
and a man's right to do as he pleases with his land; these
values, together with the virtures of jobs and business
expansion, are likely to be prominently featured.

Decision makers need to know whether a proposed plan or
development is a good idea. Should it, and others like it, be
carried out? If so, how many? Should it be taken as a model
for other locations? If so, can the leaders in these commu-
nities be persuaded to accept the idea? The EIRs cannot tell
a decision maker the answers to any of these questions--
though they can offer hundreds or thousands of numbers that
bear on them in one way or another. Since the decision maker
cannot understand or assimilate thousands of numbers, all only
indirectly related to the question at hand, he has no choice
but to select a few, combine them with a large dose of intui-
tion and political savvy, and make a seat-of-the-pants
decision.

If forced to choose between no EIR and an EIR, we will
choose the latter almost every time. Fact gathering, however
dull it may be, is indispensable to everything that comes
after. And a reasonably exhaustive compendium of relevant
facts about a plan can, in principle and sometimes in practice,
be used by a decision maker to find out whatever he really
wants to know.

But we feel that fact gathering in itself has two severe
deficiencies as an evaluation method. The first, already
indicated, is that too many facts are almost as difficult to
use for decision making as too few. Indexing, summarizing,
and information-retrieval techniques tend to be the weaknesses
of every EIR evaluation. And the more remote the decision
maker is from the scientists who collected the EIR data or
the builder-developer who proposed the action or the environmentalists who oppose it, the more severe the difficulty
becomes. This, we feel, explains one of the paradoxes of our
time: that in a government in which practically everything
is studied, restudied, and evaluated to death, most decision
makers feel simultaneously inundated with information they
cannot effectively use and unable to obtain the rather small
set of simple answers they need in order to make wise decisions. No one (not even the librarians or the computer-

6

memory experts) feels other than queasy about the information
explosion.

The other difficulty of the EIR approach to evaluation, of
course, is the one we keep harping on: It has virtually
nothing to say about values. Almost inevitably these will
escape the EIR number dredge because they reside in the
decision makers' heads (or, more often, in the collective and
disagreeing heads of the various pressure groups and individuals with a say or a stake in the decision), not in the
detailed facts of the program itself.

## FOLKWAY 4: THE MUSHROOM APPROACH TO EVALUATION

The basic tenet of this approach is to "keep 'em in the
dark." For a number of reasons, the decision makers may not
want anyone to know how they actually evaluate plans and
arrive at public decisions. First, the decision maker may be
unable or unwilling to articulate his evaluation process
because of incomplete awareness of the problem or issues involved or inability (or disinclination) to spend enough time
and effort on the task. Second, the decision maker may fear
the wrath of his constituency or of special-interest support
if he makes explicit and open to public scrutiny his evaluation procedures. This wrath could very well be felt at the
next election or could lead interested parties with an ax to
grind to generate conflict or threats. Finally, many public
decision makers fear that explicit evaluation procedures will
make more difficult their execution of the traditional
American political skills of logrolling, horse trading, and so
on. Though we understand this fear, we do not share it. For
one thing, we feel that it underestimates the talents that
politicians bring to their profession. Every administrative,
political, or bureaucratic procedure can be and ultimately
will be exploited by those talented at such exploitation. Our
hope is to design procedures having the property that such
exploitation serves the public interest. We believe that
anyone entering into a horse trade would be wise to find out
the value both of the horse he is trading and of whatever he
is getting for it.

## FOLKWAY 5: AGENDAMANSHIP

Hearings, like other public meetings, have agendas and
rules of procedure. Both can be and are exploited by those
with axes to grind. For example, early items on an agenda
are usually examined rather thoroughly, while later ones get
attention that typically ranges from slipshod to rubber-stamp.
Consequently, the applicant whose application is likely to

profit from careless consideration may engage in complicated maneuvers to have his case considered at the end of the day rather than the beginning.

Maneuvering to have a particular decision made while someone especially hostile to it is absent often occurs. It may be instigated by the applicant, but often it is instigated by members of the regulatory body who are biased in favor of the application.

The rules of procedure before regulatory agencies tend to be loose and permissive, leaving less room for advantages to accrue to those expert at using *Robert's Rules of Order* as a weapon. Nevertheless, such expertise can be useful even in a regulatory hearing. It is especially useful in snarling up the process of voting; incredible tangles can often be created by motions to reconsider, points of personal privilege, and the like.

The extreme of procedural expertise is, of course, expertise in the law creating the regulatory body. Exploitation of loopholes in badly drafted laws is a standard tool of the legal profession, as applicable in land-use-regulation contexts as in any other. And, as usual, the law turns out most often to be on the side of whoever can afford, or obtain without affording, the most able lawyers.

Everyone prefers to exclude variables like these from the decision process--except when their inclusion is to his advantage. A reformer's ideal would be to design procedures that make them irrelevant. That hope is, of course, quixotic.

AN OVERVIEW OF DECISION ANALYSIS AS IT APPLIES TO PLANNING AND EVALUATION

The following paragraphs will make decision analysts snore (or, preferably, skip or skim), but they may contain ideas unfamiliar to some planners.

Figure 1 is a block diagram, or flow chart, indicating the processes that lead up to a decision. In this and following block diagrams, rectangles enclose operations, and circles enclose the informational inputs to or outputs from operations. Arrows, of course, indicate direction of information flow. Only one instance exists within Figure 1 (and none in the other flow charts) in which informational outputs combine without intervening operations to produce other informational outputs. The list of available acts combines with the list of states relevant to outcomes of acts to generate the table of outcomes without any intervening processing because an outcome is, by definition, the intersection of an act and a state; or, in less mathematical language, an outcome is what

Block Diagram of a Decision System

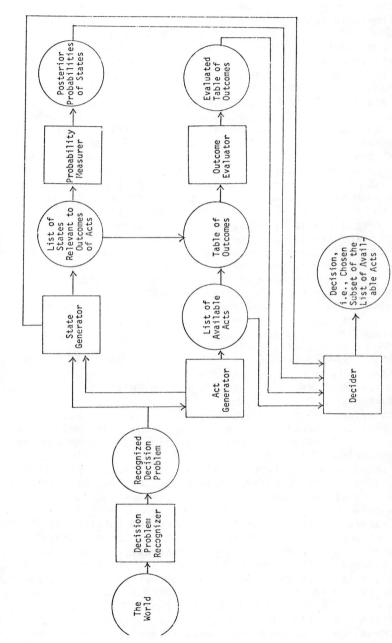

Fig. 1. The processes that lead up to a decision.

9

happens if a given act is chosen and a particular state of the world turns out to obtain.

The main conclusion to which an initial look at Figure 1 must inevitably lead is that decision making, fully analyzed, is complicated. It is divided into four phases. The first consists of recognition of the decision problem and definition of its nature and dimensions--the raw materials of a decision process. The second is called probability evaluation in Figure 1; other names used for the same process in other contexts are diagnosis, intelligence evaluation, data gathering and interpretation, and so on. It is itself a complicated process. Figure 1 indicates, in typical Bayesian fashion, that the output is a set of posterior probabilities of states, but less formal judgments of probability, like those contained in such intuitive processes as conventional medical diagnosis and such formal ones as the acceptance or rejection of statistical hypotheses, also fit here and might be substituted for the Bayesian version of the process by those less convinced than we of the Bayesian point of view.

A more detailed Bayesian version of what goes on in probability evaluation is given in Figure 2, which translates into flow-diagram form some of the basic ideas of an information-processing system called PIP (see Edwards, Phillips, Hays, & Goodman, 1968), but applies just about equally well to any formal application of Bayesian ideas that distinguishes between priors and likelihoods.

We believe that Bayesian techniques have much to offer evaluation--unfortunately, too much to go into here. For expositions of the Bayesian position in statistics itself, see Edwards, Lindman, and Savage (1963) or Phillips (1973). For illustrations of how to use Bayesian inference in decision making, see Raiffa (1968), Schlaifer (1969), or any of a dozen recent texts on the subject, mostly addressed to business-school audiences. For an exciting example of application of Bayesian tools for evaluating alternative options in medical diagnosis, see Fryback (1974). The essence of what these procedures have to offer evaluators, we think, is flexibility. They do not make use of artificial devices such as null hypotheses.

The third phase of decision making, as outlined in Figure 1, is outcome evaluation. "Evaluation" here means literally that--the attachment of values, preferably in numerical form, to outcomes. These values are explicit, numerical answers to the question "Is that particular outcome good or bad, and how good or how bad?" Another way of putting the question to be answered in outcome evaluation is "Suppose I could know for certain that this particular act would lead to this particular outcome, and suppose I then chose this act. How attractive

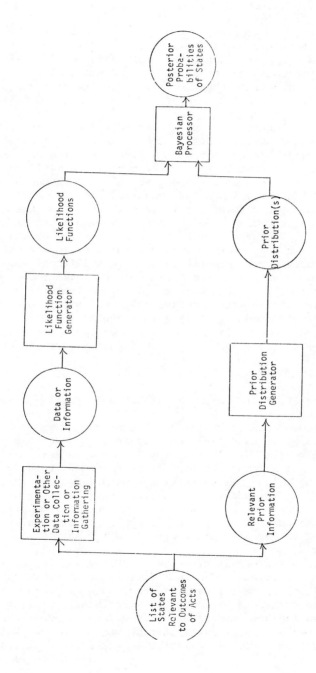

Block Diagram of a Probability Measurer

Fig. 2. The processes involved in probability evaluation. This is an elaboration of the probability-evaluation block of Figure 1.

11

would its outcome be to me, or to someone, or to some collec-
tion of people?"

Note that outcomes, not acts, are evaluated. We often
think of values as being attached to acts. That is in a
sense appropriate, since the whole purpose of obtaining values of outcomes and probabilities of states is to permit the
simple computation that associates an expected value with an
act. In the special case of no uncertainty (that is, some
state has probability 1, or, more often, you treat it as
though it had probability 1 even though you know that unlikely
alternative states exist), each act has only one outcome, and
so the value of the outcome is also the value of the act.

The fourth phase of decision making, as outlined in Figure 1, is actual choice among acts. It is based on the
values of outcomes and the probabilities of states (or the
intuitive substitutes for these numbers). In general, it is
a rather trivial process. In a pick-one-act situation, one
simply picks the act with the highest value, or expected
value. In a pick-several-acts situation, more complex decision rules may be used, but they are still logically simple
and have essentially the character that either the acts that
have the highest values or the acts that return the most value
per unit of cost are selected. Special situations, such as
competitive games, gambler's-ruin problems, and sequential-
decision problems lead to still other, computationally more
complex decision rules, but the input numbers are still the
same.

OUTCOME EVALUATION USING MULTIATTRIBUTE-UTILITY MEASUREMENT

Outcomes can be evaluated in many direct ways. Perhaps the
most commonly used direct way is to equate outcome with price.

The remark "That's so cheap it can't be any good" is true
enough often enough to illustrate the phenomenon, and its
frequent falsity illustrates how unsatisfactory the procedure
is. Price depends more on the relation between supply and
demand than on value. Air is free--but if some predatory
corporation or country had a monopoly on it, wouldn't you be
willing to pay any amount within your means for a year's
supply?

A more reasonable procedure, often used, is simply to consider the outcome and make a direct intuitive value judgment.
We all do this every day; experts, such as diamond appraisers,
make good livings by doing it exceptionally well within a
limited field of expertise. Although such judgments are most
often phrased in language that is vague, categorical, or both,
they can be expressed directly in numbers. Miller, Kaplan,

and Edwards (1969) showed that a resource-allocation system
designed around such numbers far outperformed a system based
on intuitive judgments. Yet this, too, is an extremely primi-
tive way of making value judgments.

Most outcomes have value for a number of different reasons--
that is, on a number of different dimensions. A condominium
on the beach in Venice, California, may house a number of people in reasonable confort, give them good access to recrea-
tional facilities, return a profit to the owner, and stimulate
neighborhood businesses. It may also contribute additional
cars to Venice's constant traffic jam and its surplus of cars
over places to park them; further burden the water, electrical,
phone, and sewage systems; further crowd the schools; place
additional demands on the police and fire departments and
other municipal services; impair general public access to the
beach; and be an eyesore.

All these considerations, and many others, may enter into
a decision about whether to allow that condomimium to be built.
Clearly, this multiplicity of value dimensions presents a
multiplicity of problems. Who determines what dimensions are
relevant and how relevant each is? How is that set of judgments made and used? How is the location of each possible
outcome of each act being considered (for example, various
alternative uses of the land) on each relevant dimension of
value measured, judged, or otherwise discovered? Finally,
what combination of judgmental transformation and arithmetical
aggregation is used to translate all this input information
into outcome evaluations?

An explicit technology, or, more precisely, several competing versions of an explicit technology, exists to answer
some of these questions. Its name is multiattribute-utility
measurement, and expositions of various versions of it have
been presented by Raiffa (1969), Keeney (1972b), Edwards
(1971), and others. The version we present here, previously
published by Edwards (1971) and illustrated in this paper, is
oriented not toward mathematical sophistication or intimacy of
relation between underlying formal structures and the practical procedures that implement them but rather toward easy
communication and use in environments in which time is short
and decision makers are multiple and busy. Still, unpublished
studies strongly argue that the simple rating-scale procedures
described below produce results essentially the same as much
more complicated procedures involving imaginary lotteries.

The essence of multiattribute-utility measurement, in any
of its versions, is that each outcome to be evaluated is
located on each dimension of value by a procedure that may
consist of experimentation, naturalistic observation, judgment,
or some combination of these. These location measures

13

(perhaps further transformed, perhaps not) are combined by means of an aggregation rule, most often simply a weighted average. The weights in the weighted average are numbers describing the importance of each dimension of value relative to the others--in every application we know of, such numbers are judgmentally obtained. A flow diagram of this process is contained in Figure 3, which is an expansion of the block called "outcome evaluation" in Figure 1.

## A SIMPLE MULTIATTRIBUTE-RATING TECHNIQUE (SMART)

Our implementation of Figure 3 consists of 10 steps, which show that our technique emphasizes simplicity and rating rather than more complicated elicitation methods:

*Step 1.* Identify the person or organization whose utilities are to be maximized. If, as is often the case, several organizations have stakes and voices in the decision, they must all be identified. People who can speak for them must be identified and induced to cooperate.

*Step 2.* Identify the issue or issues (that is, decisions) to which the utilities needed are relevant. The same objects or acts may have many different values, depending on context and purpose. In general, utility is a function of the evaluator, the entity being evaluated, and the purpose for which the evaluation is being made. The third argument of that function is sometimes neglected.

*Step 3.* Identify the entities to be evaluated. We previously indicated that they are outcomes of possible actions. But in a sense the distinction between an outcome and the opportunity for further action is usually fictitious. The value of a dollar is the value of whatever you choose to buy with it; the value of an education is the value of the things the educated person can do that he could not have done otherwise. Since it is always necessary to cut the decision tree somewhere--to stop considering outcomes as opportunities for further decisions and instead simply to treat them as outcomes with intrinsic values--the choice of what to call an outcome becomes largely one of convenience. Often, in practice, it is sufficient to treat an action itself as an outcome. This amounts to treating the action as having an inevitable outcome--that is, of assuming that uncertainty about outcomes is not involved in the evaluation of that action. Paradoxically, this is often a good technique when the outcome is utterly uncertain--so uncertain that it is impractical or not worthwhile to explore all its possible consequences in detail and assign probabilities to each.

14

Block Diagram of an Outcome Evaluator

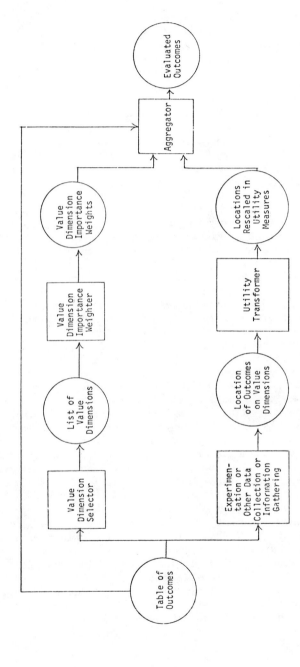

*Fig. 3. The processes involved in outcome evaluation. This is an elaboration of the outcome-evaluation block in Figure 1.*

*Step 4*: Identify the relevant dimensions of value. The first three steps were more or less philosophical. The first answered the question "Whose utility?" The second answered the question "Utility for what purpose?" The third answered the question "Utility of what entities?" With Step 4 we come to the first technical task: discover what dimensions of value are important to the evaluation of the entities we are interested in.

As Raiffa (1969) has noted, goals ordinarily come in hierarchies. But it is often practical and useful to ignore their hierarchical structure and instead to specify a simple list of goals that seem important for the purpose at hand.

It is important not to be too expansive at this stage. The number of relevant dimensions of value should be kept down for reasons that will be apparent shortly. This can often be done by restating and combining goals or by moving upward in a goal hierarchy. Even more important, it can be done by simply omitting the less important goals. There is no requirement that the list evolved in this step be complete, and much reason to hope that it will not be.

*Step 5*. Rank the dimensions in order of importance. This ranking job, like Step 4, can be performed either by an individual, by representatives of conflicting values acting separately, or by those representatives acting as a group. Our preferred technique is to try group processes first, mostly to get the arguments on the table and to make it more likely that the participants start from a common information base, and then to get separate judgments from each individual. The separate judgments will differ, of course, both here and in the following step.

*Step 6*. Rate dimensions in importance, preserving ratios. To do this, start by assigning the least important dimension an importance of 10. (We use 10 rather than 1 to permit subsequent judgments to be finely graded and nevertheless made in integers.) Now consider the next-least-important dimension. How much more important (if at all) is it than the least important? Assign it a number that reflects that ratio. Continue on up the list, checking each set of implied ratios as each new judgment is made. Thus, if a dimension is assigned a weight of 20 while another is assigned a weight of 80, it means that the 20 dimension is one-fourth as important as the 80 dimension. And so on. By the time you get to the most important dimensions, there will be many checks to perform; typically, respondents will want to revise previous judgments to make them consistent with present ones. That is fine; they can do so. Once again, individual differences are likely to arise.

*Step 7.* Sum the importance weights, divide each by the sum, and multiply by 100. This is a purely computational step which converts importance weights into numbers that, mathematically, are rather like probabilities. The choice of a 0-to-100 scale is, of course, purely arbitrary.

At this step the folly of including too many dimensions at Step 4 becomes glaringly apparent. If 100 points are to be distributed over a set of dimensions and some dimensions are very much more important than others, then the less important dimensions will have nontrivial weights only if there are not too many of them. As a rule of thumb, eight dimensions are plenty and 15 are too many. Knowing this, you will want at Step 4 to discourage respondents from being too finely analytical; rather gross dimensions will be just right. Moreover, the list of dimensions can be revised later, and that revision, if it occurs, will typically consist of including more rather than fewer.

*Step 8.* Measure the location of each entity being evaluated on each dimension. The word "measure" is used rather loosely here. There are three classes of dimensions: purely subjective, partly subjective, and purely objective. The purely subjective dimensions are perhaps the easiest; you simply get an appropriate expert to estimate the position of that entity on that dimension on a 0-to-100 scale, where 0 is defined as the minimum plausible value on that dimension and 100 is defined as the maximum plausible value. Note "minimum and maximum plausible" rather than "minimum and maximum possible." The minimum plausible value often is not total absence from the dimension.

A partly subjective dimension is one in which the units of measurement are objective but the locations of the entities must be subjectively estimated.

A wholly objective dimension is one that can be measured rather objectively, in objective units, before the decision. For partly or wholly objective dimensions, it is necessary to have the estimators provide not only values for each entity to be evaluated, but also minimum and maximum plausible values, in the natural units of each dimension.

At this point, we can identify a difference of opinion among users of multiattribute-utility measurement. Some (for example, Edwards, 1971) are content to draw a straight line connecting maximum plausible with minimum plausible values and then to use this line as the source of transformed location measures. Others, such as Raiffa (1968), advocate the development of dimension-by-dimension utility curves. Of various ways of obtaining such curves, the easiest way is simply to ask the respondent to draw graphs. The $X$ axis of each graph represents the plausible range of performance values for the attribute under consideration. The $Y$ axis represents the ranges of values, or desirabilities or utilities, associated with the corresponding $X$ values.

Strong reasons argue for the straight-line procedure whenever the underlying dimension is conditionally monotonic (that is, either more is better than less, or else less is better than more throughout the plausible range of the dimension regardless of locations on the other dimensions). These reasons essentially are that such straight lines will produce magnificent approximations to the true value functions after aggregation over dimensions; correlations in excess of .99 are typical. Still, respondents are sometimes concerned about the nonlinearity of their preferences and may prefer to use the more complicated procedure. Additionally, preferences may not be monotone. In part for these reasons, the study reported later in this paper used nonlinear-value curves, though it avoided the elaborate techniques dependent on hypothetical indifference judgments that have often been proposed to obtain such curves.

Now all entities have been located on the relevant value dimensions, and the location measures have been rescaled. In what sense, if any, are the scales comparable? The question cannot be considered separately from the question of what "importance," as it was judged at Step 6, means. Formally, judgments at Step 6 should be designed so that when the output of Step 7 (or of Step 6, which differs only by a linear transformation) is multiplied by the output of Step 8, equal numerical distances between these products on different dimensions correspond to equal changes in desirability. For example, suppose entity A has a location of 50 and entity B a location of 10 on value dimension $X$, while A has a location of 70 and B a location of 90 on value dimension $Y$ (only $X$ and $Y$ are relevant). Suppose further that dimension $Y$ is twice as important as dimension $X$. Then A and B should be equivalent in value. (The relevant arithmetic is this: for A, $50 + 2(70) = 190$; for B, $10 + 2(90) = 190$. Another way of writing the same arithmetic, which makes clearer what is meant by saying that equal numerical differences between these products on different dimensions correspond to equal changes in desirability, is $(50 - 10) + 2(70 - 90) = 0$.) It is important that judges understand this concept as they perform both Steps 6 and 8.

*Step 9.* Calculate utilities for entities. The equation is

$$U_i = \sum_j w_j u_{ij}.$$

Remembering that $\sum_j w_j = 100$, $U_i$ is the aggregate utility for the $i$th entity, $w_j$ is the normalized importance weight of the

$j$th dimension of value, and $u_{ij}$ is the rescaled position of the $i$th entity on the $j$th dimension. Thus, $w_j$ is the output of Step 7, and $u_{ij}$ is the output of Step 8. The equation, of course, is nothing more than the formula for a weighted average.

*Step 10.* Decide. If a single act is to be chosen, the rule is simple: Maximize $U_i$. If a subset of $i$ is to be chosen, then the subset for which $\sum_i U_i$ is maximum is best.

A special case arises when one of the dimensions, such as cost, is subject to an upper bound--that is, there is a budget constraint. In that case, Steps 4 through 10 should be done ignoring the constrained dimension. The ratios $U_i/C_i$ should be chosen in decreasing order of that ratio until the budget constraint is used up. (More complicated arithmetic is needed if programs are interdependent or if this rule does not come very close to exactly exhausting the budget constraint.) This is the only case in which the benefit-to-cost ratio is the appropriate figure on which to base a decision. In the absence of budget constraints, cost is just another dimension of value, to be treated on the same footing as all other dimensions of value, entering into $U_i$ with a minus sign, like other unattractive dimensions. In effect, in the general case it is the benefit-minus-cost difference, not the benefit-over-cost ratio, that should usually control action.

An important caveat needs to be added concerning benefit-to-cost ratios. Such ratios assume that both benefits and costs are measured on a ratio scale--that is, a scale with a true zero point and ratio properties. The concepts of both zero benefit and zero cost are somewhat slippery on close analysis. A not too bad solution to the problem is to assume that you know what zero cost means and then attempt to find the zero point on the aggregate-benefit scale. If that scale is reasonably densely populated with candidate programs, an approach to locating that zero point is to ask the decision maker, "Would you undertake this program if it had the same benefits it has now but had zero cost?" If the answer is yes, the program is above the zero point on the benefit scale; if the answer is no, it is below the zero point.

The multiattribute-utility approach can easily be adapted to cases in which there are minimum or maximum acceptable values on a given dimension of value by simply excluding alternatives that lead to outcomes that transgress these limits.

## FLEXIBILITIES OF THE METHOD

Practically every technical step in the preceding list has alternatives. For example, Keeney (1972a) has proposed use of a multiplicative-aggregation rather than an additive-aggregation rule. Certain applications have combined multiplication and addition. The methods suggested above for obtaining location measures and importance weights have alternatives; the most common is the direct assignment of importance weights on a 0-to-100 scale. (We consider this procedure inferior to the one described above but doubt that it makes much practical difference in most cases.)

## INDEPENDENCE PROPERTIES

Either the additive or the multiplicative version of the aggregation rule assumes value independence. Roughly, that means that the extent of your preference for location $a_2$ over location $a_1$ of dimension A is unaffected by the position of the entity being evaluated on dimensions B, C, D, . . . . Value independence is a strong assumption, not easily satisfied. Fortunately, in the presence of even modest amounts of measurement error, quite substantial amounts of deviation from value independence will make little difference to the ultimate number $U_i$ and even less to the rank ordering of the $U_i$ values. (For recent discussions of the robustness of linear models, on which this assertion depends, see Dawes & Corrigan 1974.) A frequently satisfied condition that makes the assumption of value independence very unlikely to cause trouble is conditional monotonicity; that is, the additive approximation will almost always work well if, for each dimension, either more is preferable to less or less is preferable to more throughout the range of the dimension that is involved in the evaluation, for all available values of the other dimensions. When the assumption of value independence is unacceptable even as an approximation, much more complicated models and elicitation procedures that take value dependence into account are available.

A trickier issue than value independence is what might be called environmental independence. The traffic congestion caused by a coastal development is extremely likely to be positively correlated with the number of people served by the development. Yet these two dimensions may be value-independent; the correlation simply means that programs with both little traffic congestion and many people served are unlikely to be presented for evaluation.

Violations of environmental independence can lead to double counting. If two value dimensions are perfectly environmentally correlated, only one need be included in the evaluation process. If both are included, care must be taken to make sure that the aggregate-importance weight given to both together properly captures their joint importance. For example, if number of people served and traffic congestion were perfectly environmentally correlated and measured on the same scale after rescaling, if they had equal weights, and if one entered with positive and the other with negative sign into the aggregation, the implication would be that they exactly neutralized each other, so that any feasible combination of these two variables would be equivalent in value to any other feasible combination. The decision maker is unlikely to feel that way but may have trouble adjusting his importance weights to reflect his true feelings. His life could be simplified by redefining the two dimensions into one--for example, number of people served, taking into consideration all that it entails with respect to traffic.

The problem is trickier if the environmental correlation is high but not perfect. But the solution remains the same: Try, whenever possible, to define or redefine value dimensions so as to keep environmental correlations among them low. When that cannot be done, check on the implications of importance weights and location measures assigned to environmentally correlated dimensions to make sure that their aggregate weight properly reflects their aggregate importance.

Similar comments apply, though transparent examples are harder to construct, when the sign of the environmental correlation and the signs with which the dimensions enter into the aggregate-utility function are such that double counting would overemphasize rather than underemphasize the importance of the aggregate of the two dimensions.

A final technical point should be made about environmental correlations.[1] In general, they should be expected to be both present and negative in sign. The reason is fairly simple and is best illustrated with a two-dimensional example, though the argument applies to any number of dimensions. Consider a large set of plans, varying only on the dimensions of number of people served and traffic congestion, and suppose that you regard more people served preferable to fewer, and less congestion preferable to more. Reverse the sign of the congestion dimension (for example, by measuring $k - n$, where $k$ is a large constant and $n$ is the number of cars per hour, instead of simply measuring $n$), so that both dimensions will enter into the final value aggregation with a positive sign. Now imagine

---

[1] We are grateful to David Seaver, who first called the issue discussed in the following paragraphs to our attention.

21

that for the entire set of available plans, the two dimensions are environmentally independent, so that any combination of the two dimensions can be found (and all other relevant dimensions are constant over these combinations).

If you must choose one plan from all these possibilities, you will certainly not consider one for which number of cars is large and number of people served is small. Consider Figure 4. The only plans you will be interested in will be those at the outer boundaries of the set of available plans. In fact, every plan inside the lines connecting those plans at the outer boundary is either strictly or stochastically dominated (to borrow technical terms from decision theory), and should not be considered at all.

Consider the relation between number of people served and $k - n$ if attention is confined only to the plans at the outer boundary. The correlation between these dimensions will be large and negative, as you can see by inspection of Figure 4. The argument generalizes easily to any number of dimensions. In the technical language of decision theory, the point is simply that the undominated set of acts must lie on the convex boundary and so are necessarily negatively correlated with one another. This point becomes much less significant when one is selecting a number of plans rather than just one, since the selection of each plan removes it from the choice set, redraws the convex boundary of the remaining plans, and probably thus reduces the negative correlation.

Unfortunately, the higher the negative environmental correlation among value dimensions, the less satisfactory becomes the use of the value-independence assumption as an approximation when value correlations are actually present. At present we know of no detailed mathematical or simulation study of the effect of size of the environmental correlation on acceptability of the value-independence approximation. This question is likely to receive detailed examination in the next few years.

*INTERPERSONAL AND INTERGROUP DISAGREEMENTS*

Nothing in the preceding discussion ensures that different respondents will come up with similar numbers--and such agreements are indeed rare.

We might expect that the magnitude of interpersonal disagreement would make this technology of questionable value. Not so. Consider the following application in a case study of coastal-zone management.

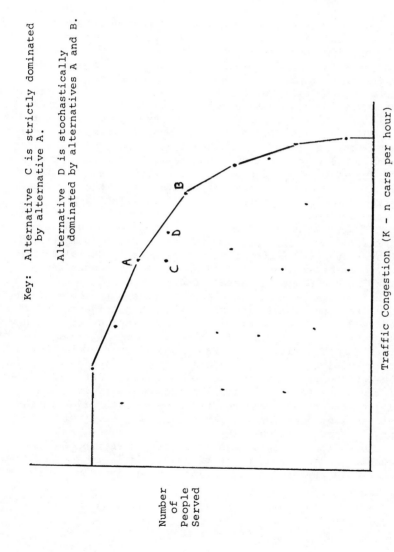

Key: Alternative C is strictly dominated
     by alternative A.

     Alternative D is stochastically
     dominated by alternatives A and B.

Fig. 4. Examples of strict and stochastic dominance of alternatives.

THE CASE STUDY[2]

A review of the national population census in 1950, 1960, and 1970 shows that there has been and continues to be population growth and concentration in the nation's coastal zone (by which we mean coastal counties). The concentration of growth in the coastal zone has produced drastic changes and fierce competition for the use of its scarce resources. The result is problems of ecology, conservation, development, land use, transportation, public access, recreation, public utilities, maintenance of ocean mineral and fish and game resources, education and science, and so forth. The growing complexity of the problems and issues involved in coastal-zone management calls for a level of sophistication that is straining the capacities of local, urban, and county governments.

Recently the state of California found itself thrust into a position of leadership in developing policies and programs for the planning and management of its coastal zone. Prior to 1972, 200 separate entities—city, county, state, and federal governments, agencies, and commissions—regulated the California coast. The citizens of California, in reviewing the performances of these 200 entities, were apparently dissatisfied. In a voter-sponsored initiative during the general election of 1972, the voters approved legislation placing coastal-zone planning and management under one state commission and six regional commissions. In passing the Coastal-Zone Conservation Act, the voters established decision makers with ultimate authority (other than appeal to the courts) to preserve, protect, restore, and enhance the environment and ecology of the state's coastal zone.

The Coastal-Zone Conservation Act charges the commissioners of each regional commission with evaluating the worth of each development request submitted and then either approving or disapproving. A major problem results, since the Act does not specify just how this very large and difficult evaluation and decision-making task is to be accomplished. The permit requests consist of information on many different importance dimensions that are specified (at the abstract, conceptual level) by the Act. Decisions taken on permits prior to the development of a master plan are to be consistent with the eventual planning output.

Although the Act specifies that certain attributes should be considered in making evaluations, it fails to specify just how they are supposed to enter into the evaluation process.

---

[2]For a complete discussion of this case study, see Gardiner (1974).

Nor does the Act specify how the commissioners are to balance
the conflicting interests affected by their decisions.  In
effect, the Act implies that individual commissioners assigned
to a commission will represent the interests of all affected
parties with respect to that coastal zone.  How this is to be
accomplished in practice is left unspecified.  In practice,
attempts to include the preferences and value judgments of
interested groups and individuals occur when the commission
holds public-advocacy hearings on permit requests.  Under these
procedures, opposing interest groups express their values and
viewpoints as conclusions--often based on inconsistent sets
of asserted facts or no facts at all--in the form of verbal
and written presentations at the open hearings.

Fourteen individuals involved in coastal-zone planning and
decision making agreed to participate in this study.  Included
were two of the current commissioners for Region V (Los
Angeles and Orange Counties), a number of active conservation-
ists, and one major coastal-zone developer.  The purpose of
this study was to test the consequences of using multiattribute-utility-measurement processes by having participants in
or people close to the regulatory process with differing views
rather than the usual college sophomores make both individual
and group evaluations of various proposals for development in
a section of the California coastal zone.  Evaluations were
made both intuitively and by constructing multiattribute-
utility-measurement models.

To provide a common basis for making evaluations, a sample
of 15 hypothetical but realistic permit requests for development were written.  The types of permits were limited to those
for development of single-family dwellings and duplex, triplex,
or multifamily dwellings (owned or for renting).  Dwelling-
unit development (leading to increased population density) is
a major area of debate in current coastal-zone decision making.
Most permit applications submitted to the Region V Commission
thus far fall into this class.  Moreover, permits granted in
this class will probably generate further permit requests.
Housing development tends to bring about the need for other
development in the coastal zone, such as in public works,
recreation, transportation, and so on.  The permit applications provided eight items of information about the proposed
development that formed the information base on which subjects
were asked to make their evaluations.  These eight items were
abstracted from actual staff reports currently submitted to
the Region V commissioners as a basis for their evaluations
and decision making on current permit applications.  The
commissioners' staff reports do have some additional information, such as the name of the applicant and so on, but the
following items are crucial for evaluation:

1. *Size of development*. Measured in the number of square feet of the coastal zone taken up by the development.
2. *Distance from the mean high-tide line*. The location of the nearest edge of the development from the mean high-tide line measured in feet.
3. *Density of the proposed development*. The number of dwelling units per acre for the development.
4. *On-site parking facilities*. The percentage of cars brought in by the development that are provided parking space as part of the development.
5. *Building height*. The height of the development in feet (17.5 feet per story).
6. *Unit rental*. Measured as the dollar rental per month (on the average) for the development. If the development is owner occupied and no rent is paid, an equivalent to rent is computed by taking the normal monthly mortgage payment.
7. *Conformity with land use in the vicinity*. The density of the development relative to the average density of adjacent residential lots. Measured on a 5-point scale from much less dense to much more dense.
8. *Aesthetics of the development*. Measured on a scale from poor to excellent.

Each of the invented permits was constructed to report a level of performance for each item. They were as realistic as possible and represented a wide variety of possible permits.

Each subject answered seven questionnaires. In general, the participants had five days to work on each of the questionnaires. Throughout, the procedures of the Delphi technique were used.[3] In the process of responding to the seven questionnaires, each subject (1) categorized himself on an 11-point continuum that ranged from very conservationist oriented to very development oriented, (2) evaluated intuitively (wholistically) 15 sample permit requests by rating their overall merit on a 0-to-100-point scale, (3) followed the steps of multiattribute-utility measurement outlined previously and in so doing constructed individual and group value models,[4] and (4) re-evaluated the same 15 sample permit

---

[3]The use of this technique has become fairly common. It was developed by Norman Dalkey and Olaf Helmer in the 1960s (see Dalkey, 1968).

[4]The evaluation and decision making in this study were assumed to be riskless. Decisions involving permit requests, by the nature of the permits themselves, suggest that the consequences of approval or disapproval are known with certainty. The developer states on his permit what he intends to do if the permit is approved and is thereby constrained if

requests intuitively a second time. Subjects did not know that the second batch of permits was a repetition of the first.

The location of the proposed developments was Venice, California, which is geographically part of the city of Los Angeles located between Santa Monica and Marina del Rey. Venice has a diverse population and has been called a microcosm--a little world epitomizing a larger one (Torgerson, 1973). In many ways, Venice presents in one small area the most controversial issues associated with coastal-zone decision making.

After the initial questionnaire round in which the subjects categorized themselves according to their views about coastal-zone development, the 14 individuals were divided into two groups. We called the eight more conservationist-minded subjects Group 1 and the other six subjects (whose views, by self-report, ranged from moderate to strongly pro-development) Group 2.

In both the intuitive-evaluation and the multiattribute-utility-measurement task, the subjects reported no major difficulty in completing the questionnaires. An example of one participant's value curves and importance weights is shown in Figure 5. The abscissas represent the natural dimension ranges, and the ordinates represent worth, ranging from 0 to 100 points. Although the value curves shown are all monotone, and could therefore be linearly approximated as indicated earlier, 11 of the 14 subjects produced at least one nonmonotone value curve. This study therefore used the actual value curves for each subject rather than the linear approximation.

To develop group intuitive ratings and group value models, each individual in a group was given, through feedback, the opportunity of seeing his group's initial responses on a given task (intuitive ratings, importance weights, and so on). These data were fed back in the form of group means. Averaging individual responses to form group responses produced the results shown in Table 1.

Table 1 shows in column 2 test-retest wholistic evaluations of the 15 sample permits. These correlations are computed by taking the mean group ratings for each permit on the initial (test) intuitive evaluation and the second (retest) intuitive evaluation. The test wholistic-SMART evaluation correlations are computed by comparing a group value model's ratings of the 15 sample permits with the group's initial intuitive

---

approval is granted. If the request is disapproved, there will be no development. Outcomes are known with certainty, and this is the requirement for riskless decision making.

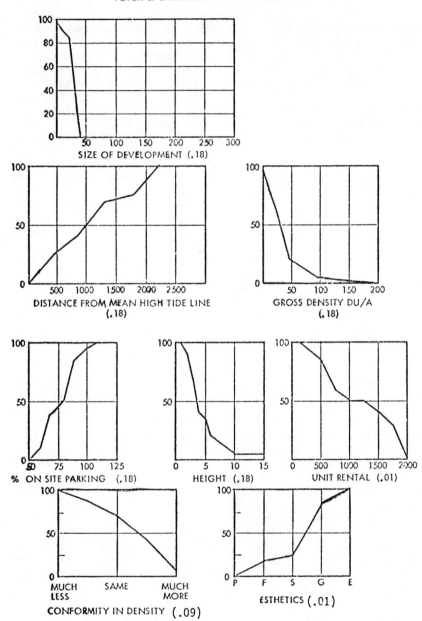

*Fig. 5. An example of value curves and importance weights (parentheses) for permit items for a Group 1 subject.*

evaluations. The group value model is found by computing the mean importance weights and mean value curves for the group and then evaluating each permit using the group's value model. The retest wholistic–SMART evaluation correlations are similar except that the second intuitive evaluation is used.

TABLE 1
*Group Product-Moment Correlations*

| Group | Test–Retest wholistic evaluations (reliability) | Test wholistic–SMART evaluations | Retest wholistic–SMART evaluations |
|---|---|---|---|
| 1 | .9485(001) | .9437(001) | .9167(001) |
| 2 | .8672(001) | .6645(007) | .8731(001) |

As can be seen from Table 1, each group's value model, constructed using the procedures of multiattribute–utility measurement, apparently captured the wholistic evaluations of the group. The interesting question is then "What is the effect of using a group's value model versus a group's intuitive evaluation?"

To answer this question, a two–way analysis of variance was conducted of permit worths by group by permit. The results are shown in Table 2. These results indicate that the two groups initially (that is, by intuitive evaluations) represented differing viewpoints (that is, were drawn from differing populations), although the differences were not dramatic. Substantial percentages of variance were accounted for both by group main effects and by permit–group interactions for the first–test wholistic evaluations. (Results for the retest were similar and are not presented here.) Both findings indicate differing viewpoints between the two groups. The main effect could have been caused, however, by a constant evaluation bias alone. The key indication of differing viewpoints is the interaction term. Notice that use of each group's value–model evaluations instead of their intuitive evaluations causes the percent of variance accounted for by the interaction to drop from 12% to 2%. Figure 6 shows this difference dramatically.

In other words, use of the multiattribute–utility technique has turned modest disagreement into substantial agreement. Why? We suggest a plausible answer. When making wholistic evaluations, those with strong points of view tend to concentrate on those aspects of the entities being evaluated that most strongly engage their biases (recall the advocacy folkway). The multiattribute procedure does not

TABLE 2

ANALYSIS OF VARIANCE SUMMARY

TWO-WAY ANALYSIS OF VARIANCE (PERMIT X GROUP) FOR WHOLISTIC
EVALUATION PERMIT WORTH

| Source | d.f. | MS. | Error d.f. | F | P |
|---|---|---|---|---|---|
| Main Effect | | | | | |
| Permits | 14 | 4274.6668 | 180 | 9.91 | 0.0005 |
| Group | 1 | 13675.2366 | 180 | 31.70 | 0.0005 |
| Interaction | | | | | |
| Permit/group | 14 | 1536.8741 | 180 | 3.56 | 0.0005 |
| Within Cells | 180 | 431.3517 | | | |

TWO-WAY ANALYSIS OF VARIANCE (PERMIT X GROUP) FOR SMART
EVALUATION PERMIT WORTH

| Source | d.f. | MS. | Error d.f. | F | P |
|---|---|---|---|---|---|
| Main Effect | | | | | |
| Permits | 14 | 1853.0008 | 180 | 17.47 | 0.0005 |
| Group | 1 | 2128.5143 | 180 | 20.06 | 0.0005 |
| Interaction | | | | | |
| Permit/group | 14 | 77.6310 | 180 | 0.73 | 0.741 |
| Within Cells | 180 | 106.0942 | | | |

PERCENT OF VARIANCE ACCOUNTED FOR

| Rating | Source | Percent in Sample | Percent in Population (estimate) |
|---|---|---|---|
| Wholistic | Permit | 0.34 | 0.31 |
| SMART | Permit | 0.53 | 0.49 |
| Wholistic | Group | 0.08 | 0.08 |
| SMART | Group | 0.04 | 0.04 |
| Wholistic | Interaction | 0.12 | |
| SMART | Interaction | 0.02 | |
| Wholistic | Within Cells | 0.45 | |
| SMART | Within Cells | 0.39 | |

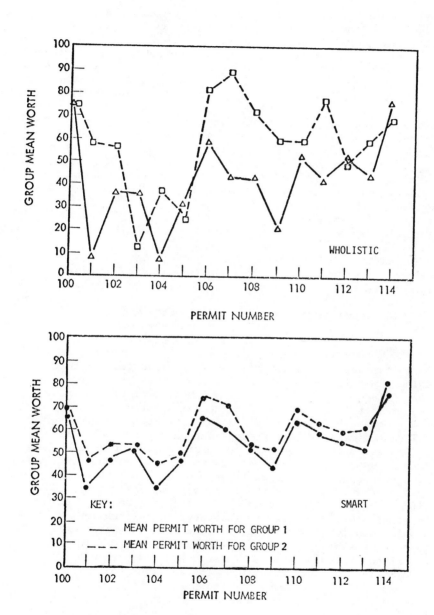

*Fig. 6. SMART-fostered agreement.*

permit this; it separates judgment of the importance of a dimension from judgment of where a particular entity falls on that dimension. These applications varied on eight dimensions that are relevant to the environmentalist-versus-builder arguments. Although these two views may cause different thoughts about how good a particular level of performance on some dimensions may be, evaluation on other dimensions will be more or less independent of viewpoint. Agreement about those other dimensions tends to reduce the impact of disagreement on controversial dimensions. That is, multiattribute-utility-measurement procedures do not foster an opportunity for any one or two dimensions to become so salient that they emphasize existing sources of conflict and disagreement. Multiattribute-utility measurement cannot and should not eliminate all disagreement, however; such conflicts are genuine, and any value-measurement procedure should respect and so reflect them. Still, in spite of disagreement, social decisions must be made. How?

We distinguish between two kinds of disagreements. Disagreements at Step 8 seem to us to be essentially like disagreements among different thermometers measuring the same temperature. If they are not too large, we have little compunction about taking an average. If they are, then we are likely to suspect that some of the thermometers are not working properly and to discard their readings. In general, we think that judgmentally determined location measures should reflect expertise, and typically we would expect different value dimensions to require different kinds of expertise and therefore different experts. In some practical contexts, we can avoid the problem of disagreement at Step 8 entirely by the simple expedient of asking only the best available expert for each dimension to make judgments about that dimension.

Disagreements at Steps 5 and 6 are another matter. These seem to us to be the essence of conflicting values, and we wish to respect them as much as possible. For that reason, we feel that the judges who perform Steps 5 and 6 should be either the decision maker(s) or well-chosen representatives. Considerable discussion, persuasion, and information exchange should be used in an attempt to reduce the disagreements as much as possible. At the least, this process offers a clear set of the rules of debate and an orderly way to proceed from information and data to values, to decisions which represent quite an improvement over the folkways.

Even this will seldom reduce disagreements to zero, however. For some organizations, we can at this point invoke former President Truman's desk sign, "The buck stops here." One function of an executive, boss, or decision maker is to resolve disagreements among subordinates. He can do this in various ways: by substituting his judgment for theirs, by picking one of them as "right" and rejecting the others, or, in the weighted-averaging spirit of multiattribute-utility measurement, by assigning a weight to each of the disagreeing subordinates and then calculating weighted-average importance weights.

If there is no individual or group decision maker to resolve disagreement, we can carry through the evaluation separately for each of the disagreeing individuals or groups, hoping that the disagreements are small enough to have little or no action implications. And if that hope is not fulfilled, we have no suggestions to offer beyond the familiar political processes by means of which society functions in spite of conflicting interests. We offer technology, not miracles!

Fortunately, in the land-use-management context decision-making bodies exist and will continue to exist regardless of any foreseeable technological changes in their mode of operation.


A PUBLIC TECHNOLOGY FOR LAND-USE MANAGEMENT

We conclude with a rather visionary discussion of how these agencies could carry out the task of land-use management by fully exploiting SMART or some similar value-measurement technique.

The statutes would define, at least to some degree, the appropriate dimensions of value, as they do now. They might, but probably should not, specify limits on the importance weights attached to these dimensions. They might, and perhaps should, specify boundaries beyond which no value could go in the undesirable direction.

The main functions of the regulatory agency would be four: to specify measurement methods for each value dimension (with utility functions or other methods for making the necessary transformations at Step 8); to specify importance weights; to define one or more bounds on acceptable levels of aggregated utility, and perhaps also lower bounds not specified by statute on specific dimensions; and to hear appeals. Perhaps two bounds on acceptable levels of aggregated utility would be appropriate. Requests falling above the higher bound would be automatically accepted; requests falling below the lower bound would be automatically rejected; requests falling in between would be examined in old-style hearings. Presumably the regulatory agency would also have to hear appeals from the automatic decisions, perhaps with the provision that the appellant must bear the cost of the hearing if the appeal is rejected.

The regulatory agency could afford to spend enormous amounts of time and effort on its first two functions, specification of measurement methods and of importance weights. Value considerations, political considerations, views of competing constituencies and advocates, the arts of logrolling and compromise--all would come into play. Public hearings would be held, with elaborate and extensive debate and full airing of all relevant issues and points of view.

The regulatory agency would have further responsibilities in dealing with measurement methods for wholly or partly subjective value dimensions. Since such measurements must be judgments, the regulatory agency must make sure that the judgments are impartial and fair. This could be done by having staff members make them, or by offering the planner a list of agency-approved impartial experts, or by mediating among or selecting from the conflicting views of experts selected by those with stakes in the decision, or by some combination of these methods. We consider the first two of these approaches to be most desirable but recognize that the third or fourth may be inevitable.

The reason that the costs of prolonged and intensive study of measurement methods and of importance weights could be borne is that they would recur infrequently. Once agreed-on measurement methods and importance weights have been hammered out, most case-by-case decisions would be automatically made by means of them. Only in response to changed political and social circumstances or changed technology would reconsideration of the agreed-on measurement methods and importance weights be necessary--and even such reconsiderations would be likely to be partial rather than complete. They would, of course, occur; times do change, public tastes and values change, and technologies change. Those seeking appropriate elective offices could campaign for such changes--an election platform consisting in part of a list of numerical importance weights would be a refreshing novelty.

The decision rules would, of course, be public knowledge. That fact probably would be the most cost-saving aspect of this whole approach. Would-be developers and builders would not waste their time and money preparing plans that they could easily calculate to be unacceptable. Instead, they would prepare acceptable plans from the outset. Once a plan had been prepared and submitted to the regulatory agency, its evaluation would consist of little more than a check that the planner's measurements and arithmetic had been done correctly. Delay from submission to approval need be no more than a few days.

Changes in the decision rules can be and should be as explicit as the rules themselves. Such explicitness would permit regulators and those regulated alike to know exactly what current regulatory policies are, and if they have changed, how and how much. Such knowledge would greatly facilitate both enlightened citizen participation in deciding on policy changes and swift, precise adaptation of those regulated to such changes once they have taken effect.

In short, multiattribute-utility measurement allows value conflicts bearing on social decisions to be fought out and resolved at the level of decision rules rather than at the level of individual decisions. Such decision rules, once specified, define and thus remove nearly all ambiguity from regulatory policy without impairing society's freedom to modify policies in response to changing conditions. Possible savings in financial and social costs, delays, frustrations, and so on are incalculable, but cost reduction in dollars alone could be 90% or more.

We consider the idea of resolving value conflicts at the level of decision rules rather than at the level of individual decisions to have the potential of revolutionary impact on land-use management--and many other public-decision contexts as well. Any revolutionary idea is bound to be full of unexpected consequences, booby-traps, and surprises. For a while, therefore, the wise innovator would want to run old and new systems in parallel, comparing performance of the two and building up experience with the new system. The mechanism we have suggested above of defining an upper and a lower bound, with automatic acceptance above the upper bound, automatic rejection below the lower one, and hearings in between, provides a convenient administrative device for operation of such parallel procedures. Initially the upper bound could be very high and the lower bound very low so that most cases fall in between and are handled by the traditional hearing mechanism. Our candidate number for the lower bound, at least initially, is the utility of the do-nothing (that is, *status quo*) alternative, for obvious reasons. If what the applicant wants is not clearly better than the *status quo*, why does he deserve a hearing? As experience and confidence in the multiattribute-utility-measurement system develop, the two bounds can be moved toward each other, so that more and more cases are handled automatically rather than by means of hearings. This need work no hardship on any rejected applicant; he can always appeal, accepting the delays, costs, and risk of losing implicit in the hearing process rather than the cost of upgrading his plan. And the regulatory agency, by moving the boundaries, can in effect control its caseload, thus gradually shortening what under current procedures are frequently inordinate delays.

At present, we know of no public context in which even limited experimentation with the methods we advocate is occurring. But we have hopes.

## REFERENCES

Dalkey, N. C. *Delphi*. Santa Monica, Calif.: The RAND Corp., 1968.

Dawes, R. M., & Corrigan, B. Linear models in decision making. *Psychological Bulletin*, 1974, *81*, 97-106.

Edwards, W. Social utilities. *The Engineering Economist*, Summer Symposium Series, 1971, *6*.

Edwards, W., & Guttentag, M. Experiments and evaluations: A re-examination. In C. Bennet & A. Lumsdaine (Eds.), *Experiments and evaluations*. New York: Academic Press, in preparation, 1975.

Edwards, W., Guttentag, M., & Snapper, K. Effective evaluation: A decision theoretic approach. In M. Guttentag (Ed.), *Handbook of evaluation research*. In preparation, 1975.

Edwards, W., Lindman, H., & Savage, L. J. Bayesian statistical inference for psychological research. *Psychological Review*, 1963, *70*, 193-242.

Edwards, W., Phillips, L. D., Hays, W. L., & Goodman, B. C. Probabilistic information processing systems: Design and evaluation. *IEEE Transaction on Systems Science and Cybernetics*, 1968, *SSC-4*, 248-265.

Fryback, D. Subjective probability estimates in a medical decision making problem. Unpublished doctoral dissertation, The University of Michigan, 1974.

Gardiner, P. C. The application of decision technology and Monte Carlo simulation to multiple objective public policy decision making: A case study in California coastal zone management. Unpublished doctoral dissertation, University of Southern California, 1974.

Keeney, R. L. *Multiplicative utility functions*. (Technical Report No. 70) Cambridge: Operations Research Center, Massachusetts Institute of Technology, 1972. (a)

Keeney, R. L. Utility functions for multi-attributed consequences. *Management Science*, 1972, *18*, 276-287. (b)

Miller, L. W., Kaplan, R. J., & Edwards, W. JUDGE: A laboratory evaluation. *Organizational Behavior and Human Performance*, 1969, *4*, 97-111.

Phillips, L. D. *Bayesian statistics for social scientists*. New York: Crowell, 1973.

Raiffa, H. *Decision analysis: Introductory lectures on choices under certainty.* Reading, Mass.: Addison-Wesley, 1968.

Raiffa, H. Preferences for multi-attribute alternatives. (Memorandum RM-5968-DOT/RC) Santa Monica, Calif.: The RAND Corp., April 1969.

Schlaifer, R. *Analysis of decisions under uncertainty.* New York: McGraw-Hill, 1969.

Torgerson, D. Venice: Everything is changing, middle-income hippies moving in where poor are moving out. *Los Angeles Times*, November 18, 1973.

## 2. DECISION PROCESSES IN RECOGNITION MEMORY

*Steven Schwartz*
University of Texas Medical Branch

Decision and Memory: A Hypothetical Mechanism for the
Influence of Semantic Memory on Episodic Recognition–
Memory Tasks | 41
  What Is Remembered in Recognition Memory? | 41
  Filtering and Pigeonholing in Memory | 43
  The Decision Model | 44
The Decision Model: Evidence from Experiments on the
Recognition of Words and Names | 47
  The Effect of Name Frequency | 47
  The Effect of Word Frequency | 48
  The Effect of Input Modality | 50
The Decision Model: Evidence from Experiments on the
Recognition of Word Strings and Sentences | 51
Relationships between the Decision Model and Other Views
of Memory | 56
  A Levels-of-Analysis Framework | 56
  The Importance of Encoding Specificity | 57
Conclusions | 58
References | 59

Many of the chapters in this volume are concerned with issues of obvious social importance--overpopulation, ecology, and large-scale evaluation research. There are, however, social decisions which, though not of such cosmic importance, may prove quite troublesome. Consider the common experience of being confronted with what appears to be a familiar face at a party or at a convention. All things being equal, most of us would probably approach the individual with a casual "Haven't we met before?" or "Aren't you Mary Smith?" If we discount the possibility of some mild temporary embarrassment, there are few costs attached to being wrong in such a situation. In some instances the potential costs are greater. A similar approach taken to a female on a subway platform, for example, could result in a painful rebuke. There is, of course, the possibility that even on a subway platform such an approach could lead to certain rewards. The important point is that the decision to approach an uncertainly recognized individual depends not only on how clearly the person's face is remembered but also on the relative rewards and costs attached to making such an approach.

Precisely the same analysis holds for any decision that must be made in the face of uncertainty. In the psychological laboratory, subjects are frequently called upon to decide whether a test object, word, or nonsense syllable was encountered previously or is new. Performance in such tasks is a function of how well the item is remembered and of the relative odds, rewards, and costs attached to making errors in the testing situation. In many laboratory experiments no explicit rewards or penalties are attached to performance, but the odds in favor of or against certain responses can still be calculated. That is, one important influence on behavior in the recognition task when the material to be recognized is meaningful is the subject's *a priori* knowledge of the language and of what words and relationships are probable. Such knowledge has been assigned by Tulving (1972) to an information-processing system known as semantic memory. Semantic memory consists of an organized library containing all of the information one possesses about the language, including the meaning of words as well as a set of useful algorithms and heuristics for linguistic processing. In addition to the semantic system, an episodic-memory system which receives and stores information concerning the perceptible attributes of temporally dated events is thought to be operative in many laboratory situations.

Although not necessarily physically distinct, these two systems do differ in several important ways. For our present purposes, it is enough to note that the two memory systems differ in the nature of the information stored within them and in the ways in which this information is retrieved.

In some situations the semantic-memory system may function more or less independently of the episodic store (on a final examination in chemistry, for example), whereas in other situations (recognizing someone's face, for example), the episodic memory may primarily retain and retrieve information. In a great many, if not most, situations, however, both memory systems are involved, and it is these situations which are the focus of this chapter. Specifically, this chapter is concerned with the influence of semantic memory on decision making in memory recognition tasks.

There are many types of recognition tasks. The sort of situation focused on in this chapter is one in which individuals are presented with single test "probes" and required to determine whether each probe appeared in some earlier learned list. A model for decision making in such situations is developed, followed, in turn, by a discussion of word and sentence recognition. For both types of tasks, the decision-making model is used to separate and account for the respective contributions of episodic and semantic memory. The relationships between the current model and other views of memory are explored, and implications for future research are discussed.

DECISION AND MEMORY: A HYPOTHETICAL MECHANISM FOR THE INFLUENCE OF SEMANTIC MEMORY ON EPISODIC RECOGNITION-MEMORY TASKS

*WHAT IS REMEMBERED IN RECOGNITION MEMORY?*

Even common laboratory tests of episodic memory may involve the semantic-memory system when the items to be remembered are meaningful words. What is unclear is the precise nature of the information retained and tested in typical recognition-memory experiments. One widely accepted view is that verbal material is held in a modality-specific form for a brief time during which it is encoded into an enduring, semantically coded, long-term trace (Neisser, 1967). From this point of view, recognition memory for verbal material depends upon a specific semantic interpretation of the material rather than upon memory for its physical form (Bransford & Franks, 1971; Reder, Anderson, & Bjork, 1974). There is good reason to believe, however, that memory for the physical aspects of verbal material may, under certain conditions, last longer than just a few seconds.

"S," the mnemonist studied by Luria (1968), relied almost exclusively on visual images and a "memory walk" retrieval strategy. Furthermore, recent experiments conducted by

41

Anderson (1974); Hintzman, Block, and Inskeep (1972); Kirsner (1973, 1974); Kolers (1973); Nelson and Brooks (1974); and Schwartz and Witherspoon (1974) indicate that even non-mnemonists can retain for rather long periods fairly detailed information about the physical (visual-temporal-acoustic) aspects of verbal material. The relative influence of such physical cues on recognition is most certainly related to the context in which both learning and testing take place (Tulving & Thomson, 1973). That is, the importance of physical cues may be affected by such factors as orienting tasks assigned at the time of learning (Hyde & Jenkins, 1973) and retrieval cues given at the time of recall (Thomson & Tulving, 1970).

Evidence in support of the notion that the physical properties of verbal material are remembered for some time after input answers only part of the question posed earlier. Certainly, words are semantically coded as well. In addition, one's *a priori* knowledge of the language also influences recognition-memory performance. That is, knowledge of such things as the frequency of words in the language (Kintsch, 1970) or the structure of syntactical relationships (Slamecka, 1969) will have a strong effect on recognition-memory performance. The manner in which such *a priori* knowledge is combined with the sensory-temporal data and the semantic information stored in episodic memory to produce recognition decisions is decidedly unclear. One intuitively reasonable, if deceptively simple, hypothesis is to assume that the episodic and semantic memory systems interact to create a memory "trace" with both episodic and semantic features. The precise features encoded, of course, depend on the learning context. It is not difficult to conceptualize episodic features because they are essentially the physical (sensory-temporal) characteristics of input events and the meaning of words. The remaining semantic features are more difficult to comprehend because these features are not physical qualities but rather information about the meaning of words, the relationships among words, and the interconnections between words, concepts, and other symbolic referents. It is difficult to think of such semantic qualities in terms of "features." One could categorize words as to their part of speech or perhaps as members of various semantic categories, but such classification schemes hardly do justice to the complexities of memory. Memory, whether in the form of words, sentences, or longer passages, involves a complicated knowledge structure, all or part of which can come into play in trying to remember even a single word (Brockway, Chmielewski, & Cofer, 1974). Any particular language input calls forth a great deal of stored information, both about the word and about many related words and concepts. The complexity of

42

these linguistic relationships goes far beyond the notion of features (at least the sort of easily describable features one associates with episodic memory).

It is easier, therefore, on a purely rational basis, to view the single-probe recognition experiment as based on a judgment concerning the familiarity of only the stored episodic trace, without the inclusion of information stored in semantic memory. The model to be developed here does just that. In order for the model to predict recognition performance, however, some provision must be made for the effects of one's *a priori* knowledge of the language. These effects are incorporated into the model in the form of response biases which influence the likelihood of particular responses. These response biases are the contribution of semantic memory.

It is now possible to form a preliminary hypothesis as to the nature of what is remembered in recognition-memory experiments. What is always remembered is a representation in the form of an episodic-memory trace of the physical-temporal characteristics of the input material. When conditions permit (appropriate input context, enough time between learning and testing, and so on); the input is also encoded semantically. As a result of this semantic processing, a semantic code is added to the episodic trace. Equally important, a bias toward certain, but not other, responses is established. This bias is only indirectly related to the episodic trace and may be influenced by various motives and many other factors influencing the organism's general state.

The mechanism underlying the interaction of semantic and episodic memory is discussed further and the model expanded in the next section.

## FILTERING AND PIGEONHOLING IN MEMORY

Consider the situation in which a subject is required to recall from a list of mixed words only the names of colors. This task requires the creation of a subvocabulary "response set," and errors may often consist of color names not on the original list. Clearly, semantic memory is operating in this situation. It is, according to the present thesis, not only providing appropriate verbal labels but also producing a bias toward certain responses, even toward some words not presented in the original list. Given the definition of the task, the semantic-memory system sets a lower criterion for such color-name responses. The mechanism by which the organism adjusts its decision rules in accord with current risks and benefits (which may, by the way, be partially determined by the context) has been called "pigeonholing" by Broadbent (1971). Pigeonholing, then, is, according to the present formulation, an important aspect of semantic memory.

Turning from recall to recognition, we can see that it is possible to examine pigeonholing rather precisely by deriving an operating characteristic relating the probability of an accurate recognition response to the probability of an incorrect response (false alarm). Pigeonholing would be mirrored by an increase in correct responses accompanied by an increase in false alarms (responding to color names not presented). In signal-detection-theory terms (Tanner & Swets, 1954), pigeonholing would be mirrored by changes in the subject's response criterion.

Now let us consider the situation in which one is required to recall only the words printed in gothic letters from a list of mixed words. The subject must here choose the items to be remembered on the basis of some common feature (in this case, type font) and ignore those items in the store without this feature. Broadbent (1971) has labeled such a strategy "filtering." Within the present model, filtering should be important in retrieval of physical information from episodic memory. On a recognition task an increase in filtering will result in an increase in correct detections not accompanied by an increase in false alarms. Therefore, in the recognition situation, filtering is mirrored by changes in the signal-detection parameter of sensitivity. The subject in a recognition experiment may rely on either filtering or pigeonholing to accomplish his task. Most often, however, he will use some combination of the two. It is these situations that are the focus of the present model.

*THE DECISION MODEL*

Figure 1 depicts the basic theoretical orientation of the model. The input probe is stored in a transitory sensory buffer during which perceptible features are extracted. It is assumed that any particular stimulus is made up of sensory-temporal features, each of which is the product of discrete sensory components, and that the perception of a component allows one to infer not only the presence of a particular feature but the presence of some of the other components as well. The probability that a particular component will be attended to and a particular feature inferred is a function not only of stimulus complexity but also of such variables as the time available to study the stimulus (stimulus duration), the rate of information processing, and the amount of distracting (competing) stimuli. The perceptible features of the test probe are compared with the stored episodic-memory trace (the extracted perceptible features of the original item) in what is called a "familiarity check." Familiarity

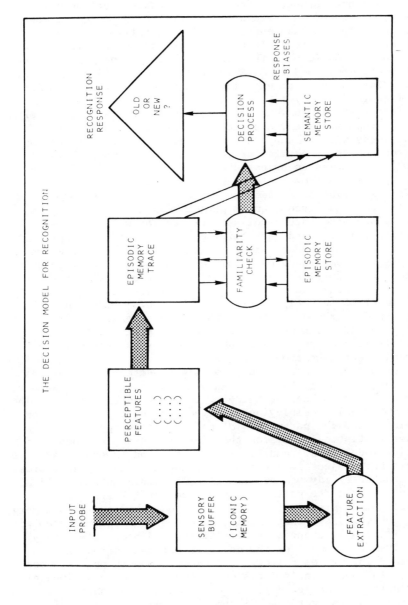

Fig. 1. *The decision process for single-probe recognition memory. See the text for a detailed description.*

45

is assumed to be greater for presented than for nonpresented items, and the difference between the familiarity of each type (both of which vary in a Gaussian fashion) is equal to $d'$ (see Tanner & Swets, 1954). The signal-detection parameter, $d'$, then, is taken as a measure of retention independent of response bias and reflecting in this model stored episodic information. In some situations, a decision can be made on the basis of a familiarity check, alone. Such situations are described by Atkinson and Juola (1974) as generally occurring early in an experiment in which the test items are well learned.

In situations in which the test words are less well learned or the test words and distractors less easily discriminable, test words will be subject to further, semantic, processing. In such cases, a particular decision (for example, "old or new") is assumed to be based not only on the episodic features inferred from the presented stimuli but also on *a priori* information already resident in semantic memory.

If time and circumstances permit semantic processing to take place, the outcome of such processing will influence both familiarity and the position of the criterion applied to determine the response made. That is, semantic processing allows the comparison of a name as well as a sensory code in determining familiarity. Such processing also allows the subject to make use of what he knows of the language. In the remainder of this paper, criterion bias will be taken to be the ratio of the ordinates of the trace-strength distributions of presented and nonpresented items, or that point on the familiarity (*strength*) axis above which a subject will make a positive recognition response.

The successes and failures of signal-detection theory as an approach to memory have been chronicled by many (for example, Banks, 1970; Lockhart & Murdock, 1970; Broadbent, 1971). The current model is employing signal-detection theory as a convenience and the parameters $d'$ and $\beta$ as descriptive indexes. Other statistical decision theories (for example, Luce's choice model, 1959) can be used as well and in some instances (when the subject is required to recognize one of many words, for instance) may be more useful. The important theoretical point is that the underlying processes of filtering and pigeonholing are identified with episodic and semantic memory, respectively, and that changes in one or the other system will be mirrored by changes in sensitivity and bias selectively.

Given this model of the decision process in recognition, certain inferences follow. If semantic memory operates so as to influence one's decision criterion, then experimental manipulations designed to affect semantic processing (orienting instructions, distractions, and so on) should

46

primarily affect response-bias indexes. On the other hand, manipulations that make nonpresented test words difficult to differentiate from presented words should affect only sensitivity.

We next turn to the results of some experiments that bear upon the model.


THE DECISION MODEL:  EVIDENCE FROM EXPERIMENTS ON THE RECOGNITION OF WORDS AND NAMES

*THE EFFECT OF NAME FREQUENCY*

Evidence directly applicable to the model developed here has been provided by Ingleby (1973a), who investigated memory for common English surnames when these names belonged to the characters in brief, meaningful stories. In both a recall and a recognition test, common names were more easily remembered than rare names. Knowledge of what constitutes a rare or common name is the sort of information one would expect to reside in semantic memory. Thus, the advantage of common names is the result of semantic memory's contribution to the task.

The predictions of the decision model in this situation are clear. Assuming that common and rare names do not differ much in their pronounceability or in any other temporal or physical quality (about this, more later), we should not expect to find any differences in the familiarity of their episodic-memory traces $(d')$. Rather, the advantage found for common names should be the result of a lower criterion for the recognition of such names. Indeed, Ingleby's results support such a view. Common names were more accurately recognized not because they were easier to retain (in fact, $d'$ was actually lower for such names) but because of a lower value of $\beta$. The influence of semantic knowledge resident in memory before the experiment was not to alter the strength of the episodic-memory store but rather to bias the respondent toward certain, but not other, responses.

Ingleby's finding was replicated for American surnames and extended in the author's laboratory (Schwartz, 1974a). Reasoning that any interference with processing the stories semantically would be mirrored by changes in $\beta$, the author repeated the experiment but added moderate or loud white noise during the period when subjects were first listening to the stories. If the noise made it more difficult to hear the stories, then the subjects would have to spend a great deal of processing time and capacity trying to make out and encode the episodic information. Thus, they would have little

47

time for semantic processing; and if semantic processing is not accomplished, semantic memory cannot tribute the bias toward common names reported by Ingleby. That this was indeed the case is illustrated in Figure 2. Whereas β was lower for common than for rare names in the no-noise condition, the biases were equal for both types in the high-noise condition. The results of both Ingleby's and Schwartz's studies support the view that semantic memory contributes, in recognition experiments, criterion values for recognition decisions. In the same vein, interference with semantic processes has the effect of influencing the value of the decision criterion.

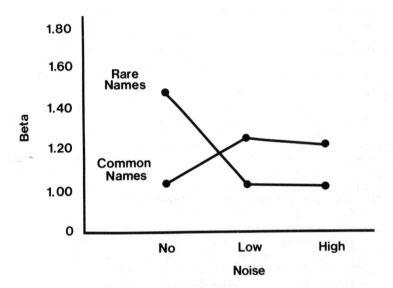

*Fig. 2. Beta as a function of name type and noise (reprinted from Schwartz, 1974a, Journal of Experimental Psychology, with permission).*

## THE EFFECT OF WORD FREQUENCY

That word recognition of common names should be superior to recognition of rare names seems consistent with most research on the perception of words (for example, Howes & Solomon, 1951). In memory, however, it has been widely reported (see, particularly, Kintsch, 1970) that rare words are more easily recognized than common words. Granted, there

48

are some differences between surnames and meaningful words, but there are many similarities as well, and the effect of word (or name) frequency deserves closer scrutiny.

The decision model employed here would predict better memory for rare than for common names or words when recognition is based primarily on the filtering of episodic information. The reason for such a prediction will become clear if we re-examine the results of Ingleby's study more closely. In his experiment the advantage given to common names was solely a function of response bias (rare names were reluctantly used as responses). Without this bias, rare names would have been recognized more accurately than common names because the former were better preserved ($d'$ was higher for rare names).[1] Thus, in those circumstances in which differences in $d'$ are very large or when the differences in criterion for rare and common names are small, the model predicts better recognition for rare than for common names. In other situations (Ingleby's, for one), common names are better recognized. Therefore, if we employ the present model, we would expect both types of results; and, in fact, the literature is contradictory with regard to the word-frequency effect in recognition memory, with some studies reporting better recognition of common (or familiar) words (for example, Kinsbourne & George, 1974).

As the poor recognition of common names and words (when such recognition occurs) is dependent, in the present view, on a lower sensitivity for common than for uncommon items, it is important to determine what support other than Ingleby's finding for names exists for such a contention. Support can be found not only in experiments employing both rare and common words (for example, Schulman, 1974, in Figure 2 reported a lower level of $d'$ for common than for rare words) but also in the results of experiments in which the situational frequency of words was manipulated. For example, Kinsbourne and George (1974) noted that words exposed for an ostensibly unrelated reason prior to a learning task were poorly recognized in comparison to words not pre-exposed. In a very similar experiment Ingleby (1973b, Exp. III) found the result to be due to a lower level of $d'$ for previously presented words. It seems well established, then, that whether frequency is taken to be the result of a word's probability

---

[1]In Schwartz's study, $d'$ for rare and common names did not, as in Ingleby's study, differ. Unfortunately, Schwartz did not control for size or difficulty in pronouncing names. The failure to control for such differences resulted in the rare names' being considerably more difficult to pronounce and makes the findings with respect to $d'$ problematic.

of appearance in the language or whether frequency is manipulated within an experiment, the result is to produce a lower level of sensitivity for frequent words.

The reason that $d'$ should be lower for common than for rare words is not at all clear. One possibility is that individuals are more skilled at encoding the perceptible aspects of common words because they have done so more often and, therefore, devote more time to the details of rare words. One pre-exposure, however, is all that is necessary to create the word-frequency effect (see, for example, Kinsbourne & George, 1974), and it is not obvious that one presentation can result in this sort of "habituation." Moreover, frequent words are better *recalled* than rare words (Kintsch, 1970) and, therefore, must be encoded at least as well. The possibility of some complex proactive-inhibition (PI) mechanism cannot be discounted, although none of the present PI theories can account for the observed pattern of results (Ingleby, 1973b).

One thing is clear. For whatever reason, common words and names are recognized poorly because of lower levels of $d'$ for such items. It is still possible that common names and words will, in the present model, be better remembered than rare ones when the response bias in favor of such (common) responses over-rides the effects of lowered sensitivity. One way in which to accomplish such a result is to use as rare words only those that subjects find truly unfamiliar, thus eliminating the effect of semantic memory. That is, words whose correct meaning is unclear should be used. Such words should have very low biases in comparison with familiar words and will not be recognized as well as common words. Lowenthal and Gibbs (1974) have, in fact, reported better recognition for familiar than for unfamiliar words, with the bias in favor of common words primarily responsible for the result.

The results of recognition experiments using single words or names support the decision model for recognition proposed here. Knowledge about the language and about the meaning of words influences recognition by determining the value of the decision criterion applied to the familiarity axis of episodic traces in order to determine the response made.

## THE EFFECT OF INPUT MODALITY

The effect of the modality of input (that is, auditory or visual) on subsequent memory has long been a topic of interest to cognitive psychologists. For the most part, this research has focused on such questions as, do the visual and acoustic features of linguistic material persist for more than just a brief time, and, if so, for how long? As noted earlier, recent research indicates that under certain circumstances such modality information does indeed persist.  The results of these studies leave open the question of whether modality information persists as a literal copy of the sensory experience or as some abstract, perhaps semantic, proposition bearing only an indirect relationship to the stimulus.  A recent study by Kirsner (1974) was designed to shed light on this question.

In a continuous-recognition task some words were repeated either in the same modality or in another modality.  In general, intramodality-recognition performance was found superior to intermodality performance.  Arguing that such repetition should be unimportant if modality is stored in some abstract form, Kirsner took these results as evidence in support of a representational, literal coding hypothesis.  According to the present view, the facilitative effect on recognition of repeating a word in the same modality should be due to filtering (increasing $d'$).  Kirsner's experiment was replicated in the author's laboratory with the addition of requiring that subjects give confidence ratings in their recognition judgments.  In this manner it was possible to estimate $d'$ for both words presented in the same modality and words presented in different modalities.  The results scored for accuracy mirrored Kirsner's, with the same modality presentations producing a facilitative effect.  The signal-detection analysis indicated that higher levels of $d'$ (.83 and .70 for intra and inter modality words respectively) for such words were responsible for the results.  This finding supports the present model.


THE DECISION MODEL:  EVIDENCE FROM EXPERIMENTS ON THE RECOGNITION OF WORD STRINGS AND SENTENCES

The results of experiments concerned with words and names in the preceding section supported the decision model proposed at the outset.  Semantic memory was seen to influence the setting of the decision criterion.  The present section describes experiments dealing with strings of words rather than single words and names.  Similar relationships between semantic memory and criterion and between episodic memory and $d'$ should be demonstrable.

First, let us examine studies concerned with the recognition of word strings which vary with respect to their conformity with linguistic rules.  This sort of research is well typified by an experiment by Marks and Miller (1964). They found normal sentences to be better remembered than anomalous sentences having grammatical structure but no coherent meaning (for example, "Rapid bouquets deter sudden

51

neighbors") and "anagram strings" formed by scrambling the
order of words in normal sentences. Poorest recall was
obtained for lists of haphazardly ordered random words. The
decision model developed here would see this result as reflecting the input of semantic memory and, therefore, should
be mirrored by a lower criterion for sentences than for
anomalous sentences and anagram strings and a much lower
criterion than for random-word lists. A recognition-memory
version of this experiment (using three of the four types
of word strings but omitting anagram strings) reported by
Slamecka (1969), however, reported that sensitivity differed
for the various types of word strings and that this was
responsible for the finding that grammatical sentences were
better recalled than anomalous sentences or word strings. As
this result appears to be in conflict with the decision model,
it deserves closer scrutiny. Slamecka did not report estimates of $\beta$, but these are relatively easy to obtain from his
MOC curves, and they appear in Table 1. (The values of $\beta$
calculated from group data only offer approximations to the
actual values obtained when individual subject's data are
used.)

TABLE 1
*Estimates of Beta from Slamecka's MOC Curves (1969)*

| Criterion level | Sentence type | | |
| --- | --- | --- | --- |
| | Grammatical | Ungrammatical (random words) | Anomalous |
| 1 | 2.31 | 2.67 | 3.90 |
| 2 | .90 | 1.33 | 1.44 |
| 3 | .74 | .88 | 1.00 |
| 4 | .45 | .67 | .55 |

Note.--These values are estimated from graphs of MOC curves
and may, therefore, be slightly inaccurate. Lower values
represent more risky criteria.

Table 1 indicates that at each of the four criterion levels
subjects employed a riskier criterion for sentences than for
either anomalous sentences or random-word strings. Contrary
to expectation, however, subjects did not show a response bias
toward anomalous sentences. In fact, $\beta$ was in three out of
four cases actually higher (more conservative) for anomalous
sentences than for random-word strings. Memory for normal
sentences, then, was facilitated by a greater sensitivity for
such sentences and by a response bias in their favor, whereas

memory for anomalous sentences was superior to random-word strings because of a greater sensitivity to the anomalous sentences.

According to the current model, response bias is the contribution of semantic memory. The sensitivity differences obtained for normal and anomalous sentences must be due to some features of their episodic traces. The current thesis is that it is not the semantic components of normal and anomalous sentences that resulted in the obtained differences in $d'$ but their syntactic structure--their word order. If word order can be viewed as an episodic feature, with certain word orders easier to retain than other word orders (even when meaning is missing, as in the case of anomalous sentences), then interference with semantic processing should adversely affect normal-sentence recognition by eliminating response bias but should not affect the recognition of anomalous sentences. In another study performed in the author's laboratory (Schwartz, 1974b), all four types of visually presented strings were used in a recall task. One-half of the subjects viewed the strings with a background of loud, extraneous, unpredictable white noise, while the other half viewed the strings in silence. Noise reduced the ability subsequently to recall normal sentences to the level of recall for anomalous sentences (see Figure 3). A second recognition test using the same procedure produced similar results, with the effects clearly due to a diminishing of the bias toward sentences in noise. These findings, in total, support the contention that in recognition memory, semantic memory serves to bias the respondent toward certain (in this case, meaningful sentences) responses.

Perhaps an even better example of the same phenomenon is illustrated by a study reported by Schwartz and Witherspoon (1974). This study involved the replication and modification of experiments originally reported by Bransford and Franks (1971). In the study complex sentences (henceforth referred to as "level-four," or L-4, sentences because each expressed four independent ideas) were broken down into simpler constituent sentences, each expressing either one (L-1), two (L-2), or three (L-3) of the original four ideas. Some of these sentences were presented during an acquisition phase and some, including the original L-4 sentences, were presented only in a recognition phase. New sentences (those appearing only in recognition) were frequently misidentified as having appeared during acquisition. In addition, subjects were most confident of having previously encountered those new sentences that contained all of the semantic information acquired during acquisition. Thus, L-4 sentences, containing four of the ideas conveyed in simpler form during acquisition,

53

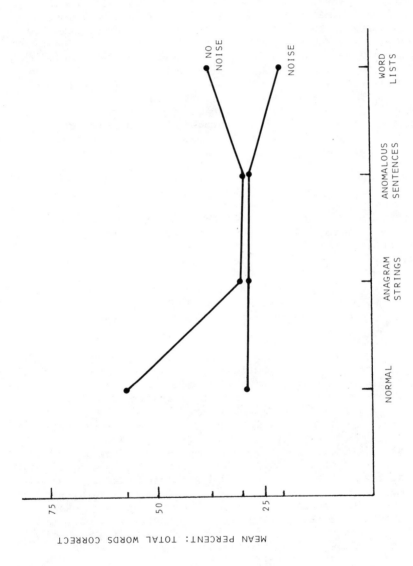

MEAN PERCENT: TOTAL WORDS CORRECT

*Fig. 3. Mean percent of the total words correct for each sentence type in each noise condition. (Each point represents the mean taken across trials.)*

54

although never actually presented, were likely to be mis-identified as "old" with high confidence. New sentences expressing three of the ideas (L-3's) were misidentified with somewhat less confidence, L-2's with still less confidence, and L-1 sentences with the least confidence of all. Replications of this study by Cofer and his associates (1973) have demonstrated the reliability of this finding.

The present decision model also predicts that the sentences from the various levels should differ in response bias. As the sentences are processed by semantic memory, the information contained in these sentences is related to knowledge already resident in memory. Inferences from and interpretations of the input sentences are also made (Bransford & Johnson, 1973). These inferences and interpretations will result in a bias toward recognizing any sentence that conveys the ideas of the original sentences. Schwartz and Witherspoon also found evidence for just such a bias in favor of more complex (informative) sentences (see Figure 4). Additional support for the decision model derives from another experiment (Schwartz & Maney, 1975). Meaningful stories were presented aurally, one sentence at a time. In a subsequent recognition task, sentences that were never presented in the original story were misrecognized if they were deductions from these stories (see Bransford & Johnson, 1973). The misrecognition rate was, as one would expect from the present model, the result of a response bias in favor of such deductions and not to any differences in $d'$.

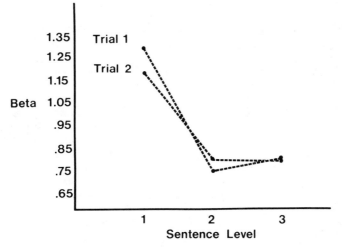

*Fig. 4. Beta as a function of sentence level for two trials (reprinted from Schwartz and Witherspoon, 1974, Bulletin of the Psychonomic Society, with permission).*

Experiments on word strings, then, yield results consistent with experiments on words and names and in line with the decision model. In both cases the episodic store contributes a trace which consists of the perceptible and temporal qualities of the input, as well as, in some cases, a semantic code and the semantic store contributes a criterion for responding.

## RELATIONSHIPS BETWEEN THE DECISION MODEL AND OTHER VIEWS OF MEMORY

### A LEVELS-OF-ANALYSIS FRAMEWORK

In several recent articles (Craik, 1973; Craik & Lockhart, 1972), Craik and his colleagues have developed a levels-of-analysis framework for memory research. Within this framework, input events are seen as undergoing a hierarchical series of analyses. At each level of analysis, different information is extracted, and different encoding procedures are performed. The hierarchy runs from the early analysis of physical features to later, more complex analyses involving semantic processing. One of the products of these analyses is a memory trace which endures in memory as a function of the depth of the analyses performed.

The present decision model also sees input as passing through stages of analyses and also sees semantic analyses as usually following an analysis of perceptual features. The decision model presented here is somewhat more explicit as to the precise contribution of semantic memory.

There are some important differences between the two points of view, however. For instance, whereas Craik (1973) seems to think of the products of superficial (perceptual) analyses as usually transitory, the present view is quite the contrary. Moreover, and perhaps more important, the idea that the more analyses (actually, to be precise, the greater depth of analyses) performed on input material the better one's memory for such material will be does not follow from the decision model developed here. That is, for rare names and words, at least, the result of more complete semantic processing is not better recognition (when compared with common words). Moreover, semantic processing (a deep level of analysis) may result, in some circumstances, in a large number of errors in recall (see, for example, Bransford & Franks, 1971; Schwartz & Witherspoon, 1974) not easily discriminable from the material actually presented.

*THE IMPORTANCE OF ENCODING SPECIFICITY*

It is clear that the ability to recognize a word studied earlier is highly dependent on both the context during learning and the context during testing. In attempting to explain the effect of context, Tulving and Thomson (1973) introduced their encoding-specificity principle, which asserts that "only that can be retrieved which has been stored, and how it can be retrieved depends on how it was stored (p. 359)." To-be-remembered words are thought to be stored (in a manner similar to the present view) as higher-order episodic units, and only elements of the episodic unit can access the unit (see Tulving, 1972). This view has been challenged by others, most recently be Reder, Anderson, and Bjork (1974). In experiments employing both rare and common words, they found that changing the cues accompanying to-be-remembered words during testing from those present during learning will adversely affect the recognition of common (when the change is from a cue that suggests an obscure meaning of the word to one suggesting a common meaning) but not rare words. This finding was taken to indicate that recognition involves remembering a particular sense of a word rather than the phonemic or orthographic characteristics of the word.

Ultimately, the question of what is retained can only be answered by examining signal detection measures, since, in many situations false-positive reports and omissions may also contribute to the accuracy score, simple-recognition accuracy does not tell us whether the effect of changing cues accompanying to-be-remembered words affects retention or response bias. From the point of view of the present model, such information is, of course, crucial because both types of information are thought to affect accuracy, but in quite different ways.

In a similar study, Hunt and Ellis (1974) found that changing the cues accompanying to-be-remembered words adversely affected recognition (at least as compared with an unchanged cue condition). In this study, however, no difference was found between new cues which altered the meaning of a to-be-remembered word and new cues which left the original meaning unchanged. These findings suggest that more than just the meaning of words is involved in recognition memory. From the point-of-view of the present model, both sets of findings are explicable and quite predictable. If we assume that what is remembered in the situation are both the sensory-temporal characteristics of the cue and the target word and their meanings a change in one or the other would be expected to adversely affect recall. In the experiments reported by Reder et al. all to-be-remembered words were paired with weak cues during learning in order to give common words obscure interpretations. As rare words, or at least, rare meanings, were all that were encountered during learning, subjects may have been reluctant to give common word meanings as responses during testing. Such a response bias could have resulted in greater recognition accuracy for rare words, not because such words were better retained (because their meanings were unchanged), but because of a cautious decision criterion for common words at the time of testing. The Hunt and Ellis study did not employ only rare meanings and, therefore, no such bias developed. Without such a selective response bias, the change in meaning exerted no greater effect on recognition accuracy than any other change in cue.

## CONCLUSIONS

In summary, the decision model developed here is suggested as an appropriate framework for the study of recognition. The present chapter has not addressed itself to other types of memory tasks. Needless to say, the simple model developed here will have to be expanded and made more complicated if it is to deal with the complexities of behavior in other memory situations. In recall, for example, it is clear that semantic memory can be searched and the information contained therein used as responses. Even in recall, however, some of the same mechanisms described in this chapter with respect to recognition operate.

Among the questions that remain to be answered are these: First, how is information stored in semantic memory transformed into response biases? Second, how can these biases be modified? Also unknown are the factors determining how response biases are related to input contextual events. Nevertheless, the model as described here accounts for a variety of experimental results and can serve as a framework for further theoretical development.

A more complete mathematical presentation has been foregone here because of the difficulties involved in judging (beforehand) the influence of semantic memory. It may be possible, for small vocabularies, in well-learned situations, to describe a model that can be tested. Such work, however, must await future efforts.

## REFERENCES

Anderson, J. R.  Verbatim and propositional representation of sentences in immediate and long-term memory. *Journal of Verbal Learning and Verbal Behavior*, 1974, *13*, 149-166.

Atkinson, R. C., & Juola, J. F.  Search and decision processes in recognition memory.  In D. H. Krantz, R. D. Luce, R. C. Atkinson, & P. Suppes (Eds.), *Learning, memory and thinking*. San Francisco:  W. H. Freeman, 1974.

Banks, W. P.  Signal detection theory and human memory. *Psychological Bulletin*, 1970, *74*, 81-99.

Bransford, J. D., & Franks, J. J.  The abstraction of linguistic ideas.  *Cognitive Psychology*, 1971, *2*, 331-350.

Bransford, J. D., & Johnson, M. K.  Considerations of some problems of comprehension.  In W. G. Chase (Ed.), *Visual information processing*.  New York:  Academic Press, 1973.

Broadbent, D. E.  *Decision and stress*.  London:  Academic Press, 1971.

Brockway, J., Chmielewski, D., & Cofer, C. N.  Remembering prose:  Productivity and accuracy constraints in recognition memory.  *Journal of Verbal Learning and Verbal Behavior*, 1974, *13*, 194-208.

Cofer, C. N.  Constructive processes in memory.  *American Scientist*, 1973, *61*, 537-543.

Craik, F. I. M.  A "levels of analysis" view of memory. In P. Pliner, L. Krames, & T. Alloway (Eds.), *Communication and affect:  Language and thought*.  New York:  Academic Press, 1973.

Craik, F. I. M., & Lockhart, R. S.  Levels of processing:  A framework for memory research.  *Journal of Verbal Learning and Verbal Behavior*, 1972, *11*, 671-684.

Hintzman, D. L., Block, R. A., & Inskeep, N. R.  Memory for mode of input.  *Journal of Verbal Learning and Verbal Behavior*, 1972, *11*, 741-749.

Howes, D. H., & Solomon, R. L.  Visual duration threshold as a function of word probability.  *Journal of Experimental Psychology*, 1951, *41*, 401-410.

Hunt, R. R., & Ellis, H. C.  Recognition memory and degree of semantic contextual change.  *Journal of Experimental Psychology*, 1974, *103*, 1153-1159.

Hyde, T. S., & Jenkins, J. J.  Recall for words as a function of semantic, graphic, and syntactic orienting tasks. *Journal of Verbal Learning and Verbal Behavior*, 1973, *12*, 471-480.

Ingleby, J. D.  A test of current explanations of the effect of item familiarity on memory.  *Quarterly Journal of Experimental Psychology*, 1973, *25*, 378-386.  (a)

Ingleby, J. D.   The use of the $d'$ statistic in interpreting the nature of proactive interference in short-term memory. *British Journal of Psychology*, 1973, *64*, 521-529.   (b)

Kinsbourne, M., & George, J.   The mechanism of the word-frequency effect on recognition memory.   *Journal of Verbal Learning and Verbal Behavior*, 1974, *13*, 63-69.

Kintsch, W.   Models for free recall and recognition.   In D. A. Norman (Ed.), *Models of human memory*.   New York:   Academic Press, 1970.

Kirsner, K.   An analysis of the visual component in recognition memory for verbal stimuli.   *Memory and Cognition*, 1973, *1*, 449-453.

Kirsner, K.   Modality differences in recognition memory for words and their attributes.   *Journal of Experimental Psychology*, 1974, *102*, 579-584.

Kolers, P. A.   Remembering operations.   *Memory and Cognition*, 1973, *1*, 347-355.

Lockhart, R. S., & Murdock, B. B.   Memory and the theory of signal detection.   *Psychological Bulletin*, 1970, *74*, 100-109.

Lowenthal, K., & Gibbs, G.   Word familiarity and retention. *Quarterly Journal of Experimental Psychology*, 1974, *26*, 15-25.

Luce, R. D.   *Individual choice behavior*.   New York:   Wiley, 1959.

Luria, A.   *The mind of a mnemonist*.   New York:   Basic Books, 1968.

Marks, L. E., & Miller, G. A.   The role of semantic and syntactic constraints in the memorization of English sentences.   *Journal of Verbal Learning and Verbal Behavior*, 1964, *3*, 1-5.

Neisser, U.   *Cognitive psychology*.   New York:   Appleton-Century-Crofts, 1967.

Nelson, D. L., & Brooks, D. H.   Relative effectiveness of rhymes and synonyms as retrieval cues.   *Journal of Experimental Psychology*, 1974, *102*, 277-283.

Reder, L. M., Anderson, J. R., & Bjork, R. A.   A semantic interpretation of encoding specificity.   *Journal of Experimental Psychology*, 1974, *102*, 648-656.

Schulman, A. I.   The declining course of recognition memory. *Memory and Cognition*, 1974, *2*, 14-18.

Schwartz, S.   Arousal and recall:   Effects of noise on two retrieval strategies.   *Journal of Experimental Psychology*, 1974, *102*, 896-898.   (a)

Schwartz, S.  The effects of arousal on recall, recognition, and the organization of memory.  Unpublished paper, Northern Illinois University, 1974.  (b)

Schwartz, S., & Maney, J.  Individual differences in cognitive processes:  Some relationships between verbal ability and memory for prose.  Paper presented at the annual meeting of the Midwestern Psychological Association, Chicago, May, 1975.

Schwartz, S., & Witherspoon, K. D.  Decision processes in memory:  Factors influencing the storage and retrieval of linguistic and form information.  *Bulletin of the Psychonomic Society*, 1974, *4*, 127-129.

Slamecka, N. J.  Recognition of word strings as a function of linguistic violations.  *Journal of Experimental Psychology*, 1969, *79*, 377-378.

Tanner, W. P., & Swets, J. A.  A decision-making theory of visual detection.  *Psychological Review*, 1954, *61*, 401-409.

Thomson, D. M., & Tulving, E.  Associative encoding and retrieval:  Weak and strong cues.  *Journal of Experimental Psychology*, 1970, *86*, 255-262.

Tulving, E.  Episodic and semantic memory.  In E. Tulving & W. Donaldson (Eds.), *Organization of memory*.  New York: Academic Press, 1972.

Tulving, E., & Thomson, D. M.  Encoding specificity and retrieval processes in episodic memory.  *Psychological Review*, 1973, *80*, 352-373.

## 4.   FORMAL MODELS OF DILEMMAS IN SOCIAL DECISION-MAKING

*Robyn M. Dawes*
University of Oregon and Oregon Research Institute

Introduction                                          88
Social Dilemma: A Formal Definition                   89
The Commons Dilemma                                   97
References                                            106

## INTRODUCTION

Social dilemmas are easy to invent. Consider a game in which each of three participants must place either a blue poker chip or a red poker chip in an envelope in private. Each participant who places a blue chip in the envelope receives $1, and his choice has no effect on the other two participants. Each one who places a red chip in the envelope receives $2, and the other two are fined $1 each for this choice. (Equivalently, that individual receives $3 and then pays his share of a $3 fine assessed on the group as a whole.) Which chip should each participant choose? No matter what the other two people do, each is $1 better off choosing a red chip; moreover, the choice of the red chip is the only guarantee against losing money. But if all choose the red chip, no one gets anything; while if all had chosen the blue, each would have received $1.

Social dilemmas--which are often described as involving a conflict between "individual rationality" and "group rationality"--have become of increasing interest to both social scientists and laymen. Overpopulation and pollution are two dramatic examples of particular interest. Mathematically oriented psychologists and sociologists have developed formal models (usually algebraic or geometric) of social dilemmas. This chapter attempts a systematic review and integration of such models. Drawing heavily on the work of Hamburger (1973) and Schelling (1973), the chapter is an attempt both to integrate their work and to delineate its relationship to a "commons-dilemma game" devised by the author. In particular, three dilemma games discussed by other authors and the commons-dilemma games are proved to be equivalent.

The simplest social dilemma is one involving two people, the well-known *prisoner's dilemma*. In the example from which it draws its name, the dilemma concerns two men who are known to have robbed a bank, who have been taken prisoner, but who cannot be convicted without a confession from one or both. The law-enforcement people offer each an identical proposition: If you confess and your partner does not, you will go free, and he will be sent to jail for 10 years. If you both confess, you will both be sent to jail for five years. If neither of you confesses, you will both go to jail for a single year on a lesser charge. Each prisoner is now asked to consider his own best interests in light of what the other may do. If the other confesses, each is better off confessing, for then he will go to jail for five years rather than 10; if the other does not confess, each is still better off confessing, for then he will go free rather than go to jail for a year. Hence, the strategy of confessing is better in both circumstances; it is termed a *dominating strategy*. Both prisoners would be better off, however, if neither confessed; hence, simultaneous choice of the dominating strategies (confession) leads to a *deficient equilibrium*, a result that is less preferred by both prisoners than is the result that would occur if neither chose his dominating strategy--that is, if neither confessed. This result is termed in "equilibrium" because neither prisoner is motivated to change his choice given that the other has confessed.

In the game considered at the beginning of this chapter, the dominating strategy is choosing the red chip, and the resulting deficient equilibrium is that no one gets anything-- while if all had chosen the blue chip, all would have received a dollar.

## SOCIAL DILEMMA: A FORMAL DEFINITION

In general, a *social dilemma* can be defined as *a situation in which each player has a dominating strategy and in which the choice of dominating strategies results in a deficient equilibrium*. This definition can easily be stated formally when each player has a choice between two strategies (or choices of action) and all players have the same payoff structure, one that depends only on the number of people who choose the dominating strategy [condition (1) in Schelling's 1973 article]. Although the concept of social dilemma does not require that choice is limited to two alternatives or that all players have the same payoff structure, most formal theoretical work is within this framework.

Consider that each of $N$ players has a choice between two strategies, $D$ and $C$ ($D$ for "defecting" and $C$ for "cooperating"). Let $D(m)$ be the player's payoff for a $D$ choice when $m$ players choose $C$, and let $C(m)$ be the payoff for a $C$ choice when $m$ choose $C$.[1] A *social-dilemma game* is one in which:

$$D(m) > C(m + 1); \qquad\qquad (1)$$

[Hamburger's condition P3,
Schelling's condition (2)]

---

[1]The $m$ refers to the *number* of players who choose $C$, not to a particular set of $m$ players. When $m$ players choose $C$ (that is, cooperate), $N - m$ choose $D$ (that is, defect). Payoffs could be expressed in terms of the number of defectors rather than the number of cooperators--and such a choice has seemed more natural to many readers of earlier versions of this paper--but number of cooperators has been chosen in order to be consistent with past authors.

that is, whenever any number $m$ of other people choose $C$, each player is better off choosing $D$ than choosing $C$ and becoming the $m + 1$st cooperator, and

$$C(N) > D(0). \tag{2}$$

(Hamburger's condition P7)

Conditions (1) and (2) guarantee that $D$ is a dominating strategy that results in a deficient equilibrium.

Hamburger (1973) has discussed these conditions at length in relation to other conditions.

Two other aspects of most social dilemmas are that both the individuals in the society and the society as a whole are better off the more people who cooperate. In the present context of two-choice games with identical outcome structure across players, these conditions can be expressed as:

$$D(m + 1) > D(m) \tag{3}$$

and

$$C(m + 1) > C(m),$$

[Schelling's condition (3)]

and

$$(m + 1)C(m + 1) + (N - m - 1)D(m + 1) \tag{4}$$
$$> mC(m) + (N - m)D(m).$$

(Hamburger's condition P12)

Conditions (1) and (2) guarantee only that $D$ is a dominating choice for everyone and that the *end result* of everyone's choosing $D$ is deficient. They do not in and of themselves imply conditions (3) and (4). In fact, as will be demonstrated shortly, games can satisfy (1), (2), and (3) but not (4), or they can satisfy (1), (2), and (4) but not (3).

Two-person prisoner's dilemmas do necessarily satisfy condition (3) because by conditions (1) and (2), $D(0) > C(1)$, $D(1) > C(2)$, and $C(2) > D(0)$; it follows that $C(2) > C(1)$ and $D(1) > D(0)$. They do not, however, necessarily satisfy condition (4).[2]

---

[2]Some theorists, for example, Rapoport and Chammah (1965) in their classic book on prisoner's dilemmas, require that $2C(2) > C(1) + D(1)$--in which case condition (4) is satisfied. The reason for this requirement is that the outcome yielding $C(1)$ and $D(1)$ may be preferable to that yielding $C(2)$ to each player if the subjects are permitted to redistribute the payoffs after the game or if the subjects may play the game many times and alternate who gets the $C(1)$ payoff and who gets the

As shown by Schelling (1973), two-choice games can be simply and neatly characterized by graphing $D(m)$ and $C(m)$ as a
function of $m$, an empirical demonstration appearing in Kelley
and Grzelak (1972).  Condition (1) is then that the curve for
$D$ at point $m$ must always lie above that for $C$ *at point* m + 1.
[There is occasionally some confusion here; it is not enough
that the curve for $D$ simply dominate that for $C$; rather, it is
at the point at which a player may choose to become the
$m$ + 1st cooperator that $D(m)$ must dominate.]  Condition (2) is
that the end point on the $C$ curve must be higher than the 0
point on the $D$ curve.  Condition (3) stipulates that both
curves must be monotone, and condition (4) involves a rather
complex averaging property.  An example of $C$ and $D$ curves'
satisfying conditions (1) through (4) is given in Figure 1.
[Note that it is necessary to specify some metric on the
absyssa in order to ensure that condition (1) is satisfied.]

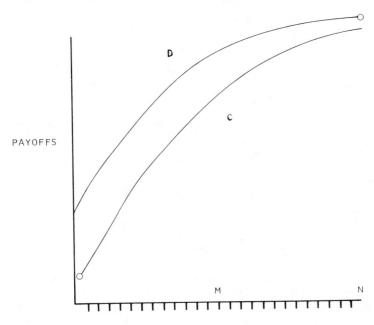

*Fig. 1.  A social-dilemma game satisfying
conditions (1) through (4).*

$D(1)$ payoff.  Neither possibility is considered in this
chapter; hence, this inequality is not used in the definition
of a prisoner's dilemma.

Figure 2 represents a game in which conditions (1), (2), and (3) are met but (4) is not.

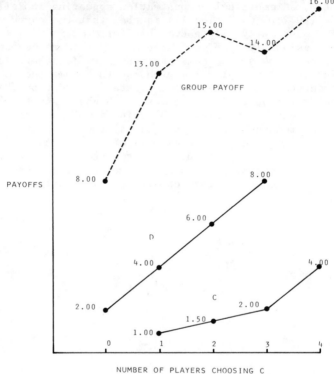

Fig. 2.  A four-person social-dilemma game satisfying conditions (1), (2), and (3) but not (4).

In contrast, condition (4) implies condition (2).

*Proof*:  By condition (4), society as a whole is better off if one player chooses $C$ than if none does.  That is, $C(1) + (N - 1)D(1) > ND(0)$.  Again by condition (4), society is better off if two players choose $C$ than if one does.  That is, $2C(2) + (N - 2)D(2) > C(1) + (N - 1)D(1)$.  Iterating and combining inequalities yield $NC(N) > ND(0)$, which reduces to (2) by dividing by $N$.

Figure 3 represents a game in which conditions (1), (2), and (4) are met but (3) is not.

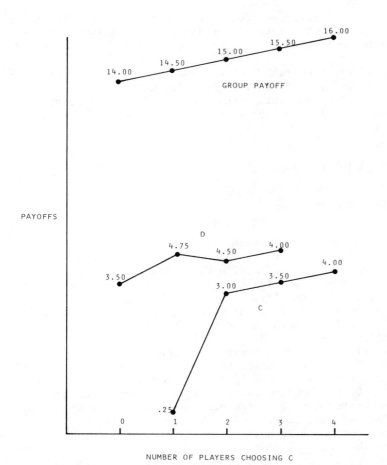

*Fig. 3.   A four-person social-dilemma game
satisfying conditions (1), (2), and (4) but
not (3).*

One type of social-dilemma game of particular interest is
that which generalizes a two-person *separable prisoner's
dilemma*.  A prisoner's dilemma is defined as *separable* if and
only if:

$$D(1) - C(2) = D(0) - C(1).    \qquad (5)$$

(This is a restriction of Hamburger's
condition P9 to a situation of identical payoff structure for both
players.)

93

That is, the increment for defection is constant whether the other player cooperates [in which case the player receives $D(1)$ for defecting and $C(2)$ for cooperating] or defects [in which case the player receives $D(0)$ or $C(1)$].

The term "separable" comes from Evans and Crumbaugh (1966), Pruitt (1967), and Messick and McClintock (1968), who independently noted that when condition (5) is satisfied, each player's choice of $C$ or $D$ can be conceptualized as choosing between the two options:

$C$:  Give the other player $C(2)$; give me nothing.

$D$:  Give the other player $C(1)$; give me $D(0) - C(1)$.

The outcome is the result of these two *separable* options if and only if:

$$D(1) = D(0) - C(1) + C(2), \qquad (5')$$

which is just a restatement of condition (5)--that is, if and only if the payoff to a single defecting player can be expressed as the sum of $D(0) - C(1)$ from his or her own choice and $C(2)$ from that of the other player. Clearly it is also true that if both players choose $C$, both get $C(2)$ (as a result of the other's choice); if both choose $D$, both receive $D(0)$ [$D(0) - C(1)$ as a result of their own choice and $C(1)$ as a result of the other's], and a single cooperating player gets only $C(1)$ (from the defector's choice).

Consider, for example, the separable two-person prisoner's dilemma game in which $D(1) = 9$, $C(2) = 6$, $D(0) = 3$, and $C(1) = 0$.  A $C$ choice can be conceptualized as having the experimenter give 6 to the other player and a $D$ choice as having the experimenter give the chooser 3 and the other player nothing.  If both choose $D$, both get 3; if one chooses $D$ and the other chooses $C$, the $D$ chooser gets 9 and the other player 0; if both choose $C$, both get 6.  The term "separable" refers to the fact that each choice can be conceptualized as yielding one payoff for the chooser and another for the other player in such a way that the final payoffs are simply the sum of these payoffs.  If, for example, $D(1) \neq 9$ but $C(2)$, $D(0)$, and $C(1)$ were still 6, 3, and 0, respectively, the game could not be separated in the above manner.

Condition (5) can also be restated as

$$D(1) - D(0) = C(2) - C(1), \qquad (5'')$$

which implies that the graph of the game consists of two straight lines of equal slope, as illustrated in Figure 4A. Figure 4B is a graph of a generalization to an $N$-person game in which $C(m)$ and $D(m)$ are linear functions of $m$ with equal slopes.

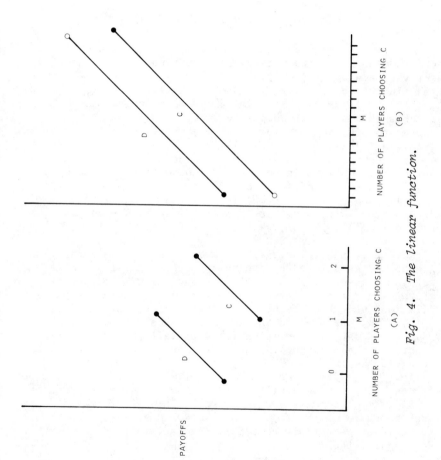

PAYOFFS

NUMBER OF PLAYERS CHOOSING C

(A)

NUMBER OF PLAYERS CHOOSING C

(B)

Fig. 4. The linear function.

Hamburger (1973, p. 38) has proved that games characterized by a graph in which $C(m)$ and $D(m)$ are linear functions correspond to simultaneous prisoner's dilemma games in which each of the $N$ players plays against each of the $N - 1$ others. The payoffs for each of these pairwise prisoner's dilemmas are $D(0)$, $D(1)$, $C(1)$, and $C(2)$ [subject to the usual constraints that $D(0) > C(1)$, $D(1) > C(2)$, and $C(2) > D(0)$], and the equations for $C(m)$ and $D(m)$ are given by

$$C(m) = [C(2) - C(1)]m + C(1)N - C(2) \qquad (6)$$

and

$$D(m) = [D(1) - D(0)]m + D(0)(N - 1).$$

*Proof*: First, each individual who cooperates when $m - 1$ others also cooperate receives $C(2)$ for those games and $C(1)$ for the remaining $(N - 1) - (m - 1) = N - m$ games. Hence, that individual's payoff is $(m - 1)C(2) + (N - m)C(1) = [C(2) - C(1)]m + C(1)N - C(2)$. Similarly, each individual who defects when $m$ others cooperate receives $D(1)$ for those $m$ games and $D(0)$ for the remaining $N - m - 1$; that is, he or she receives $(m)D(1) + (N - m - 1)D(0) = [D(1) - D(0)]m + D(0)(N-1)$. Conversely, if $\alpha$ is the intercept of the $C(m)$ function and $\beta$ the slope, it is possible to solve for $C(1)$ and $C(2)$ in the first part of (6). Specifically, $C(1) = (\alpha + \beta)/(N - 1)$, and $C(2) = (\alpha + N\beta)/(N - 1)$. Similarly, if $\gamma$ is the intercept of $D(m)$ and $\delta$ its slope, $D(0) = \gamma/(N - 1)$, and $D(1) = [\gamma + (N - 1)\delta]/(N - 1)$.

Note that the relationship between games as defined by the graphs and as defined by the pairwise prisoner's dilemmas is *not* independent of $N$; that is, for any pairwise structure there is a different graph depending on $N$, and for graphs with different values of $N$ there are different values of $D(0)$, $D(1)$, $C(1)$, and $C(2)$ in the pairwise games. Note also that such games satisfy condition (3) (trivially, since linear functions are monotone). They need not, however, satisfy condition (4).

*The linear functions* C(m) *and* D(m) *will have the same slope if and only if* C(2) - C(1) = D(1) - D(0)--*that is, if and only if the pairwise games are separable.* It will be proved later that games in which $C(m)$ and $D(m)$ are linear functions with the same slope satisfy condition (4) (a result implicit in Hamburger's theorem 2, p. 34).

An essential equivalence has now been established. *Games described by graphs in which* C(m) *and* D(m) *are linear functions with equal slopes are identical to games in which each player simultaneously plays separable prisoner's dilemmas with each of the remaining N - 1 players.* This equivalence has previously been proved by Hamburger, but it is reiterated here with slightly different proof and terminology because of its importance in what follows.)


## THE COMMONS DILEMMA

Another approach to $N$-person social dilemmas has been taken by Dawes (1973), who proposed a simple algebraic structure for the *commons dilemma* as expounded by Hardin (1968). (This dilemma is based on a somewhat minor point made by Lloyd in 1833 in an essay on population; its exposition and development are due mainly to Hardin.) In the example from which it draws its name, each of 10 people owns one 1,000-pound bull, and all 10 bulls graze upon a common pasture that is capable of sustaining them all. If an additional bull is introduced, the weight of each bull would decrease to 900 pounds; that is, with the introduction of an additional bull, the pasture could support only 9,900 pounds of cattle rather than 10,000. Any individual who introduces an additional bull has increased his wealth by 800 pounds because he now has two 900-pound bulls rather than one 1,000-pound bull. But the total wealth has been reduced by 100 pounds, as has the wealth of each of the other individuals.

This commons dilemma, gain to self with loss shared by everyone, is ubiquitous—especially in large societies. In its most dramatic form it may cause each single soldier to flee from a battle because each reasons that his own participation makes little difference in the final outcome, yet it makes a great difference to him personally, and he thereby ensures rout and disaster for all the soldiers—including himself (unless the soldiers on the other side are equally rational). In a milder form it may result in an academician's securing a job offer from another institution solely to achieve a better salary at his or her own institution. If he or she is successful, colleagues will, of course, suffer through restrictions of funds available to grant them raises, although the adverse effect on each individual will be quite small in a large institution. An intermediate form of the dilemma can be found in people's decisions to obtain unrealistically high payoffs from insurance companies because "after all, the company can afford it" (with the result that everyone's premiums skyrocket). Even the decision to have children can be regarded as involving a commons dilemma (Dawes, Delay, & Chaplin, 1974):

> With the world as our commons, each of us may believe
> he stands to gain (fulfillment, "eternal life,"

companionship and perhaps wealth) by having children, while the loss of each "consumatory and polluting agent" to the commons is clearly distributed among all the living creatures in it, and particularly the other people. That this one type of pollution may underlie most other pollution problems makes the study and resolution of the class of such problems particularly timely [p. 3].

These commons dilemmas all clearly involve two principles: Gain for defection accrues directly to self, and loss, which is greater than gain, is spread out among all the members of the group (for example, commons, society, or world).[3]

Again within the context that each player has a choice between two actions and each has the same payoff structure dependent only on the number of cooperators and defectors, Dawes (1973) has defined the *commons-dilemma game* as follows:

(i)   Each player who chooses $D$ rather than $C$ has his payoff incremented by an amount $d > 0$ above the payoff $C(N)$ for total cooperation.

(ii)   Players are collectively fined $d + \lambda$ ($\lambda > 0$) for each choice of $D$, each player's share of the fine being $(d + \lambda)/N$.

(iii) $d > \lambda/(N - 1)$.

Condition (iii) simply guarantees that the individual's increment for defection is not so small that it is offset by his or her share of the fine.

*Theorem 1:   The commons-dilemma game as defined by conditions (i) through (iii) satisfies conditions (1) through (4).*

Condition (1):   $D(m) = C(N) + d - \dfrac{(N - m)(d + \lambda)}{N}$,

while

$$C(m + 1) = C(N) - \frac{(N - m - 1)(d + \lambda)}{N}.$$

Hence,

$$D(m) - C(m + 1) = d - \frac{d + \lambda}{N} = \frac{(N - 1)d - \lambda}{N},$$

which is greater than 0 by condition (iii).  Note that $D(m) - C(m + 1)$ is independent of $m$.

---

[3]If the loss to society as a whole did not outweigh the benefits to the defector, the result would be merely a redistribution of wealth--perhaps with a net increase.  Such a situation would scarcely constitute a dilemma.

Condition (2): $D(0) = C(N) + d - \dfrac{N(d + \lambda)}{N} = C(N) - \lambda$

$< C(N)$.

Condition (3): $C(m + 1) = C(N) - \dfrac{(N - m - 1)(d + \lambda)}{N}$

$> C(N) - \dfrac{(N - m)(d + \lambda)}{N} = C(m)$

and

$$D(m + 1) = C(N) + d - \dfrac{(N - m - 1)(d + \lambda)}{N}$$

$$> C(N) + d - \dfrac{(N - m)(d + \lambda)}{N} = D(m).$$

Condition (4): Each choice of $D$ decreases the outcome for the players as a whole by an amount $\lambda$.

For example, the game proposed at the beginning of this chapter is a commons-dilemma game in which $C(N) = \$1$, $d = \$2$, and $\lambda = \$1$.

The following theorem establishes that the commons-dilemma game is identical to the two equivalent ones described earlier.

*Theorem 2: Commons-dilemma games, games described by graphs in which* C(m) *and* D(m) *are linear functions with equal slopes, and games in which each player simultaneously plays separable prisoner's dilemma games with each of the* N - 1 *remaining players are all identical.*

*Proof*: Given the previous equivalence, it is necessary only to establish the identity of commons-dilemma games and those described by graphs in which $C(m)$ and $D(m)$ are linear functions with equal slopes.

$$C(m) = C(N) - \dfrac{(N - m)(d + \lambda)}{N} = \left(\dfrac{d + \lambda}{N}\right)m + [C(N) - (d + \lambda)]$$

and

$$D(m) = C(N) + d - \dfrac{(N - m)(d + \lambda)}{N} = \left(\dfrac{d + \lambda}{N}\right)m + [C(N) - \lambda],$$

which shows that $C(m)$ and $D(m)$ are linear functions with equal slopes. Conversely, if $\beta$ is the slope of $C(m)$ and $D(m)$, $\alpha$ is the intercept of $C(m)$, and $\gamma$ is the intercept of $D(m)$, it is possible to solve for $d$, $\lambda$, and $C(N)$. Specifically, $d = \gamma - \alpha$, $\lambda = N\beta + \alpha - \gamma$, and $C(N) = N\beta + \alpha$.

*Corollary 2.1: Since the commons-dilemma game satisfies condition (4), the other two do as well.*

The relationships between the parameters of the three equivalent social-dilemma games are outlined in Table 1.

The commons-dilemma game has a property not found in the other two. Even though it is strictly equivalent for any value of $N$, variation of $N$ defines a whole additional dimension. Thus, while each commons-dilemma game with a given $N$ can be conceptualized as a game whose graph consists of linear functions with equal slopes, the entire class of commons-dilemma games with $d$, $\lambda$, and $C(N)$ fixed but $N$ allowed to vary can be conceptualized as a graph consisting of planes in 3-space--the dimensions being $m$, $N$, and the resulting values of $C(m)$ and $D(m)$.

Moreover, the class of commons-dilemma games formed by fixing $d$, $\lambda$, and $C(N)$ and letting $N$ vary has the property that the degree to which $D(m)$ dominates $C(m + 1)$ increases as a function of $N$. That is,

$$[D(m) - C(m + 1)] \uparrow N. \tag{7}$$

*Proof*: As pointed out in the first part of theorem 1, $D(m) - C(m + 1) = d - (d + \lambda)/N$.

How can the commons-dilemma game have property (7) given that the difference in the intercepts of $D(m)$ and $C(m)$ is always $d$? The answer is that the slope of both functions, $(d + \lambda)/N$, decreases with increasing $N$. [This reason sounds a bit paradoxical at first, but a few moments' thought will reveal that for any given intercept difference, the smaller the slope the larger the difference between $D(m)$ and $C(m + 1)$.]

Property (7) is considered crucial to many people analyzing real-world commons dilemmas--particularly Hardin (1972). The more people among whom the bad consequence of defecting behavior is spread out, the less each individual "suffers the consequences" of his or her own defection.

Another specific game of some interest is *Messick's union game* (Messick, 1973). This game is defined by the following three conditions:

(a) Each member of a potential union of size $N$ must pay a fixed cost $c$ to join.

(b) If the union succeeds in its goal, each member of the potential union (*not* just each member who pays the cost $c$ to join) receives a prize $P$, otherwise nothing.

(c) The probability that the union succeeds in its goal is equal to the number of members of the potential union who join (and pay $c$) divided by $N$.

TABLE 1
*Relationships between the Parameters of Three Social-Dilemma Games*

| Graph Parameters | Pairwise Prisoner's-Dilemma Parameters | Commons-Dilemma Parameters |
| --- | --- | --- |
| $\alpha$ | $C(1)N - C(2)$ | $C(N) - (d + \lambda)$ |
| $\beta$ | $C(2) - C(1) = D(1) - D(0)$ | $(d + \lambda)/N$ |
| $\gamma$ | $D(0)(N - 1)$ | $C(N) - \lambda$ |
| $\delta$ | $C(2) - C(1) = D(1) - D(0)$ | $(d + \lambda)/N$ |
| | | |
| $(\alpha + N\beta)/(N - 1)$ | $C(2)$ | $C(N)/(N - 1)$ |
| $(\alpha + \beta)/(N - 1)$ | $C(1)$ | $C(N)/(N - 1) - (d + \lambda)/N$ |
| $[\gamma + (N - 1)\delta]/(N - 1)$ | $D(1)$ | $(d + \lambda)/N + [C(N) - \lambda]/(N - 1)$ |
| $\gamma/(N - 1)$ | $D(0)$ | $[C(N) - \lambda]/(N - 1)$ |
| | | |
| $N\beta + \alpha$ | $(N - 1)C(2)$ | $C(N)$ |
| $\gamma - \alpha$ | $N[D(0) - C(1)] - C(2) - D(0)$ | $d$ |
| $N\beta + \alpha - \gamma$ | $(N - 1)[C(2) - D(0)]$ | $\lambda$ |

Note.—Throughout, $\beta = \delta$. Further, given that $D(1) - D(0) = D(0) = D(2) - C(1)$, there are only three free parameters in each game.

Suppose, Messick reasons, that $m$ other people have joined the union. The expected value of joining the union when $m$ others have joined is equal to:

$$\left(\frac{m+1}{N}\right) P - c.$$

The expected value of not joining is equal to:

$$\left(\frac{m}{N}\right) P.$$

An expected-value maximizer will then join if and only if:

$$\left(\frac{m+1}{N}\right) P - c - \left(\frac{m}{N}\right) P > 0;$$

that is, if and only if:

$$\frac{P}{N} - c > 0,$$

or equivalently, $P/N > c$ or $P/c > N$.
Note that this result does not depend on $m$.

Now let us reformulate the problem. Let $c$ be regarded as the amount saved by not joining the union (that is, a defecting payoff), and let $(m+1)/N)NP - (m/N)NP = P$ be the expected loss to all the potential union members together from each defection. Thus, $c$ is identified with $d$ in the commons-dilemma game, and $P$ with $d + \lambda$. Hence, the expected-value maximizer will join if and only if:

$$\frac{d + \lambda}{N} - d > 0.$$

That is, the player will refuse to join if and only if:

$$d - \frac{d + \lambda}{N} > 0,$$

or if and only if:

$$d > \frac{\lambda}{N - 1},$$

which is condition (iii) of the commons-dilemma game. That is, condition (iii) guarantees that the result of joining or not on the basis of maximizing expected value is no joining--which establishes a dilemma, because if all joined, all would receive $P - c = d + \lambda - d = \lambda$, whereas if none joined, none would receive anything.

The following theorem has been established:

*Theorem 3: The Messick union game results in a social dilemma for expected-value maximizers if and only if it is equivalent to a commons-dilemma game (hence equivalent to a game whose graph consists of linear functions C(m) and D(m) with equal slopes, hence equivalent to simultaneous separable prisoner's dilemmas in which each player plays against the N - 1 remaining ones).*

*Corollary 3.1: If the Messick union game results in a social dilemma for expected-value maximizers, it satisfies conditions (3), (4), and (7).*

Actually, conditions (3) and (4) are immediate, and condition (7) can be derived easily from Messick's formulation. Messick himself, who is concerned with when his game results in a dilemma for expected-value maximizers, points out that when $P$ and $c$ are held constant, some $N$ is reached at which a dilemma occurs (p. 148).

Olsen (1965) has made a similar argument both with respect to the difficulty of getting laborers to join a union in an open-shop situation and with respect to the difficulty of getting people to contribute to a public good or venture when a large number of contributions is necessary for success. The logic of Olsen's argument is essentially the same as that of Messick's. The main difference in mathematical development is that Olsen proceeds from differential equations (pp. 24-28) and hence considers a larger class of possible functions for determining whether or not an individual should join a union or contribute to a public effort. (Toward the end of his paper, Messick also broadens his scope--by considering probabilities of union success that are monotonic in $m$ but not necessarily linear.) Moreover, Olsen supports his argument with examples from the history of the labor-union movement. The importance and influence of Olsen's work far outweigh its space in this chapter.

Messick and Olsen reach the same conclusions--especially with respect to the importance of $N$. Frolich and Oppenheimer (1970) have challenged the idea that the type of social dilemma discussed by Olsen and others (and outlined in this chapter) necessarily becomes more acute as $N$ increases. They argue that the probability of failing by exactly $k$ units of effort (for example, contributions) should be unrelated to $N$--unless certain assumptions are made about "how subjective probabilities vary from situation to situation [p. 113]." Such an assumption is explicit in Messick's union model and is certainly reasonable in the contexts discussed by Olsen. The probability of failing by exactly $k$ units should decrease with $N$. Isn't it reasonable to assume, for example, that a candidate for the city council has a higher probability of failing by three votes than does a candidate for mayor of the city, who in turn has a higher probability of failing by three votes than does the candidate for governor of the state? Voters are clearly reasonable in assuming that their vote has less

103

effect on the probability of victory for their favorite
gubernatorial candidate than on the probability of victory
for their favorite city-council candidate. Hence, as Messick
and Olsen argue, granted a certain amount of negative value
involved in bothering to go to the poll, the expected value
of voting for a city-council candidate should be greater than
that of voting for a gubernatorial candidate if the success
of each candidate is equally valued.

The four equivalent games (hence single game) described
above are (is) rather restricted. The way in which various
constraints can be relaxed (hence the game generalized) can
best be seen by considering the graph of the functions $C(m)$
and $D(m)$. First, these functions can remain linear but not
have equal slopes; if so, the game is equivalent to one in
which each player is engaged in a *nonseparable* prisoner's
dilemma game with each of the $N - 1$ remaining players.
Monotone but nonlinear functions can describe social dilemmas
which cannot correspond to pairwise prisoner's dilemmas. And
then, of course, it is possible to consider the functions
that do not satisfy one or both of the social-dilemma conditions [(1) and (2)], functions which describe games that lie
beyond the scope of this chapter. Schelling (1973) has
described a wide variety of such functions.

Also, it is possible to relax the assumption that the
payoff structure is the same for all players. If such a
relaxation is made, it is necessary to examine the game in
some detail to see whether in fact it constitutes a social
dilemma. For example, some players may profit so much by
engaging in a defecting strategy and pay so little of the
penalty that the resulting equilibrium is not deficient--
that is, it benefits them although it hurts others severely.
Such players may be analogous, for example, to industries
that share the dirty air they create with the rest of us
but profit much more greatly per unit of pollution they create
than we could by creating the same unit. Or perhaps their
unit profit is the same, but they pay the same fraction of
the price as do the other "players," despite owning more units.

In general, it is possible to create a wide variety of
$N$-person social-dilemma games; all that must be guaranteed
is that conditions (1) and (2) are met. The game discussed
in the bulk of this chapter captures many characteristics of
the real-world social dilemmas that motivate the study of
experimental dilemmas; for example, conditions (3) and (4)
seem ubiquitous in these real-world dilemmas--as does condition (7) when size varies. Moreover, the game can be presented in a variety of ways: in terms of the graph of the
payoff function for $C(m)$ and $D(m)$, in terms of the prisoner's
dilemma, or in terms of the gain-for-self-loss-spread-out

principle. (Whether different presentations result in different behaviors is an empirical question which may be of interest at least to propagandists.) As Goehring (1974) has noted,
"a parsimonious representation of the $N$-player prisoner
dilemma game matrix is possible if restrictions are imposed
upon payoffs such that the incentive for defection and the
payoff decrement incurred by individual players per player
choosing his defection strategy are constant values independent of player identifications and of the distribution of
player choices." These characteristics are precisely those
of identity of payoff structure and of the independence of
$D(m) - C(m + 1)$ of $m$, which of course guarantees that if $C(m)$
and $D(m)$ are linear functions, then their slopes are equal.

A final note. As Amnon Rapoport (1967) has so persuasively
argued in the context of prisoner's dilemma games, a social-
dilemma game that is repeated (iterated) may not constitute
a dilemma at all. If there is the possibility of "tacit
collusion [p. 140]" or "that each player believes that his
decision at Time $t - u$ can partly effect what will happen at
Time $t$ [p. 141]," then it is no longer clear that defection
is a dominating strategy. In fact, the situation can become
horribly complicated—even more complicated than envisioned
in Rapoport's "optimal strategies." We have a situation in
which people are attempting to control the future behavior of
others by dispensing rewards and punishments which simultaneously determine—in a complex interactive way—their own
present rewards and punishments. It should not be surprising
that few, if any, simple generalizations about "cooperative"
or "competitive" behavior have arisen from studying people
faced with such a complicated task, despite literally thousands of attempts to do so. In contrast, the social-dilemma
games discussed in this chapter do not involve iteration.
They face the subject with a rather simple though compelling
dilemma.[4] Perhaps subjects' behavior in these game situations—and the effect of such variables as communication and
humanization—can shed some light on behavior in the real-
world dilemmas the games were constructed to represent.

---

[4]My experience has been that moderate-sized groups of
students participating for moderate amounts of money [for
example, $N = 8$, $C(N) = \$2.50$, $d = \$5.50$, $\lambda = \$2.50$] do take
the commons dilemma very seriously indeed.

## ACKNOWLEDGMENTS

This research was supported by the Advanced Research
Projects Agency of the Department of Defense (ARPA Order No.
2449) and was monitored by ONR under Contract No. N00014-75-
C-0093. I have received many valuable criticisms of earlier
drafts of this paper. I would like to thank particularly:
Baruch Fischhoff, Lita Furby, Sundra Gregory, Paul Hoffman,
Len Rorer, Mick Rothbart, and Harriet Shaklee.

## REFERENCES

Dawes, R. M. The commons dilemma game: An $n$-person mixed-motive game with a dominating strategy for defection. *Oregon Research Institute Research Bulletin*, 1973, *13*(2).

Dawes, R. M., Delay, J., & Chaplin, W. The decision to pollute. *Journal of Environment and Planning*, 1974, *6*, 3-10.

Evans, G. W., & Crumbaugh, C. M. Effect of prisoner's dilemma format on cooperative behavior. *Journal of Personality and Social Behavior*, 1966, *3*, 486-488.

Frolich, N., & Oppenheimer, J. A. I get by with a little help from my friends. *World Politics*, 1970, *23*, 104-120.

Goehring, D. J. Number of players and matrix competitiveness in prisoner's dilemma. Paper presented at the meeting of the Western Psychological Association, San Francisco, April 1974.

Hamburger, H. $N$-person prisoner's dilemmas. *Journal of Mathematical Sociology*, 1973, *3*, 27-48.

Hardin, G. The tragedy of the commons. *Science*, 1968, *162*, 1243-1248.

Hardin, G. *Exploring new ethics for survival: The voyage of the spaceship* Beagle. New York: Viking Press, 1972.

Kelley, H. H., & Grzelak, J. Conflict between individual and common interest in an $n$-person relationship. *Journal of Personality and Social Psychology*, 1972, *21*, 190-197.

Lloyd, W. F. *Two lectures on the checks to population.* Oxford: Oxford University Press, 1833.

Messick, D. M. To join or not to join: An approach to the unionization decision. *Organizational Behavior and Human Performance*, 1973, *10*, 145-156.

Messick, D. M., & McClintock, C. G. Motivational bases of choice in experimental games. *Journal of Experimental Social Psychology*, 1968, *4*, 1-25.

Olsen, M. *The logic of collective action.* Cambridge, Mass.: Harvard University Press, 1965.

Pruitt, D. G. Reward structure and cooperation: The decomposed prisoner's dilemma game. *Journal of Personality and Social Psychology*, 1967, *7*, 21–27.

Rapoport, Amnon. Optimal policies for the prisoner's dilemma. *Psychological Review*, 1967, *74*, 136–148.

Rapoport, Anatol, & Chammah, A. M. *Prisoner's dilemma: A study in conflict and cooperation*. Ann Arbor: University of Michigan Press, 1965.

Schelling, T. S. Hockey helmets, concealed weapons, and daylight saving time: A study of binary choices with externalities. *Journal of Conflict Resolution*, 1973, *17*, 381–428.

## 5. AN INFORMATION-INTEGRATION ANALYSIS OF RISKY DECISION MAKING

*James Shanteau*
Kansas State University

| | |
|---|---|
| Introduction | 110 |
| Information-Integration Theory | 110 |
| Integration Models | 110 |
| Integration Operations | 111 |
| Multiplying Model | 112 |
| Basic Results | 112 |
| Subjective Values | 116 |
| Preference Judgments | 116 |
| Individual-Subject Analyses | 118 |
| Analyses of Other Studies | 120 |
| Adding Model | 124 |
| Basic Results | 124 |
| Response-Scale Linearity | 125 |
| Subadditivity | 126 |
| Studies of Commodity Bundles | 129 |
| Explanations of Subadditivity | 130 |
| Discussion | 130 |
| Empirical Overview | 130 |
| Traditional Utility Approach | 131 |
| Multiple-Regression Approach | 132 |
| Information-Integration Approach | 133 |
| References | 134 |

## INTRODUCTION

The purpose of this chapter is to present an information-processing analysis of risky decision making using the theory of information integration (Anderson, 1974; also see the Kaplan chapter). Toward this goal, the results of a series of studies on gambling judgments are reviewed and evaluated. The chapter is organized into four sections. The first is a discussion of the application of information-integration theory to risky decision making. Next, the success of this approach with simple one-part gambles is discussed. The third section is an evaluation of the approach with more complex two-part gambles. The last section contains a discussion of implications for other approaches to risky decision making together with comparisons to the integration approach.

## INFORMATION-INTEGRATION THEORY

Many judgment tasks require a subject to combine, or integrate, diverse pieces of information into one overall judgment. In integration theory each piece of information is characterized by a scale value $s$ and a weight, or importance, value $w$. The response is then taken to be a weighted sum:

$$R = \Sigma w_i s_i. \tag{1}$$

The sum is over all relevant pieces of information, with the subjective value of each being weighted by its subjective importance. In the present applications no context effects are assumed, so that the value of any piece of information is constant no matter what else it is combined with. The response $R$ is taken to be on a continuous, or numerical, scale.

*INTEGRATION MODELS*

The application of Eq. (1) to risky decision making is straightforward. Simple one-part gambles can be characterized as "$P$ to get \$," where $P$ is the probability of getting outcome \$. The subjective value of the outcome, \$, is represented by its scale value, $s$, and the subjective likelihood of getting the outcome, $P$, is represented by its weight value, $w$. Therefore, Eq. (1) reduces to:

$$R = ws. \tag{2}$$

110

This is a *multiplying* model in which the worth of the bet is determined by a product of subjective likelihood and subjective value.

In general, gambles can have more than one part. This is illustrated by two-part gambles, which can be characterized as "$P_1$ to get $\$_1$ *and* $P_2$ to get $\$_2$." The two parts are usually independent, so that subjects can get both, either, or neither of the outcomes. The subjective values of the outcome, $\$_1$ and $\$_2$, are represented by scale values, $s_1$ and $s_2$, and the subjective likelihood of getting the outcomes, $P_1$ and $P_2$, by weight values, $w_1$ and $w_2$. For this case, Eq. (1) can be stated as:

$$R = w_1 s_1 + w_2 s_2. \tag{3}$$

This implies a multiplying model for each part of the bet and an *adding* model for the combination of the two parts.

## *INTEGRATION OPERATIONS*

According to integration theory, two basic psychological operations are involved in making decisions about gambles. The first is the *valuation* operation, by which the probabilities and outcomes come to have psychological values. The second is the *integration* operation, by which these values are combined into a single judgment. The study of these two operations goes hand in hand. To estimate the psychological values, it is necessary to know how these values combine to form a judgment. Conversely, evaluation of the integration rule requires estimates of the values being combined.

This simultaneous determination of psychological values and the integration rule has probably been the central problem in research on risky decision making. However, procedures from functional measurement provide a general solution to this problem (Anderson & Shanteau, 1970; Shanteau, 1974a). In particular, these procedures lead to a joint validation of the psychological values and the multiplying and adding models. Although precise goodness-of-fit tests have been developed (Anderson & Shanteau, 1970; Shanteau & Anderson, 1972), functional measurement readily lends itself to simple graphical analyses. Accordingly, results are presented here in graphical form to allow visual inspection. The supportive statistical analyses can be found in the cited studies.

## MULTIPLYING MODEL

*BASIC RESULTS*

   The multiplying model in Eq. (2) can be directly examined
in one-part bets. Such bets were employed by Anderson and
Shanteau (1970) in a study on numerically defined gambles. In
one condition, subjects were asked to rate the subjective
worth of positive one-part bets, such as "5/6 to win 25¢."
The bets were varied in a 5 × 4, $P \times \$$ factorial design. The
subjects were run individually through four replications on
four successive days; a preliminary day was used for famil-
iarizing subjects with stimuli and for practice in using the
response scale. The worth responses were recorded on an
unmarked graphic rating scale with anchors used to define the
end points; the responses were read by the experimenter from
the rear side with a meter stick. This general procedure is
typical for the studies reported here.
   The mean worth responses are plotted in the upper left
panel (single-positive) in Figure 1. The outcomes are listed
as curve parameters. The probabilities along the horizontal
axis are spaced according to their subjective values. This
method of plotting allows a direct graphical assessment of the
multiplying model. If the model is correct, then the four
curves should form a diverging fan of straight lines. Moreover, the slope of each line should be proportional to its
subjective value. Figure 1 shows that the curves do diverge
and are very nearly linear. This support for the multiplying
model was substantiated by statistical tests based on
bilinear-trend analyses for each subject.
   The remaining panels in Figure 1 show the results for three
other stimulus designs. In the upper right panel (single-
negative), the bets all involve losses rather than wins. As
can be seen, the linearity of the results is substantially
the same as in the single-positive design. The bottom two
panels are of special interest because two-part duplex bets
were used (similar to those in Slovic & Lichtenstein, 1968).
These bets contain independent win and loss parts--for
example, "3/6 to win 5¢ *and* 4/6 to lose 25¢." The results
in the lower left panel (duplex-positive) show the mean worth
ratings for the win part averaged over the loss part. Conversely, the results in the lower right panel (duplex-
negative) show the means for the loss part averaged over the
win part. In each case the curves show the same general
pattern as in the upper panels. This is significant, since
two-part duplex bets require a more complex judgment than
one-part single bets.

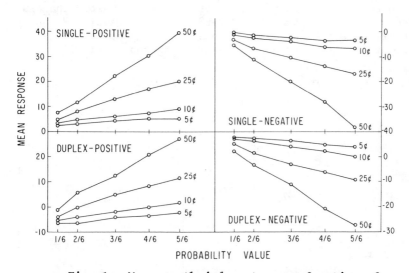

*Fig. 1. Mean worth judgments as a function of probability and outcome for single-positive and single-negative and for duplex-positive and duplex-negative designs. Duplex-positive (negative) values are averaged over the loss (win) part of the duplex bet. The probabilities are spaced along the horizontal according to their subjective values; the outcome amounts are shown as curve parameters. The multiplying model predicts that the curves should form a diverging fan of straight lines. From Anderson and Shanteau (1970).*

The gambles in Figure 1 were defined in traditional terms with numerical parameter values. However, it can be argued that real-life gambles are seldom so precisely specified. Accordingly, subjects in Shanteau's study (1974a; also see 1970b) judged the subjective worth of bets defined entirely by verbal phrases, such as "somewhat unlikely to win sandals." In addition to these one-part bets, subjects also rated the worth of two-part verbal bets, such as "highly probable to win watch *and* tossup to win bicycle." In both cases, probability and outcome for each part should combine by multiplying. For two-part bets, the worth of the parts should combine by adding.

The results appear in Figure 2 for one-part bets (single bet) and the first part of two-part bets (double bet). In both panels the curves very nearly form the diverging fan of straight lines predicted by the multiplying model. This

113

is noteworthy in that it was not initially obvious that subjects would interpret these verbal bets as gambles.  Though
the results are not quite as neat as for numerical bets
(Figure 1), the processes appear to be substantially the same.

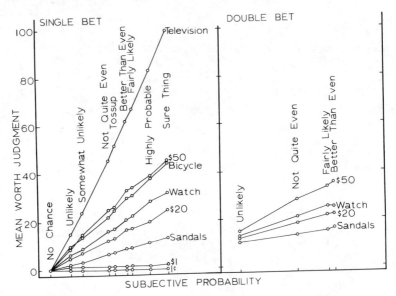

Fig. 2.  Mean worth judgments as a function of
verbally defined probability and outcome for single-
bet and double-bet designs.  Double-bet values are
averaged over the second part of the two-part bets.
The probabilities are spaced according to their
subjective values; the outcomes are shown as curve
parameters.  The multiplying model predicts a
diverging fan of straight lines.  From Experiment I
in Shanteau (1974a).

In a follow-up experiment Shanteau (1974a) directly
compared numerical and verbal bets; the three stimulus designs
used are shown in Table 1.  A clear diverging fan of straight
lines was found for all three designs.  As might be expected,
the numerical-value bets had the cleanest results.  The data
for the low-value and high-value designs revealed a clearly
bilinear pattern despite wide differences in the range and
distribution of probabilities and outcomes.

TABLE 1
*Subjective Values of Probabilities and Payoffs*[a]

| | | Probabilities | | Outcomes | | |
| --- | --- | --- | --- | --- | --- | --- |
| Design | Stimuli | Weight value | Direct rating | Stimuli | Scale value | Direct rating |
| Numerical value | No chance | .00 | .00 | Nothing ($0) | 0.0 | 0.0 |
| | One quarter | .26 | .25 | $1 bill | 2.9 | 1.3 |
| | One third | .32 | .30 | $5 bill | 7.3 | 4.3 |
| | Tossup | .50 | .50 | $10 bill | 11.6 | 10.9 |
| | Two thirds | .67 | .69 | $20 traveler's check | 20.7 | 18.7 |
| | Three quarters | .71 | .77 | $50 gift certificate | 48.4 | 49.3 |
| | Sure thing | 1.00 | 1.00 | $75 cash | 75.0 | 75.0 |
| Low value | No chance | .00 | .00 | Nothing ($0) | 0.0 | 0.0 |
| | Highly improbable | .13 | .06 | Pen | 7.5 | 4.3 |
| | Somewhat unlikely | .34 | .29 | Sunglasses | 7.7 | 3.7 |
| | Worse than even | .38 | .38 | Sandals | 10.1 | 6.4 |
| | Not quite even | .45 | .45 | Clock | 23.5 | 19.1 |
| | Fairly likely | .72 | .68 | Watch | 41.3 | 37.7 |
| | Sure thing | 1.00 | 1.00 | $75 cash | 75.0 | 75.0 |
| High value | No chance | .00 | .00 | Nothing ($0) | 0.0 | 0.0 |
| | Unlikely | .19 | .12 | Sandals | 10.0 | 6.4 |
| | Not quite even | .47 | .45 | Camera | 27.4 | 28.0 |
| | Better than even | .60 | .59 | Radio | 35.4 | 36.5 |
| | Highly probable | .92 | .90 | Suitcase | 37.6 | 37.9 |
| | Almost certain | .93 | .92 | Bicycle | 48.4 | 51.9 |
| | Sure thing | 1.00 | 1.00 | $75 cash | 75.0 | 75.0 |

[a]From Shanteau (1974a), Experiment II.

## SUBJECTIVE VALUES

One of the main purposes of the second experiment reported in Shanteau (1974a) was to derive subjective values of probabilities and outcomes. The weight and scale values given in Table 1 were obtained by recalibrating the marginal means of the factorial designs (Anderson & Shanteau, 1970). In each design the convergence of curves to a common point (as in Figure 2) justified assignment of 0.0 to "no chance" and "nothing"; arbitrary values of 1.0 and 75.0 were assigned to "sure thing" and "$75 cash," respectively. The other means were rescaled accordingly. For comparison, direct ratings of the stimuli are also given. These direct ratings were obtained by asking subjects to define the probabilities on a 0-to-1 unmarked rating scale; the outcomes were rated similarly on a scale of $0 to $75 in worth.

Several comparisons of interest can be derived from Table 1. First, "not quite even" and "sandals" appeared in both low-value and high-value designs. As can be seen, "sandals" had nearly the same value (10.1 and 10.0) in the two designs; similar values were also obtained for "not quite even" (.45 and .47). This invariance lends strong support to the functional-measurement approach to scaling. A second comparison can be made between the objective and subjective values for the numerical-value design. Although the probability values are quite similar, the scale values for low monetary amounts are overvalued relative to higher amounts. This is consistent with the negatively accelerated utility function typically used in economic applications (Coombs, Dawes, & Tversky, 1970). Finally, direct ratings can be compared to derived weight and scale values. Although there are some significant differences, the discrepancies do not appear to be systematic. Direct ratings may, therefore, provide a reasonable approximation of subjective values.

## PREFERENCE JUDGMENTS

The results reported to this point have all been based on worth ratings of single one-part or two-part gambles. In contrast, subjects in most previous research had been asked to make choices between pairs of gambles. There is evidence to suggest that different processes are employed in the two tasks (Lichtenstein & Slovic, 1971; Tversky, 1969).

To check this possibility, subjects in a series of studies were asked to make preferential choice ratings between pairs of gambles. In Shanteau (1972b), for example, subjects were told to choose between bets such as "4/6 to win 25¢ *or* 1/6 to win 50¢." Consistent with earlier results for nonpreferential

116

bets, a diverging fan of straight lines was clearly evident.

Similar results have been found in two other studies. In Shanteau and Phelps's study (1975), subjects were asked to make preference ratings between two verbal gambles (like those in Figure 2). The mean results, collapsed across the various alternatives, are shown in Figure 3. A clear bilinear trend is apparent.

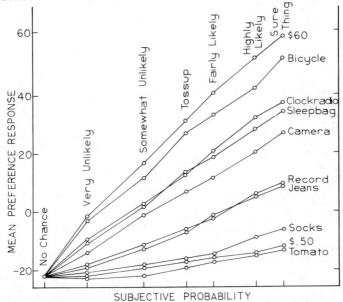

*Fig. 3. Mean preference ratings as a function of probability and outcome for one alternative. Values are averaged over other alternatives. The verbal probabilities are spaced according to their subjective values; the outcomes are shown as curve parameters. Data from Shanteau and Phelps (1975).*

In a rather different task, Shanteau and Nagy (1974) had female subjects make preferences between pairs of possible male dates. Each date was described by a photograph and the probability that the date would be willing to go out with the subject. The combination of probability and attractiveness of the picture was assumed to follow Eq. (2). As can be seen in Figure 4, the results were largely in accord with the multiplying model.

An interesting comparison can be made between the proba- bilities in Figures 3 and 4. Identical phrases were used in both studies, but the subjective spacing is quite different.

This suggests that the evaluation of probability depends on the context. Of particular interest is the "no chance" probability. Unlike those in Figures 2 and 3, the curves do not quite converge at "no chance." This apparently indicates that subjects believed that there was still some possibility of getting a date even when they were told that there was "no chance."

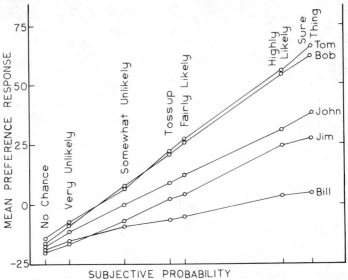

*Fig. 4. Mean preference ratings for dates described by a photograph and the probability of going out with the subject. Values are averaged over alternative dates. The probabilities are spaced according to their subjective values; the photograph names are shown as curve parameters. From Shanteau and Nagy (1974).*

## INDIVIDUAL-SUBJECT ANALYSES

All the results reported up to this point have been based on group data. However, it is well known that group analyses can mask model discrepancies for individual subjects (see, for example, Shanteau & Anderson, 1969). Accordingly, each of these studies was also analyzed at the single-subject level. For the most part, these analyses have substantiated the group results in support of the multiplying model. Where discrepancies have occurred, they tend to be small with no consistent trends.

118

Fairly typical results are presented in Figure 5 for a
single subject in the Anderson and Shanteau (1970) study on
duplex bets. Although the data are naturally more variable
than the group results shown in Figure 1, the bilinear trend
in the right-hand panel is clearly evident. This support for
the multiplying model was substantiated by statistical analyses for this subject. Of some interest is the plot of the
same data in the left-hand panel. In this case the horizontal
axis is spaced according to the objective probability values.
Based on the curvature in this plot, it might appear that the
multiplying model had failed. However, when the subject's
own subjective values are used in the right-hand panel, the
results can be seen to be linear and clearly multiplicative.
This emphasizes the importance of using psychological values,
since objective values can often lead to erroneous conclusions
when one is evaluating a model (Birnbaum, 1973).

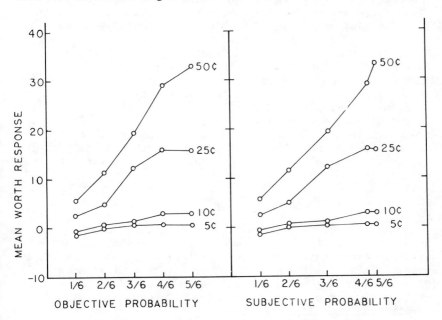

*Fig. 5. Mean worth judgments for S9 in a single-
negative design from Anderson and Shanteau (1970). The
numerical probabilities in the left-hand panel are
spaced according to their objective values; the probabilities in the right-hand panel are spaced according
to their subjective values. The monetary outcomes are
shown as curve parameters. The same data are plotted
in both panels. The response scale has been inverted
for ease of comparison. From Shanteau (1972b).*

Although the results of most single-subject analyses are comparable to those shown in Figure 5, occasionally there are large individual differences in processing strategies. In studying choices among bets, for instance, Shanteau (1972b) found indications of four distinct strategies. Some subjects, as shown by S6 in the upper left panel of Figure 6, were very close to the expected value (EV) of the bets; this can be seen in both the orderly multiplicativeness of the results and the near identity of the subjective values with the objective values. A related strategy of subjectively expected utility (SEU) was apparently followed by several subjects, as shown for S11 in the upper right panel; the results are clearly multiplicative, although the subjective values are quite different from the objective values. A number of subjects followed the adding-multiplying strategy shown for S2 in the lower left panel; though the overall results are multiplicative, there are tendencies toward parallelism, as shown in the 10¢, 25¢, and 50¢ curves. Such parallelism suggests an adding component in the combination of probabilities and outcomes. Finally, S4 in the lower right panel followed what has been labeled a high-low strategy; such subjects appeared to dichotomize each bet into being either good or bad, depending on the alternative. Although this interactive strategy is difficult to display graphically, one consequence can be seen in the displacement of high probabilities toward 6/6 and low probabilities toward 0/6. It should be emphasized that these categorizations were based not only on graphical analyses of the sort shown here but also on statistical analyses of the entire set of data.

## ANALYSES OF OTHER STUDIES

All the studies described thus far have involved the author. It is important to ask whether results obtained by other investigators are also in agreement with the multiplying model. This is difficult to answer for several reasons. First, adequate goodness-of-fit tests are seldom used in other risky-decision-making studies. Second, the data are rarely presented directly; instead, the results are typically described in terms of the parameters of some model. And even when the raw data are available, they are difficult to interpret because factorial designs are seldom used to specify stimuli. Though factorial designs are not essential for functional-measurement analyses, they do greatly simplify the procedures.

In spite of these difficulties, the author has successfully reanalyzed the results of two well-known studies. Tversky (1967b), using a procedure similar to functional measurement, found support for a multiplying model with simple one-part gambles. As exemplified by the results for a good, a median, and a bad subject in Figure 7, the bilinear analyses support Tversky's conclusions.

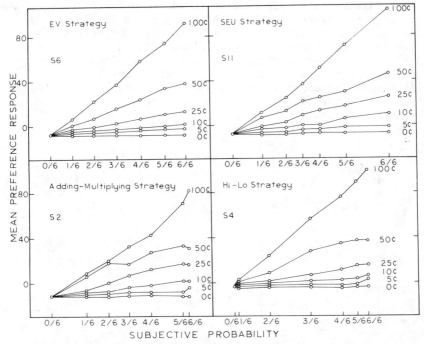

*Fig. 6. Mean preference ratings for four subjects from Shanteau (1972b). The results in the upper left panel for S6 (and one other subject) approximate expected value (EV). The results in the upper right panel for S11 (and four other subjects) are compatible with subjectively expected utility (SEU). The results in the lower left panel for S2 (and three other subjects) suggest an adding-multiplying strategy. The results in the lower right panel for S4 (and three other subjects) reveal the high-low strategy of dichotomizing each alternative bet into either good or bad. One of 16 subjects could not be classified.*

The data in Figure 7 are of particular interest in that Tversky (1967a), using similar data, made one of the initial applications of conjoint measurement. This approach, as in functional measurement, emphasizes the analysis of psychological-combination rules through simultaneous scaling of independent and dependent variables (Coombs et al., 1970).

A successful application of this nonmetric (ordinal) approach has been made by Coombs to the study of risk (see the chapter by Coombs). In nonmetric terms, however, multiplicative data such as those in Figure 7 cannot generally be distinguished from additive data. Therefore, in addition to conjoint measurement, Tversky analyzed his data by taking logarithms and applying analysis of variance (much in the spirit of functional measurement). This illustrates one difficulty of analyzing processing strategies with conjoint measurement. Another difficulty is the lack of a definitive goodness-of-fit test. Therefore, for analysis of the present results, conjoint measurement would not seem to be as useful as functional measurement.

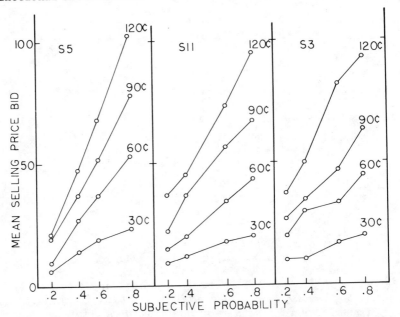

*Fig. 7. Mean selling-price bids for three subjects from Set 1 of Tversky's study (1967b). The left-hand panel shows a highly multiplicative subject, the middle panel shows a median subject, and the right-hand panel shows one of the least multiplicative subjects. Bilinear statistical support for the multiplying model was found for all three subjects.*

An often-cited study by Slovic and Lichtenstein (1968) has been widely interpreted to suggest that probabilities and outcomes combine by adding rather than multiplying (Payne, 1973). Based on a multiple-regression analysis, Slovic and

Lichtenstein applied an adding model to duplex bets. Although
the model correlated an average of .86 with both bidding and
rating responses, such correlations do not provide an adequate
index of fit for a model (Anderson, 1969; Birnbaum, 1973).
In fact, reanalyses of their preliminary data (in Shanteau,
1970b) revealed consistent multiplicative results. As shown
for a good, a median, and a bad subject in Figure 8, the
results clearly show the bilinear fan of a multiplying model
(as opposed to the parallelism of an adding model). Further,
analysis-of-variance tests revealed significant Probability ×
Outcome interactions, contrary to the adding model.

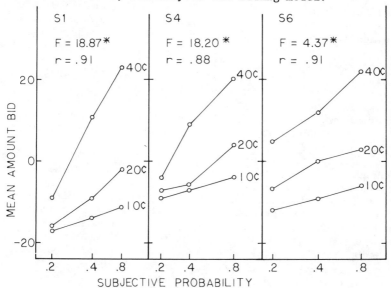

*Fig. 8. Mean amounts bid for three preliminary
subjects from Slovic and Lichtenstein (1968). The
left-hand panel shows a highly multiplicative subject,
the middle panel shows a median subject, and the
right-hand panel shows one of the least multiplicative subjects. All subjects have high correlations
(r) with an additive model, but all subjects also
reveal significant Probability × Outcome interactions (F), as noted by asterisks. Also note the
deviation of the subjective-probability spacing from
the objective values listed on the horizontal;
regression analysis assumes subjective values equal
to objective values.*

Overall, the existing data provide consistent evidence of a diverging bilinear fan. This provides impressive support for the hypothesis that probability and outcome combine by multiplying.

## ADDING MODEL

*BASIC RESULTS*

The adding model for the combination of two-part bets was also tested in a number of the above experiments. However, in sharp contrast to the success of the multiplying model, the adding model has failed repeatedly for risky decision judgments. This failure was surprising, since a large number of experiments have obtained the parallelism predicted by the adding model (Anderson, 1974). For instance, Shanteau and Anderson (1969) found parallelism in the combination of sandwiches and drinks into a lunch. In this and many other experiments, however, the combination rule can be better described by an averaging model than an adding model (Oden & Anderson, 1971).

In the initial analysis of risky decision making (Anderson & Shanteau, 1970), good support was obtained for the multiplying model (Figure 1), but equivocal support was obtained for the adding model. Further, analyses of variance revealed significant interactions, although the graphical analyses failed to reveal any pattern in the discrepancies from parallelism. It now appears that these patterns were masked, in part, by the use of both positive and negative outcomes in the duplex bets. At the time, however, there was no reason to expect deviations from additivity, and the success of the multiplying model gave hope that the adding model would be supported in later work. In fact, quite the opposite has turned out to be true.

In an extensive examination of the adding model, Shanteau (1974a) included several two-part bet designs. In these, subjects rated the worth of verbal bets, such as "highly probable to win watch *and* tossup to win bicycle." According to Eq. (3), such bets should lead to a multiplying model for each part and an adding model for the combination of the parts. As shown previously (in Figure 2), the multiplying model did quite well. However, the predicted parallelism of the adding model was not observed. The deviations from additivity appeared to be concentrated in an interaction between outcomes for the two parts. As shown in Figure 9, the curves show a convergence to the right for two different two-part bet designs; in both cases the values have been

124

averaged over the various probability phrases.  This deviation from parallelism seems to indicate that the value of the outcome for one part depends on the value of the other outcome.

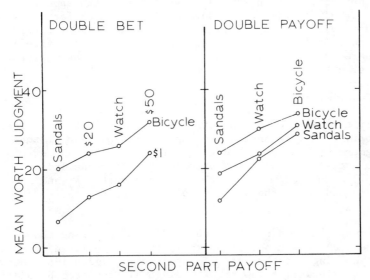

*Fig. 9.   Interaction between outcome payoffs for two-part bets in double-bet and double-payoff designs.  First-part outcomes are shown as curve parameters; second-part payoffs are shown  along the horizontal.  Values are averaged over probability levels.  The adding model predicts a parallel set of lines.  From Experiment I of Shanteau (1974a).*

## RESPONSE-SCALE LINEARITY

These conclusions depend crucially on the validity of the response scale; it could be argued that the interactions were due to a nonlinear distortion of the response scale.  This seems unlikely, since any such distortion should influence the fit of both adding and multiplying models.  Yet the multiplying model has already been supported in Figure 2, and that tends to validate the response scale.  Further, the multiplying model worked equally well for double bets and for single bets in which no adding operation was involved.  As a final check, a power-series expansion was used to transform the response scale; but this had practically no impact on the fit of the adding model (Shanteau, 1974a).  It seems clear, therefore, that the adding model itself is inadequate.

Further analyses of the adding model in the second experiment reported in Shanteau (1974a) revealed similar interactions. However, the results did extend the generality of the nonadditivity in several ways. First, the same results were found for riskless ("sure thing") bets as for risky bets (Figure 9). Second, similar results were found for verbally and numerically defined bets. Finally, the nonparallelism appeared to be greatest when the payoffs had the greatest value.

## SUBADDITIVITY

If the value of one payoff does interact with the other payoff, then this should show up in a comparison of the judgments of one-part and two-part bets. This was examined with a test of *additivity* proposed by Thurstone and Jones (1957). The judgments of the separate parts, $R_1$ and $R_2$, should add up to the judgment of the combination, $R_{12}$:

$$R_{12} = R_1 + R_2. \tag{4}$$

This was analyzed by Shanteau (1974a) by plotting the (observed) double-bet means against the (predicted) sum of the two single-bet means. The points in Figure 10A can be seen to lie well below the 45° diagonal predicted by additivity. Thus, there appears to be a less than additive or subadditive relation between one-part and two-part bets.

This *subadditivity* effect was examined in detail in the second experiment of Shanteau (1974a). To start with, the results shown in Figure 10B replicated the marked deviation from additivity found in Figure 10A. This is noteworthy because all the points in Figure 10B represent riskless ("sure thing") bets. Moreover, subadditivity can be generalized across a broad value range, as shown by the similarity of high-value and low-value two-part bets. Subadditivity was also found for both monetary outcomes (filled points) and actual objects (open points) in Figure 10B. Finally, detailed analyses revealed that the size of the effect varied with the outcomes used; for example, "watch" produced over three times the subadditivity effect of "camera."

It is possible that subadditivity is an artifact of the worth-rating task used by Shanteau (1974a). To check this, Shanteau and Phelps (1975) tested for subadditivity in preferential choice judgments. Subjects were asked to make preference ratings between a two-part bet and an alternative one-part bet. The results shown in Figure 11A closely resemble previous findings of subadditivity in two-part bets. Interestingly enough, the slope of the points is quite similar to the slopes in Figure 10. From these analyses,

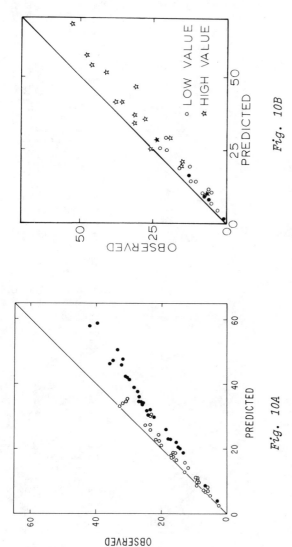

*Fig. 10A*

*Fig. 10B*

*Fig. 10. Predicted versus observed mean worth judgments for two-part bets as a function of the sum of one-part bets. Additivity predicts that the points should fall along a 45 diagonal. The points reveal the subadditivity effect, with observed values less than predicted values. In Figure 10A the 30 filled points (out of 64) have a percentage difference in worth of the parts of 50% or less. The percentage is defined by the difference in worth divided by the sum of the worth for the two parts of each bet. In Figure 10B all the points represent riskless ("sure thing") bets for low-value and high-value double-bet designs. The filled points are bets with monetary outcomes for both parts. Adapted from Experiments I and II in Shanteau (1974a).*

127

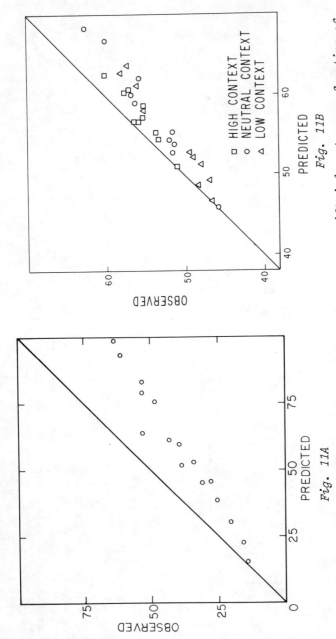

Fig. 11. Predicted versus observed values for two-part gift judgments as a function of the sum of one-part gift judgments. Subadditivity appears as a downward divergence from the diagonal. In Figure 11A both the observed two-part bet preferences and the predicted sum of the one-part bet preferences are compared to a worthless alternative; similar results were obtained with other alternatives. Data from Shanteau and Phelps (1975). Figure 11B gives the predicted versus observed ratings of riskless commodity bundles in a reanalysis of Hicks and Campbell's data (1965, p. 806). The data are plotted for high, neutral, and low context conditions. From Shanteau (1974a).

Shanteau and Phelps concluded that task and response-scale variables have little influence on subadditivity.

## STUDIES OF COMMODITY BUNDLES

Previous research on riskless decision making has been dominated by the additive-utility hypothesis (Edwards & Tversky, 1967). For instance, support for additivity has been reported for combinations of birthday gifts (Hicks & Campbell, 1965; Thurstone & Jones, 1957), foods (Gulliksen, 1956; Shanteau & Anderson, 1969), and concession goods (Tversky, 1967a).

A crucial step in much of the research on commodity bundles has been to determine the zero point of the values being combined--that is, to establish a ratio scale. Generally, zero-point estimates have been obtained by first assuming Eq. (4) and then getting an average of the best-fitting zero points over all the commodity bundles (see, for example, Thurstone & Jones, 1957). Results analyzed in this way have consistently seemed to support the additive model. Unfortunately, this procedure can easily cover up a real subadditivity effect (Shanteau, 1970b).

This led to a detailed re-examination of the previous results (Shanteau, 1974a). To serve as an illustration, the reanalysis of an extensive study by Hicks and Campbell (1965) will be described. According to Figures 10 and 11A, the lowest points appear to be the most additive and should, therefore, provide the best zero-point estimates. Thus, the lowest response in each of Hicks and Campbell's conditions (high, neutral, and low context) was used to estimate a new zero point. This led to the revised predicted-observed plot in Figure 11B for Hicks and Campbell's mean rating data (p. 806). As can be seen, there is a clear subadditivity effect in all three conditions.

Similar reanalyses of other studies on commodity bundles have consistently revealed subadditivity (Shanteau, 1970b). The effect has been found in judgments of birthday gifts (Hicks & Campbell, 1965; Thurstone & Jones, 1957), food combinations (Gulliksen, 1956), and bizarre behavior symptoms (Hicks & Campbell, 1965). In fact, just about every study reanalyzed by this author has shown the subadditivity effect. The only significant exceptions have been those studies in which an averaging rule was found.

Some additional evidence on subadditivity was offered by Shanteau (1974b). In a reanalysis of the data in Figure 10, the size of the subadditivity effect was found to depend on the difference in value of the two parts. The largest effect was observed when the two parts were closest together in value.

For instance, the 30 points (out of 64) in Figure 10A with the
least percentage difference in value are shown by filled
points. These filled points lead quite uniformly to the
greatest subadditivity effect. Therefore, the relative value
of the parts appears to play an important role in determining
the size of subadditivity.

## EXPLANATIONS OF SUBADDITIVITY

It would be helpful at this point to clarify the relation
between subadditivity and decreasing marginal utility. As
typically defined, "marginal utility" refers to a law of
diminishing returns for successive amounts of the *same* commodity (Lee, 1971). Subadditivity, on the other hand, is found
for combinations of *different* commodities. That is, subadditivity suggests the presence of a generalized law of diminishing returns that operates with as little as two nonredundant commodities. It still remains to be explained, however,
why this should occur and why there should be different results
for different combinations—as in Figure 10A, for example.

This leads to the question of how best to handle subadditivity. Unfortunately, no entirely satisfactory explanation has
as yet been proposed. However, several possibilities were
advanced by Shanteau (1974a). One is to consider overall
worth as a vector sum of part vectors, where the angle between
the parts represents the extent of subadditivity; a similar
model for combinations of odors has been used by Berglund,
Berglund, Lindvall, and Svensson (1973). A second possibility
is that overall worth may depend on the average worth of the
parts; support for this view was reported for combinations of
meals, criminals, and personality traits by Oden and Anderson
(1971). A last possibility is to represent overall worth as
a weighted sum of the parts; subadditivity might then be due
to a less valuable part   receiving little or no weight.


## DISCUSSION

### EMPIRICAL OVERVIEW

The evaluation of a gamble will, in general, involve two
kinds of operations. One operation involves the evaluation of
each part of the bet. This operation was expected to follow
a multiplying model for the combination of probability and
outcome. The other operation involves the combination of the
worths of the parts into a total worth. This combination
operation was expected to follow an adding model.

## Multiplying Model

The variety of studies supporting the multiplying model is impressive. Evidence for multiplying has been obtained in studies ranging from gambling (Figures 1 and 2) to dating choices (Figure 4). Similar evidence was found for simple one-part gambles and more complex two-part gambles (Figures 1 and 2). Support has also been found in a variety of response tasks, such as worth ratings (Figures 1 and 2), monetary bids (Figures 7 and 8), and preferential choices (Figure 3). Finally, it is worth emphasizing that these results extend to the level of individual subjects (Figures 5, 6, 7, and 8). In all, the multiplying operation is quite pervasive.

## Adding Model

Although this model has been widely assumed to hold in traditional utility theory (Edwards & Tversky, 1967), the present results provide clear and extensive evidence against the adding model. The discrepancy apparently arises from a subadditive interaction between outcomes. Support for this interpretation comes from both the interaction between payoffs (Figure 9) and the subadditivity effect in the predicted-observed plots (Figures 10 and 11). It is noteworthy that substantially identical results were obtained for a number of different types of gambles (for example, see Figure 10B). In addition, the same effects were found with worth ratings (Figures 10A and 10B) and preferential choices (Figure 11A). It should also be emphasized that similar results were obtained with risky (Figures 10A and 11A) and riskless outcomes (Figures 10B and 11B). Finally, subadditivity has been found for combinations of gambles, gifts, foods, and bizarre behavior symptoms. Therefore, it appears that subadditivity is a real and widespread effect.

## TRADITIONAL UTILITY APPROACH

The most frequently used approach to risky decision making over the past 20 years has been based on utility theory (Edwards, 1954, 1961; Rapoport & Wallsten, 1972). This leads to the familiar model of subjectively expected utility (SEU), which is shown here for two-part bets:

$$R = s(P_1)u(\$_1) + s(P_2)u(\$_2). \tag{5}$$

The terms $s(P)$ and $u(\$)$ correspond to subjective-probability and utility functions, respectively. Formally, this model is similar to Eq. (3) in predicting a multiplying operation for the combination of probability and outcome and an adding operation for the combination of the parts of a bet.

There have been numerous and often clever tests proposed for SEU (for example, Davidson, Suppes, & Siegel, 1957; Coombs, Bezembinder, & Goode, 1967; Tversky, 1967a, 1967b), but the results have been conflicting and inconclusive. This led Rapoport and Wallsten (1972) to conclude that "the conflicting evidence pertaining to SEU theory is presently irreconcilable [p. 141]." The present results may help reconcile the conflict; SEU appears to be correct in predicting a multiplying operation but incorrect in predicting an adding operation.

The additive-utility hypothesis has been so widely assumed to hold (Edwards & Tversky, 1967) that it has not been extensively tested. It is ironic, therefore, that the adding model should turn out to be incorrect. Unfortunately, this casts doubt on much of the theoretical structure used in traditional approaches to utility theory. These approaches have largely centered around a normative or prescriptive element, sometimes based on an assumption that people maximize expected utility, sometimes based on axiomatic assumptions that lead to the same conclusion. It may well prove difficult to modify the additive-utility hypothesis without compromising the normative element in these models. Thus, the results reported here raise serious questions about the descriptive adequacy of the additive-utility approach to risky decision making.

## MULTIPLE-REGRESSION APPROACH

This approach was originally applied to duplex bets by Slovic and Lichtenstein (1968) and has been used in a number of studies since then (Payne, 1973). For duplex bets, this leads to a straight additive function of the objective values:

$$R = c_1 P_W + c_2 \$_W + c_3 P_L + c_4 \$_L. \tag{6}$$

The bet parameters, subscripted by $W$ and $L$ for wins and losses, are weighted by constants $c_i$, estimated by multiple regression.

The formulation in Eq. (6) is questionable on several grounds. First, it leads to an adding model for probability and outcome. This implies parallelism in Figures 1 through 8. Instead, a multiplicative interaction is present in all eight cases, including Slovic and Lichtenstein's own subjects in Figure 8. Thus, this part of the data directly contradicts the multiple-regression model. Another problem is that Eq. (6) predicts adding between different parts of a bet. However, the subadditivity effect in Figures 9 through 11 violates this prediction.

In fairness to Slovic and Lichtenstein, it should be pointed out that their primary interest was in estimating regression weights for various stimulus dimensions. For approximate comparisons of dimensions, this may be a useful approach. However, they did not (and could not) state that the regression model provided an adequate description of risky decision making. The inadequacy of the additive model is shown by every one of the present figures. This point is worth emphasizing because of a widespread misbelief that the results of Slovic and Lichtenstein (1968) support an adding model (Payne, 1973). In all, the multiple-regression model appears to be of highly questionable validity in describing risky decision making.

## INFORMATION-INTEGRATION APPROACH

The basic elements of this approach appear in Eq. (3), which is repeated here:

$$R = w_1 s_1 + w_2 s_2. \tag{3}$$

Integration theory leads to a multiplying model for probability and outcome, and the results provide convincing evidence of a multiplying operation. In contrast, the integration approach predicts an adding model for the combination of multi-part bets. The results fail to support such a model and instead reveal the subadditivity effect.

Although the model had mixed success, the analyses did reveal a strikingly simple and uniform pattern, even with the subadditivity effect. Other approaches have not been able to uncover this pattern. Thus, it is to the credit of the integration approach to have revealed some basic features of risky decision making. Further, functional-measurement procedures appear to have resolved a longstanding problem with the simultaneous measurement of utility and subjective-probability values (as illustrated in Table 1).

Previously, integration theory has been applied to a variety of decision-making tasks, such as sequential judgments of estimation (Shanteau, 1970a), prediction (Friedman, Carterette, & Anderson, 1968), and inference (Leon & Anderson, 1974; Shanteau, 1970a, 1972a, 1975). It has also been used with preferential choices (Shanteau & Anderson, 1969) and information acquisition (Shanteau & Anderson, 1972). Together with the present results on risky decision making, these studies show that information integration has considerable promise in providing a unified approach to decision-making behavior.

Formally, the integration model in Eq. (3) is identical to the SEU model in Eq. (5). However, the two approaches have different conceptual formulations and goals. The SEU approach

133

is derived from economic theory and includes normative elements related to maximization of utility. In contrast, the integration approach is based on a psychological theory and is fundamentally descriptive. The goal of this approach has been to develop an empirical foundation for descriptive laws of behavior.

Another view of the difference between the SEU and integration theories can be seen in the interpretation of the parameters. For instance, the concept of weight in integration theory is more general than the concept of subjective probability in SEU theory. Thus, a chance of losing might be given more weight than an equivalent chance of winning. Similarly, scale value reflects more than utility, so that a crisp dollar bill might be valued more than a crumpled one. At the level of the parameters, therefore, integration theory provides a more general approach.

As far as the present data are concerned, the SEU and integration models share a similar fate. Both successfully predict the multiplying result but fail to predict the subadditivity result. Nevertheless, subadditivity may be amenable to an information-integration analysis. For instance, it may be informative to compare component ratings (Anderson, 1966) for each part of a bet with the functional-measurement values of each part. Any systematic discrepancies might help pinpoint the locus of the subadditivity effect.

## ACKNOWLEDGMENTS

Preparation of this chapter was supported in part by U.S. Public Health Service Grant MH26002 from the National Institute of Mental Health. The author wishes to express his gratitude to Norman H. Anderson for his many helpful comments on this research. The author also wishes to thank Amos Tversky and Paul Slovic for permission to use their individual-subject data. Finally, the author gratefully acknowledges the assistance of Suzanne Shuett, Deborah Spencer, Pamela White, and Charles Graber for running subjects and analyzing data in the studies reported here.

## REFERENCES

Anderson, N. H. Component ratings in impression formation. *Psychonomic Science*, 1966, *6*, 279-280.

Anderson, N. H. Comment on "An analysis-of-variance model for the assessment of configural cue utilization in clinical judgment." *Psychological Bulletin*, 1969, *72*, 63-65.

Anderson, N. H. Information integration theory: A brief survey. In D. H. Krantz, R. C. Atkinson, R. D. Luce, and P. Suppes (Eds.), *Contemporary developments in mathematical psychology*. Vol. 2. San Francisco: Freeman, 1974.

Anderson, N. H., & Shanteau, J. C. Information integration in risky decision making. *Journal of Experimental Psychology*, 1970, *84*, 441–451.

Berglund, B., Berglund, V., Lindvall, T., & Svensson, L. T. A quantitative principle of perceived intensity summation in odor mixtures. *Journal of Experimental Psychology*, 1973, *100*, 29–38.

Birnbaum, M. H. The devil rides again: Correlation as an index of fit. *Psychological Bulletin*, 1973, *79*, 239–242.

Coombs, C. H., Bezembinder, T. G., & Goode, F. M. Testing expectation theories of decision making without measuring utility or subjective probability. *Journal of Mathematical Psychology*, 1967, *4*, 72–103.

Coombs, C. H., Dawes, R. M., & Tversky, A. *Mathematical psychology: An elementary introduction*. Englewood Cliffs, N.J.: Prentice-Hall, 1970.

Davidson, D., Suppes, P., & Siegel, S. *Decision making: An experimental approach*. Stanford, Calif.: Stanford University Press, 1957.

Edwards, W. The theory of decision making. *Psychological Bulletin*, 1954, *51*, 380–417.

Edwards, W. Behavioral decision theory. *Annual Review of Psychology*, 1961, *12*, 473–498.

Edwards, W., & Tversky, A. (Eds.) *Decision making*. Baltimore: Penguin Books, 1967.

Friedman, M. P., Carterette, E. C., & Anderson, N. H. Long-term probability learning with a random schedule of reinforcement. *Journal of Experimental Psychology*, 1968, *78*, 442–455.

Gulliksen, H. Measurement of subjective values. *Psychometrika*, 1956, *21*, 229–244.

Hicks, J. M., & Campbell, D. T. Zero-point scaling as affected by social object, scaling method and context. *Journal of Personality and Social Psychology*, 1965, *2*, 793–808.

Lee, W. *Decision theory and human behavior*. New York: Wiley, 1971.

Leon, M., & Anderson, N. H. A ratio rule from integration theory applied to inference judgments. *Journal of Experimental Psychology*, 1974, *102*, 27–36.

Lichtenstein, S., & Slovic, P. Reversals of preference between bids and choices in gambling decisions. *Journal of Experimental Psychology*, 1971, *89*, 46–55.

135

Oden, G. C., & Anderson, N. H.   Differential weighting in integration theory. *Journal of Experimental Psychology*, 1971, *89*, 152-161.

Payne, J. W.   Alternative approaches to decision making under risk: Moments versus risk dimensions. *Psychological Bulletin*, 1973, *80*, 439-453.

Rapoport, A., & Wallsten, T. S.   Individual decision behavior. *Annual Review of Psychology*, 1972, *23*, 131-176.

Shanteau, J. C.   An additive model for sequential decision making. *Journal of Experimental Psychology*, 1970, *85*, 181-191.   (a)

Shanteau, J. C.   Component processes in risky decision judgments. Unpublished doctoral dissertation, University of California at San Diego, 1970.   (b)

Shanteau, J.   Descriptive versus normative models of sequential inference judgment. *Journal of Experimental Psychology*, 1972, *93*, 63-68.   (a)

Shanteau, J.   Information processing in risky decision making. Paper presented at the meeting of the Psychonomic Society, St. Louis, November, 1972.   (b)

Shanteau, J.   Component processes in risky decision making. *Journal of Experimental Psychology*, 1974, *103*, 680-691.   (a)

Shanteau, J.   Subadditivity of utility: Evidence and theoretical interpretations. Paper presented at the meeting of the Midwestern Psychological Association, Chicago, May, 1974.   (b)

Shanteau, J.   Averaging versus multiplying combination rules of inference judgment. *Acta Psychologica*, 1975, *39*, 83-89.

Shanteau, J. C., & Anderson, N. H.   Test of a conflict model for preference judgment. *Journal of Mathematical Psychology*, 1969, *6*, 312-325.

Shanteau, J., & Anderson, N. H.   Integration theory applied to judgments of the value of information. *Journal of Experimental Psychology*, 1972, *92*, 266-275.

Shanteau, J., & Nagy, G.   A decision theory analysis of dating choice. Paper presented at the meeting of the Midwestern Psychological Association, Chicago, May, 1974.

Shanteau, J., & Phelps, R.   Analysis of subadditivity in preferences between gambles defined by verbal phrases. Paper presented at the meeting of the Midwestern Psychological Association, May, 1975.

Slovic, P., & Lichtenstein, S.   Relative importance of probabilities and payoffs in risk taking. *Journal of Experimental Psychology*, 1968, *78*(3, Pt. 2).

Thurstone, L. L., & Jones, L. V.   The rational origin for measuring subjective values. *Journal of the American Statistical Association*, 1957, *52*, 458-471.

Tversky, A.  Additivity, utility, and subjective probability. *Journal of Mathematical Psychology*, 1967, *4*, 175-201.  (a)

Tversky, A.  Utility theory and additivity analysis of risky choices. *Journal of Experimental Psychology*, 1967, *75*, 27-36.  (b)

Tversky, A.  Intransitivity of preferences. *Psychological Review*, 1969, *76*, 31-48.

## 6. INFORMATION INTEGRATION IN SOCIAL JUDGMENT: INTERACTION OF JUDGE AND INFORMATIONAL COMPONENTS

*Martin F. Kaplan*
Northern Illinois University

| | |
|---|---|
| Introduction | 140 |
| The Basic Model | 140 |
| The Meaning of Information | 141 |
| The Integration of Information | 141 |
| The Judge in Social Judgment | 144 |
| Differences in Information Valuation | 145 |
| Differences in the Implications of Information | 146 |
| Differences in Integrating Information | 149 |
| Differences in Dispositional Tendencies | 152 |
| Interaction of Judge and Informational Variables | 156 |
| The Stimulus Person | 156 |
| The Situation | 159 |
| Generality or Specificity of Dispositional Effects | 162 |
| Concluding Comments | 162 |
| References | 164 |

INTRODUCTION

Broadly described, the components in any judgment consist
of the person forming the judgment, information about the
judged object, and situational requirements associated with
the judgment. In social judgment tasks, the general rules
involved in processing information have been widely studied,
whereas the processor himself has been relatively ignored.
This chapter explores the role of judge variables in the formation of social judgments and their interaction with informational and situational factors. Our understanding of any
phenomenon is never independent of a theoretical framework.
Therefore, an interpretive scheme will be outlined which has
proved well suited to the study of individual differences in
judges. Although this analysis will be limited here to
studies of social judgment, it has been applied elsewhere as
a general approach to human judgment (Anderson, 1974a, 1974b)
and decision making (see the Shanteau chapter).

THE BASIC MODEL

Judgment is based on information about the judged object.
Although this seems self-evident in tasks involving nonhuman
objects, this point has often been obscured in the study of
social judgment by affective interpretations (compare Byrne,
1971) and highly involved cognitive machinations (compare
Jones, Kanouse, Kelley, Niebett, Valins, & Weiner, 1971).
The contrast with noncognitive approaches (see Kaplan &
Anderson, 1973) and with more elaborate cognitive theories
(see Anderson, 1974c) has been treated elsewhere. It should
be noted, though, that any affect arising from social interaction, or any complex inference based on formal rules of
attribution formation, can ultimately be considered as information in itself, requiring processing and integration into
the observed judgment.

The information we receive about another may be quite
diverse in content. We may, for example, learn that a person
is kind to his friends, likes football, and cheats on his
income tax. To integrate these quite different behaviors
into a unitary judgment of a person (say, fitness for the
Presidency), we need some common means for considering each
piece of information. This common denominator is given by
the information's *scale value* (Anderson, 1974a). "Scale
value" refers to the quantitative representation of the location of the information on a particular judgment dimension.
It represents the person's subjective response to the information relative to the judgment in question. And so, income-

tax evasion may have a low value for judgments of fitness to hold the office of President but a high value for judgments of psychopathy. A first step in judgment of the stimulus object, then, is to assign value, or meaning, to the informational components. It is important to note that value is always with reference to the judgmental dimension.

## THE MEANING OF INFORMATION

The same piece of information may have several distinct meanings in the sense of possessing different values for different evaluative dimensions. This multidimensional aspect of stimuli has been explored elsewhere (for example, Rosenberg, Nelson, & Vivekananthan, 1968; Rosenberg & Sedlak, 1972); of importance here is that information influences judgment to the extent that both fall on the same response dimension (Hamilton & Fallot, 1974; Kaplan, 1975a; Rosenberg et al., 1968). This does not exclude the existence of "halo effects," whereby value on one dimension may affect value on another (Kaplan, 1975a, Exp. 1).

Similar remarks apply to the distinction between evaluative and descriptive meaning (Peabody, 1970; Rosenberg & Olshan, 1970). The former refers to the location of the information on the given judgment dimension--that is, its scale value. The latter is its descriptive referent behavior. For example, we may be informed that a person is agreeable. This may be evaluatively *positive*, and it may denote that he is friendly and obliging. Which "meaning" is used by a judge depends on the required judgment; clearly, if one is asked for a behavioral implication of given information, descriptive elements should predominate (Peabody, 1970). However, the pervasiveness of evaluative halo effects, even for tasks of descriptive inferences, has been well demonstrated (Osgood, Suci, & Tannenbaum, 1957; Thorndike, 1920). It may be fair to conclude at this stage that to the extent that a descriptive judgment contains evaluative components, evaluative meaning may exert a halo effect. The reverse effect is more difficult to demonstrate; that is, for evaluative judgment tasks, including inconsistency resolution, the importance of descriptive meaning seems minor (Anderson & Jacobson, 1965; Kaplan, 1973, 1974, 1975a; Rosenberg & Olshan, 1970).

## THE INTEGRATION OF INFORMATION

The judge is presented with information about the target person. Typically in social-judgment research, this is in the form of adjective traits, but our analysis need not be confined to a particular type of stimulus, or presentation mode.

The judge must now assign a value to each piece of information, giving his subjective response to the information on the judgment dimension. Then, these discrete values must be integrated in some way to form a unitary, overall judgment of the person on the judgment dimension. It has been suggested that the conjunction of information stimuli in forming overall person impressions changes the value of individual components from their judgment singly (Asch, 1946; Wyer, 1974), but evidence for such value change is lacking. In fact, the bulk of the evidence (see Anderson, 1971; Kaplan, 1974, 1975a) suggests that the stimulus value of individual components is unchanged in compound judgments.

In considering the manner in which people integrate information, a second attribute of information (the first is *value*) must be noted. This is the *weight* of the piece of information. "Weight" refers to the functional importance of a given stimulus for the required judgment. Weight is always in reference to the particular judgment; if a person wears an attractive article of clothing (that is, his attire has a high scale value for likableness), one might assign some moderate weight to this in judging his likableness. However, higher weight will be assigned to clothing in judging his fashionableness, since attire is more relevant (or, more precisely, more "diagnostic") for the latter dimension. Although scale value and weight may vary independently, there is evidence that higher weights are associated with more extreme scale values (Manis, Gleason, & Dawes, 1966) and with negative values (Richey, McClelland, & Shimkunas, 1967) in some tasks.

Anderson and his colleagues (Anderson, 1968, 1974a) have provided a model for the integration process which allows the consideration of judge, informational, and situational influences. Building upon the distinction between stimulus value and weight, the algebraic expression of the model, with minor changes in notation, is:

$$J = \frac{\sum\limits_{i=0} w_i s_i}{\sum\limits_{i=0} w_i}, \tag{1}$$

where the composite judgment is a weighted average of the scale values ($s_i$) of the single components. These components include a scale value for an initial impression ($s_0$), which is the judge's impression of the person prior to receiving any information about him—that is, an impression based on lack of information. The initial-impression concept will be discussed more fully in a later section. The most noteworthy implication of Eq. (1) for the integration process is that stimulus weights are constrained to sum to unity. This means that the contribution of any one piece of information to the final judgment is *relative* to the importance of other stimuli. Therefore, the relative contribution of a particular component may shift within different constellations of information components, allowing stimulus interaction and configural patterns of responding (Anderson, 1972). Instances in which people appear to be using different values of components in different contexts of other information about the stimulus object (that is, configural and context effects) may instead reflect changes in weighting (see "Effects on Integration Rules," below).

The relative-weighting rule holds, too, for the combination of stimulus information with the initial impression. That is, the scale values of information about another are averaged, each piece of information weighted by its relative importance, and this product is combined with the initial impression, each (information and initial impression) weighted by their relative importance to the judgment. Elaboration of Eq. (1) for $k$ stimuli gives:

$$J = \frac{w_1 s_1 + w_2 s_2 + \ldots w_k s_k + w_0 s_0}{w_1 + w_2 + \ldots w_k + w_0}. \tag{2}$$

If we focus on the relationship between stimulus-information value and initial impression, Eq. (2) can be restated as:

$$J = \frac{\sum_{i=1}^{k} w_i s_i}{\sum_{i=1}^{k} w_i + w_0} + \frac{w_0 s_0}{\sum_{i=1}^{k} w_i + w_0}, \tag{3}$$

where judgment is an average of the value of the stimulus information, each piece weighted by its importance, and the value of the initial impression, weighted by its importance. The contribution of either component of the judgment, information and initial impression, is relative to the contribution of the other.

Equations (2) and (3), and the theoretical analysis on which they are based, amply permit the operation of individual differences in judgment formation. The remainder of this chapter will be devoted to an examination of these phenomena within the framework of this theoretical model. The reader may refer to Anderson (1974a) for a more extensive treatment of information-integration theory and supportive evidence.

THE JUDGE IN SOCIAL JUDGMENT

The effect of a judge's personality on the social judgments he forms has long been an intriguing topic in social and personality psychology. For the most part, investigation of personality effects has employed the strategy of examining the generality, antecedents, and correlates of individual differences in judgments of other persons. In an earlier survey of personality effects, Shrauger and Altrocchi (1964) suggested that one problem in drawing conclusions has been the relative lack of systematic procedures in the study of such effects. By drawing on research in person perception and related areas and exploring implications of the information-integration model introduced by Anderson, it should be possible to derive some general conclusions regarding the role of the judge in social judgments.

The general framework, it will be recalled, is that judgment is based on the stimulus values, vis-a-vis the particular judgment dimension, of both the information about the other and the preinformation initial impression, and on situational requirements. The importance, or weight, of a particular piece of information is relative to the remaining information, and, in turn, the weight of all information is relative to that of the initial impression. From this vantage, there are four potential avenues through which individual differences in the judge can be expressed:

1. *Differences in information valuation.* Judges may differ in valuation, or placement of information on the judgment continuum. For this reason, the scale value in the integration process is considered a subjective ideographic value.

2. *Differences in attributing additional characteristics to others based on known characteristics.* These "built-in" attribute intercorrelations have been extensively studied under the rubric of "implicit personality theory."

3. *Differences in integrating the information.* These include such phenomena as ability to arrive at integrated impressions from inconsistent information, susceptibility to order effects and rigidity of first impression, differences in combinatory rules, and ability to differentiate among stimuli. Many, if not most of, these effects may reduce to differential tendencies in weighting information.

4. *Differences in pre-existing response dispositions.* These refer to both temporary and long-term generalized dispositional responses to others. Global tendencies to respond to others at a given level on a particular judgment dimension are analogous to the initial-impression term in the integration model.

144

These modes of individual differences will now be taken up in greater detail.

## DIFFERENCES IN INFORMATION VALUATION

In preceding sections it was stated that information is multidimensional in value and that a stimulus may have different information value for different judgment tasks and dimensions. Valuation may vary for individuals as well. For example, temporary deprivational or motivational states may alter value. A ham sandwich is more appealing (that is, highly valued) when one is hungry than when satiated. However, stimuli do have relatively constant values as well, and these may differ for individuals. To illustrate these points, a baked potato will always have higher gustatory value for me than Brussels sprouts, regardless of my motivational state. Yet it is entirely possible that there are some people to whom Brussels sprouts are pleasing. In describing the integration process, value is taken as a given for the information, and individual differences in valuation can be easily accommodated by assuming subjective values. However, the genesis of these valuations, and of individual differences, is a question that has been surprisingly neglected.

One possible solution to the valuation question may lie in extending the information-integration analysis to the valuing of single informational stimuli. The value of a single stimulus can be considered to be a pooled function of the evaluated experiences one has had with instances of that stimulus. These experiences leave a set of expectancies, each with scale value and weight (expressed perhaps as a probability). The value of a particular behavioral act or class of acts is determined by a pooling of these scale values and weights. For example, my encounters with acts labeled "honest" may have included a significant number of consequences painful for me. In pooling my expectancies for "honesty" (some of which have negative values), I may arrive at a less positive value than would another person who has experienced happier consequences. This analysis has the advantage of accounting for individual differences in valuation of single stimuli in a manner consistent with the integration model adopted for judging compound stimuli, but it avoids the question of what constitutes positive and negative experiences in the first place. But this is a metaphysical question which has been with psychology for a long time, and it will not be resolved here. Nor is knowing the inner nature of evaluative experiences essential for understanding the integration process.

Two more points may be worth noting. First, valuation may sometimes appear explicitly in the form of quantitative modifiers. Adverb-adjective combinations in describing persons or objects are an obvious case of this. Here the adjective may simply define the dimension of judgment, while the adverb gives its location (value) on this dimension (Anderson, 1974a). For example, "slightly honest" and "extremely honest" give values on the honesty dimension.

Second, it is possible to obtain post-hoc measures of stimulus value on an individual-subject level in order to uncover individual differences in valuation (Anderson, 1973). Given a factorial design of stimuli, functional measurement (Anderson, 1970) can be applied to derive interval scales for stimuli. If stimuli are combined in a rows-by-columns design, assuming an additive-type model, row means constitute an interval scale for row stimuli, and column means constitute the same for column stimuli. A description of and rationale for functional measurement can be found in Anderson (1970, 1974a).

## DIFFERENCES IN THE IMPLICATIONS OF INFORMATION

For more than 50 years (Thorndike, 1920, is an example) it has been observed that a judge's ratings of other people are moderately intercorrelated. One proposed source of this rating consistency is the judge's "implicit personality theory." The concept of implicit personality theory (IPT) was introduced by Bruner and Taguiri (1954) and amplified by Cronbach (1955). This concept refers to the assumptions the judge makes about the attributes which are implied by given attributes--that is, which traits go together in others and which traits do not. Whether trait implications are based on evaluative or descriptive similarities is an arguable point, although it appears to depend on the particular judgment required (Felipe, 1970; Peabody, 1970; Rosenberg & Olshan, 1970).

Strong evidence has been reported for the existence of implicit personality theory and for its stability across both stimulus persons and studies (Kuusinen, 1969; Passini & Norman, 1966). That is, similar factor structures have been found in ratings of different persons and in different studies. It is clear that the judge brings into the judgment his implicit personality theory and that there are strong common elements in individual judges' IPTs (Passini & Norman, 1966; Schneider, 1973). Furthermore, the number of dimensions judges typically use in drawing implications--that is, the factorial structure of IPT--is quite limited.

Relevant research on the general concept has been reviewed elsewhere (see Rosenberg & Sedlak, 1972; Schneider, 1973). Two questions are of immediate concern here. First, what is the evidence for individual differences in IPTs? Second, how can IPTs, and potential individual differences, be considered in relation to the model of social judgment that has been followed in the present analysis?

In his review of the evidence dealing with IPT, Schneider (1973) identified two approaches to studying individual differences. In the first, groups of judges are divided on the basis of external criteria (usually standard personality variables), and differences in IPT factor and weighting structures are sought. For example, high and low authoritarians can be compared with respect to the factors and relative factor loadings evident in the implications they draw from a wide variety of stimuli. In studies of this sort, there is only weak evidence for group differences. Such personality variables as authoritarianism (Steiner, 1954), sex (Shapiro & Taguiri, 1959), and maladjustment (Matcom, 1963) have been related to extremity of inference, while cognitive complexity (Halverson, 1970), concreteness-abstractness (Harvey, Hunt, & Schroder, 1961), and age and intelligence (Gollin, 1958) affect the ability to draw inferences and the number of dimensions used. Consistent evidence for differences in pattern and content of factor structures is lacking in this type of study.

The second method is to identify individual differences in the subjects' implicit personality theories (based on inference data) and then look for personality variables which discriminate between persons having different IPTs. Cronbach (1955) was one of the earliest researchers to represent individual judges by their position on a number of IPT dimensions. One source of individual differences is illustrated by Cronbach's work: Judges may differ in their relative usage of any particular dimension in a fixed set of such dimensions. Whereas Cronbach provided subjects with the dimensions to be used, other studies have improved upon Cronbach's beginnings by using sophisticated methods, most notably multidimensional scaling (Carroll, 1972), for detecting the dimensions used by individual judges under more natural conditions.

A number of investigators have been able to identify clusters of judges with differentiating "points of view," or factorial structures (Hamilton, 1970, 1971; Pedersen, 1965; Rosenberg & Sedlak, 1972; Sherman, 1972), providing evidence that judges differ in the implications they draw from one piece of information to another and in the way they cluster, or group, behaviors in others. However, Schneider (1973) has cautioned that these individual differences are typically quite small, particularly in relation to commonalities across judges, and that differences as yet show no systematic relationship to classic personality variables.

Thus, it is clear that subjects often go beyond the information furnished and attribute additional characteristics to stimulus persons. Particular trait implications have both universal and idiosyncratic antecedents. The former have furnished the basis for studies of trait redundancy (for example, Dustin & Baldwin, 1966; Kaplan, 1971d), or the extent to which one trait in a stimulus set implies another. Degree of trait redundancy, in turn, has important implications for the manifestation of personality dispositions, as will be shown in the section entitled "The Stimulus Person."

Surprisingly, the implications of implicit personality theories for an information-integration model have not yet been systematically explored. That is, if our response to another is based on more than the given information (that is, on additional (inferred information), the precision of predictions based only on the given stimuli should be impaired. It is likely that implicit personality theories pose no problem for the model with group data, but they may require some additional considerations when individual differences are taken into account.

Jackson and Warr (1974), in considering the relationship between information integration and inferences beyond given stimuli, have suggested that IPT may not pose a serious problem for integration models. Consider the ubiquitous trait adjective as the given stimulus. Each trait in a set contains a set of inferences, each inference possessing a scale value. Rating a set of traits amounts to rating a combination of these sets of inferences. This combination can be described by a differential weighted averaging model. In other words, the same combination rule that applies to judgments of sets of known traits may also apply to combinations of sets of inferences from the traits (see also, "Differences in Information Valuation" for similar remarks regarding stimulus valuation). Thus, the inferences provoked by each trait pose a problem only if there are marked individual differences in the range and distribution of these inferences. Even so, with careful stimulus sampling, there need not be a problem due to individual differences in IPT. Recall that scale values are ideographic. It may be reasonable to consider the subjective scale value of any single stimulus to be the weighted average of all implications of that trait. Thus, if two judges differ in the implications they draw from the same stimulus trait, they will also differ in the scale value for that trait. In the study of information integration, this suggests that stimuli should be chosen for their scale value at the individual-subject level, at least if we take individual differences in IPT seriously.

## DIFFERENCES IN INTEGRATING INFORMATION

The burden of integrating information, or, more correctly, the *scale value* of information, falls on the weighting parameter in the integration model. Information values are combined by adjusting the relative importance of the various components for the judgment at hand. Individual differences may occur in the differential weighting of information components and in the relative weighting of information and initial impression. In judgment, these weighting idiosyncracies will lead to apparent differences in information integration and in combination rules, particularly when information is internally inconsistent.

## Effects of Inconsistency and Order of Presentation

Numerous investigations have related cognitive "styles" to differences in integrating information. Such cognitive variables as cognitive complexity, leveling-sharpening, differentiation, category width, intelligence, dogmatism, authoritarianism, and field dependence have been linked with ability to arrive at integrated judgments from inconsistent information and with magnitude of order effects in sequential presentation. Main findings will be briefly characterized.

"Cognitive complexity" refers to the number of dimensions or constructs which a judge typically employs in judging others (Bieri, Atkins, Briar, Leaman, Miller, & Tripodi, 1966). Given a moderate degree of information inconsistency in serial presentation, low-complexity subjects show stronger recency effects and less ability to synthesize inconsistency (Bieri et al., 1966; Crockett, 1965; Mayo & Crockett, 1964). High-complexity subjects, on the other hand, are better able to arrive at more ambivalent impressions. Similar results obtain using conceptually similar cognitive dimensions. For example, high differentiators, defined by relative ability to discriminate between interpersonal concepts, give more integrated or ambivalent responses to inconsistent stimuli than do low differentiators (Harvey et al., 1961; Nidorf, 1961; Ware & Harvey, 1967) and discriminate more between persons described by different sets of information (Kaplan, 1968a). The degree of integration of impression is also affected by the extent of subjects' leveling tendencies (Nidorf, 1961), tolerance for ambiguity (Feather, 1967), and sex and intelligence (Gollin, 1958).

In an order-effects paradigm the extent to which subjects will change their response following the presentation of contradictory information is also influenced by authoritarianism (Steiner & Johnson, 1963), dogmatism (Kelly & Rice, 1970), field dependence (Kelly & Rice, 1970), and category width (Pettigrew, 1958; Steiner & Johnson, 1965). In general, the greatest resistance to change is shown by high authoritarians, high dogmatics, field dependents, and wide categorizers.

Yet another cognitive style proposed is that of "affective style" (Ehrlich & Lipsey, 1969). This is the extent to which individuals characteristically form strong impressions of others and is related to confidence in one's impressions (Johnson & Ewens, 1969).

Within the present framework cognitive styles in impression formation appear largely in weighting tendencies in integrating information. The presence of certain styles seems to increase the tendency to discount or ignore inconsistent information components, resulting in univalent impressions and enhanced order effects. This conclusion is consistent with decremental-weighting interpretations of order effects (Anderson, 1965; Hendrick & Costantini, 1970; Tesser, 1968). Furthermore, the observation that certain cognitive styles are associated with more extreme judgments can be handled by the notion that some people place more emphasis (weight) on the informational component of Eq. (3) than on the initial-impression component. Where information value is more extreme than the initial impression (that is, where $s_i < s_0 < s_i$), greater weighting of the former will lead to more extreme judgments.

## Effects on Integration Rules

The manner in which judges integrate information may be a source of individual differences in social judgment. It is appealing, on first impulse, to suppose that differences in how people put information together imply the use of different integration rules. This implication underlies a good deal of research aimed at demonstrating the superiority of one or another integration rule for characterizing judges and tasks (see, for example, Dawes & Corrigan, 1974; Goldberg, 1968; Hoffman, Slovic, & Rorer, 1968). But, first impulse may be misleading.

Most commonly, the distinction is made between linear and configural types of processing. Configural processing is where properties of a given stimulus are determined with reference to other stimuli in the array. Following the distinctions made earlier in this chapter, in configural processing the value or weight of a stimulus is affected by the relationships or patterning of the stimulus configuration. In linear processing, on the other hand, stimulus values are simply added (or subtracted), and patterning on the basis of the stimulus array is not invoked. While most energy has been expended in discovering *which* processing model best fits most judges--and, the linear model has not surprisingly emerged victorious in most encounters--it may be better to consider *how much* configuration a judge manifests. This point requires expansion.

There is ample evidence at the individual subject level for differences in the degree of configural processing (Einhorn, 1970; Leon, Oden, & Anderson, 1973; Wiggins & Hoffman, 1968). Although a linear model will fit almost any judge reasonably well due to its power and generality, it seems inescapable that some judges are more characteristically configural than others. But, this need not signal the use of different integration rules. The weighted averaging model represented by Eqs. (1) to (3) is inherently configural in that the *effective* weight of one stimulus is determined by reference to weights of the other stimuli--a direct consequence of the averaging form. The power of this weighted averaging rule is immediately apparent; where weights and scale values are invarient, integration will be linear, and the well known parellelism effect in stimulus combination will obtain. Thus, the integration model adopted in this chapter can handle both linear and configural integration data (Anderson, 1972). In this light, judges need not differ in *rule usage* (that is, in changing one rule for another), but in extent of configural effects on *stimulus parameters* within the same integration rule.

Strategies in assigning values to stimulus parameters may differentiate judges. Moreover, the following example, as well as studies of context effects on stimulus components (see review by Kaplan, 1974; also, "The Basic Model," above) suggests that the locus of configural effects is in the weight, and not the scale value parameter. To illustrate, consider a stimulus design incorporating physical (for example, attractiveness) and verbal (for example, personality traits) information, with two levels (positive and negative) of each. In such a factorial design, linearity would be reflected in the lack of statistical interaction between physical and verbal information, that is, in parallelism between factors. The data, however, reflect configuration, whereby the more attractive person is always judged higher, but more so when both possess positive attributes, compared to negative (Lampel & Anderson, 1968; Miller, 1972; Sigall & Aronson, 1969). This sort of stimulus interaction is in accord with Eqs. (2) and (3) where the weight $(w_i)$ of the $i$th stimulus is determined with reference to other stimuli in the array. The fact that positive physical and trait attributes are always judged higher than their negative counterparts in this illustration suggests that the locus of configural

151

effects is not on scale value changes. A pretty girl doesn't become uglier when we find that she is "selfish"; her physiognomy just becomes less important to our liking for her when other attributes are negative, compared to positive. Other configural phenomena such as inconsistency and redundancy discounting (Kaplan, 1972, 1973) are likewise understandable in terms of differential weighting (for related discussion, see Anderson, 1969, 1972).

And so, the question is not whether people use linear or configural integration rules, but the extent to which they utilize complex strategies of differential weighting, and in which tasks, and with what stimulus combinations. In this regard, it would be instructive to examine the cognitive and other personality characteristics of subjects who differ consistently in integration complexity, and also developmental changes in complexity. Efforts at identifying the first have thus far proven unsuccessful (Wiggins & Hoffman, 1968).

## DIFFERENCES IN DISPOSITIONAL TENDENCIES

Judges have dispositional tendencies which affect their responses to others. Dispositions exist prior to evaluation of the information received about a particular object, and they represent the response to that object at zero pieces of information. For Eqs. (2) and (3), disposition can be coordinated with $s_0$, the initial impression. Two sources of the initial impression can be identified: transient situational states and global dispositions. In personological terms, the first refers to states, and the second to traits in the judge (Kaplan, 1975b).

### Transient Situational States

General evaluative tendencies which affect judgment beyond the given information may stem, in part, from temporary states in the judge that result from situational conditions. A common term applied to these states is "mood." Various experimental manipulations have been shown to temporarily influence levels of evaluative judgment. Transient states have been induced by prior expectancies for the other (Kelley, 1950), instructions to assume certain roles (Jones & De Charms, 1958), physical discomfort (Griffitt, 1970), crowding (Griffitt & Veitch, 1971), and overheard propaganda (Kaplan & Major, 1973).

The last study will illustrate the effect of transient situational states on interpersonal judgments. Under the guise of participating in a new experimental technique in opinion polling, subjects compared attitudes with a

152

confederate pollster having either positive (agreeing) or negative (disagreeing) attitudes. Prior to the interaction, subjects were exposed, in an offhand manner, to one of three contrived radio broadcasts. The two experimental broadcasts were of a bogus social commentator reviewing the history of mankind who portrayed man as either a nasty creature (negative condition) or essentially good at heart (positive condition). Popular music was played for the control condition. Judgments of the confederate were more positive following the positive broadcast, and more negative following the negative broadcast, compared to control conditions, and equally so for agreeing and disagreeing attitude information.

## Global Dispositions

People also differ in their global dispositions in judging others, or in their stable tendency to evaluate objects of a given class (people, for example) in a certain way. Over the years, several investigators have noted the presence of generalized evaluative dispositions and have applied a variety of labels to them. Thus, we may speak of "halo effects" (Thorndike, 1920), "logical errors" (Newcomb, 1931), "global dispositions" (Asch, 1946; Gage & Cronbach, 1955), "elevations" (Cronbach, 1955), and finally, "response biases" (Kaplan, 1967). All labels have in common the concept of characteristic individual differences in the evaluative judgment of others. To illustrate some glaring individual differences, contrast the conceptions of people reflected in Will Rogers' statement "I never met a man I didn't like" with the world-view apparent in Dickens' Scrooge.

In keeping, therefore, with the general use of the term, "disposition" here refers to a readiness to evaluate others in a particular direction—that is, positive or negative. This readiness presumably exists prior to acquaintance with a given stimulus person and is independent of specific stimulus information (see Gage & Cronbach, 1955; Kaplan, 1971a).

The focus here is on individual differences in dispositions; this does not imply, however, that universal characteristics are unimportant. For example, a general tendency to attribute positivity to others has been proposed (Boucher & Osgood, 1969).

Two approaches to studying global dispositions have emerged. The first is a search for dispositional correlates of standard personality variables. That is, dispositions are inferred from judgments of a variety of stimulus persons and are then related to personality attributes of the judge. The second approach directly measures or manipulates the judge's dispositions and then observes their effect on person impressions.

153

## *Personality Correlates*

Several personality variables, measured by standard inventories, have been related to tendencies to form positive or negative judgments of others. In some instances general evaluative favorability was studied, while in others subjects evaluated specific attributes, such as hostility (Altrocchi, Shrauger, & McLeod, 1964; Palmer & Altrocchi, 1967) and authoritarianism (Crockett & Meidinger, 1956; Scodel & Mussen, 1953). In general, more unfavorable evaluations are elicited from sensitizers and expressers compared to repressers (Altrocchi et al., 1964; Kaplan, 1967, 1968b), from high compared to low differentiators (Rosenthal, 1961), from maladjusted subjects compared to adjusted (Matcom, 1963), and from subjects low in self-reported social desirability compared to highs (Edwards, 1959; Palmer & Altrocchi, 1967). The relationship between authoritarianism and evaluative dispositions is more complex: High authoritarians are generally more negative (Crockett & Meidinger, 1956; Scodel & Mussen, 1953) except when judging persons similar to themselves (Kates, 1959) or leaders (Jones, 1954).

Studies of evaluative dispositions associated with particular personality dimensions are essentially correlative and offer little insight into the effect of dispositions on person impressions. The problem is that dispositions are inferred from the responses to specific persons and thus cannot act as predictors of impressions. It is preferable to designate dispositions independent of the responses they are to predict, permitting the study of the interaction of dispositional and situational factors. The next section describes such a research strategy.

## A-Priori *Dispositions*

It is helpful to ask first, how dispositions are formed. It is assumed that dispositions can be considered as generalized attitudes, formed in much the same way as attitudes toward any object. That is, individuals possess various beliefs about the attributes of others. Associated with each belief is an evaluative component, which is the position of that belief on the relevant evaluative dimension—for example, likableness. Global dispositions are a pooled function of the evaluative component of all salient beliefs about people in general. This assumption underlies the method for disposition measurement used in the experiments that follow.

This reasoning suggests that dispositions can be estimated from the evaluative level of the subject's salient beliefs about others. Several studies (Kaplan, 1968a, 1970, 1971a,

1971b, 1971c, 1971e) have identified dispositional tendencies
by having subjects produce, in continued association, those
traits which characterize people in general.  Dispositions
were assessed by an index of discrepancy between the number
of traits high and low on a given dimension from among the
first 12 emitted in a six-minute span.  For example, dispositions toward positive or negative evaluations of others were
identified by subtracting number of dislikable from likable
traits; discrepancies $> \pm 4$ indicated extreme levels of positive or negative dispositions (Kaplan, 1970, 1971a, 1971e).
Similar procedures have been used in identifying high-
sociableness and low-sociableness dispositions (Kaplan, 1971b,
1971c).  That is, words denoting sociable behavior were identified among the first 12 omitted, and disposition scores
consisted of the number of sociable words emitted less the
remainder.  The implicit assumption, of course, is that the
order of emission of traits of a given response class is an
index of the relative strength of dispositional tendency for
that class.  This "order of emission" assumption has been
supported in the study of racial attitudes (K. Kaplan &
Fishbein, 1969) and word associative strength (Garskof,
Shapiro, & Brandstadter, 1967).

More recently, a check-list version of the continued-
association task has been employed (Kaplan, 1972, 1973, 1975b).
The check list contains high-, medium-, and low-likableness
traits, 12 of each, and the subject's task is to select the
12 words which he would most likely use in describing other
people.  Particular traits on the list are those most frequently emitted by normative subjects in continued association.
Again, the disposition score consists of the discrepancy
between number of high-likableness and low-likableness words
selected.  The check-list and continued-association methods
are highly comparable as assessors of disposition and yield
results that are theoretically comparable as well (see below).
For further discussion of the development and rationale of the
continued-association and check-list techniques, see Kaplan
(1975b).

Judges designated as positive in global disposition, compared to negatives, have consistently given higher judgments
of others and higher judgments across variations in stimulus
materials.  That is, dispositional differences, defined by
either the check-list or the continued-association method,
have been reflected in judgments based on trait adjectives
(Kaplan, 1970, 1971a, 1971c, 1971e, 1972, 1973) and auto-
biographical sketches (Kaplan, 1971b).  And the effects of
disposition hold true whether the disposition-and-judgment
dimension is one of sociableness or likableness.  It should be
noted that dispositional differences between judges are

dimension-specific; judges who differ in their disposition toward ascribing sociableness to others do not differ in judgments of changeableness or independence (Kaplan, 1971c).


INTERACTION OF JUDGE AND INFORMATIONAL VARIABLES

That dispositions are measurable, can be identified prior to judgment of a stimulus person, and have demonstrable effects on judgments of specific others says little about the role of dispositions in the integration process and their interaction with nondispositional variables. For example, dispositions may simply act as an additive constant, to be added to (or subtracted from) the product of the information values in the judge's personal equation. This can be done by dispositions acting as values in themselves or as antecedents to response-language differences. The integration model expressed in Eqs. (2) and (3), however, specifies that dispositions and stimulus information are combined in a weighted *average*, so that the effect of dispositions need not be constant but may vary with informational and situational factors. The next two sections explore the implications of the averaging rule for dispositional effects. The reader may have noted that the concept of disposition has been substituted for the more general term employed in Anderson's model, "initial impression." Earlier it was suggested that initial impression is a function of both state and trait variables. But, in most experimental designs, transient situational effects are presumably random, and variations in initial impressions should reflect experimental manipulations of disposition (Kaplan, 1971a, p. 283).

*THE STIMULUS PERSON*

In all the experiments reported in this and the following section, an impression-formation paradigm was followed. Judges high or low in a given disposition (that is, likableness or sociableness) rated, for that dimension, persons described by a set of traits as either high or low in value on the same dimension.

One expectation from Eq. (3) is that dispositions and information should combine linearly. Thus, in a factorial design, with disposition and trait evaluative level as main factors, both main effects should obtain, and the interaction between disposition and information value should theoretically be zero. This parallelism prediction has been strongly supported for both the likableness judgment dimension (Kaplan, 1970, 1971a, 1971e, 1972) and the sociableness judgment

dimension (Kaplan, 1971b, 1971c) and is illustrated in
Figure 1.

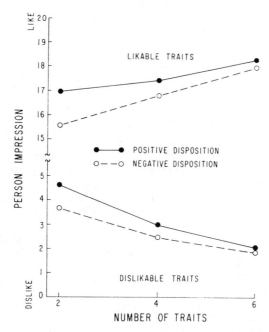

*Fig. 1. Person impression as a
function of dispositions, and likableness and number of traits. Experiment
II in Kaplan (1972).*

Although dispositional effects are parallel for stimulus
persons described by different trait values, there are some
limitations on their generality across situations and stimulus persons.  Consider first the stimulus person.  Stimulus
qualities, other than information value, may modify the effective importance of dispositions.  These include the amount,
redundancy, and inconsistency of information.
   According to Eq. (3), the relative contribution of disposition value ($s_0$) and information value ($s_k$) is a direct
function of the amount of information in the stimulus set.
That is, the summed weight ($\Sigma w_i$) of the information term ($s_i$)
is a direct function of number of stimulus components with
weight > 0.  For trait stimuli, amount of information may be
roughly coordinated with number of stimulus traits.  It is
also intuitively reasonable to expect that dispositions would
be manifested to a lesser extent given more information about
the person (see also Koltuv, 1962).  In a confirmation of this

157

prediction, increases in size of the set of traits led to
decreased impression differences due to dispositions for both
the likableness dimension (Kaplan, 1972) and the sociableness
dimension (Kaplan, 1971c). There is one important qualifica-
tion to this set-size effect, however; increases in information need to be nonredundant with earlier information (Kaplan,
1972). This modifier, too, is consistent with Eq. (3).
Redundancy tends to reduce the weight of individual stimulus
components (Kaplan, 1971d; Schmidt, 1969). This weight reduction would offset the increase in number of stimuli,
resulting in little or no net gain in the relative contribution of the stimulus term in Eq. (3). Kaplan (1972) illustrates these points. In two experiments, judges high or low
in likableness dispositions rated the likableness of persons
described by 2, 4, or 6 univalent (positive or negative)
traits. In both experiments, traits were low in intraset
redundancy, and, in one experiment, sets of redundant traits
were also rated. Redundancy was determined by norms based on
ratings of likelihood of trait co-occurrence (Kaplan, 1971d).
Increased set-size led to diminution of differences in the
ratings of disposition groups, but only for nonredundant sets
(see Figure 1). Thus, the number of traits per se is less
crucial for determining the effect of disposition than is
their informativeness. For example, three redundant traits
(say, intelligent, bright, and smart) are less diagnostic for
likableness than three nonredundant traits (intelligent,
honest, considerate). The magnitude of dispositional contribution to judgment is dependent on the informativeness of
stimuli for the required judgment.

An alternative interpretation of Figure 1 might be entertained at this point. When the response measure consists of
a metric scale, observed interactions may be an artifact of
the response scale and may not reflect real differences in
patterns of judgment. Monotone transformations can be introduced, for example, to eliminate the interaction between set
size and disposition. Similarly, the observed convergence
of curves in Figure 1 may be attributed to ceiling and floor
effects. Several pieces of evidence suggest, however, that a
scaling-artifact interpretation is not tenable. First, interactions between disposition and stimulus weighting occur,
using the same response scale, where ceiling and floor effects
are unlikely explanations (see Figures 3 and 4). Second, the
disposition by set-size interaction has been found with metric
scales on the disposition dimension, but not with similar
scales for dimensions unrelated to dispositional differences
(Kaplan, 1971c), indicating that the metric nature of the
scale is not responsible for the interaction. Third, and most
compelling, dispositional effects are found with nonmetric

response tasks involving choice of descriptive trait adjectives (Kaplan, 1968a, 1968b) and of behavioral descriptions (Kaplan, 1971b). Interactions between stimulus qualities and dispositions on nonmetric choice tasks are not readily explained by response-scale interpretations.

Studies cited thus far have presented the subject with stimulus persons described by univalent stimulus information. In the social world, however, rarely are we blessed with information so uniform; more frequently we must evaluate information which is evaluatively or semantically inconsistent. Since one response to inconsistency is stimulus discounting (Anderson & Jacobson, 1965; Hendrick & Costantini, 1970; Levin & Schmidt, 1970), we can ask, do persons with different dispositions show different patterns of discounting? For example, given both positive and negative attributes of a stimulus person, would positive-disposition subjects discount negative and negative-disposition subjects discount positive attributes? If so, impression differences due to dispositions would be enhanced when information is internally inconsistent and subjects are given an opportunity to discount. This proposition has been confirmed (Kaplan, 1973). Subjects rated their impressions of persons described by mixtures of likable and dislikable traits, and also rated the importance of each trait for forming their judgments. As predicted, subjects discounted the importance of disposition-incongruent traits under conditions favoring unequal weighting of stimuli (see Figure 2). The effect of importance discounting was to increase disposition effects on likableness ratings over equal-weighting conditions (see Figure 3). Apparently, the presence of stimulus inconsistency enhances effects due to dispositions when judges have an opportunity to attach differential importance to stimuli.

*THE SITUATION*

Consider, now, the situation. Situational factors, too, serve to reduce or enhance the effect of disposition on judgment. By influencing the weight of information ($w_i$), these factors can modify the relative contribution of information and disposition to the response. Suppose that the information about the stimulus person is supplied by an unreliable source or that an otherwise reliable source expresses little confidence that the information provided is valid. Under these conditions we would expect the information to carry little weight, and, on both intuitive and theoretical grounds, dispositional effects should be augmented. Two experiments are relevant. In one (Kaplan, 1971a), persons were described by two traits, attributed to either high-prestige or low-prestige

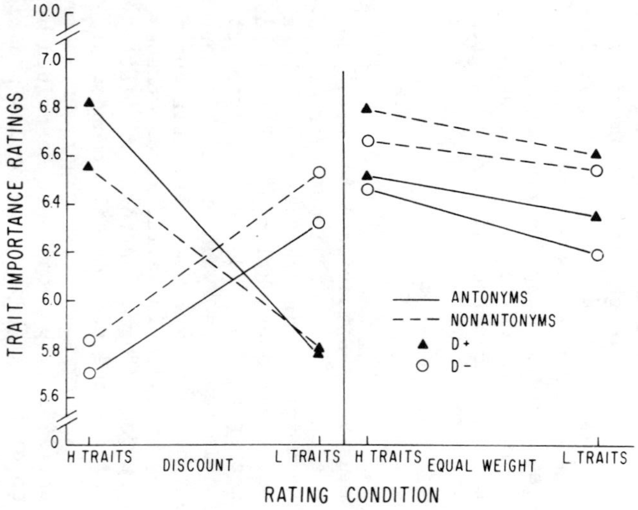

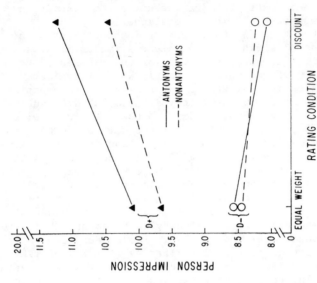

Fig. 2. Trait-importance ratings as a function of rating conditions, subject disposition, trait value, and antonymic consistency. (D+ and D− refer to positive- and negative-disposition subjects, respectively. H and L refer to highly likable and dislikable traits, respectively.) Data from Kaplan (1973a).

Fig. 3. Person impressions as a function of rating conditions, subject disposition, and antonymic consistency. Data from Kaplan (1973a).

sources. Both traits were either highly positive or highly negative in value. The second experiment (Kaplan, 1971e) was similar, except that judges were told either that the sources had rated the traits as highly characteristic of the stimulus person or that the sources were only guessing that the person possessed the traits. Findings supported the interactive prediction; impression-rating differences due to *a priori* dispositions increased when the rating situation detracted from the credence or weight of information (see Figure 4).

As a theoretical note, this implies that dispositions and information are averaged, and not added in the sense of a "constant error." The extent to which dispositions add (or subtract) from the pooled value of information depends on the relative weighting of information and disposition. The weighting by disposition interaction also rules out a response scale interpretation of disposition effects. If dispositions merely reflected idiosyncratic ways of using the response scale, rather than the underlying judgment, effects would be constant for the same scale.

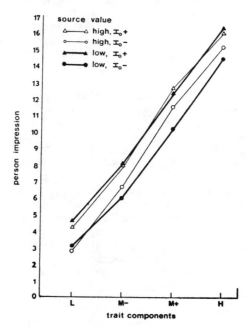

*Fig. 4. Person impressions as a function of trait components, source value, and initial impression. (L = highly dislikable, M− = moderately dislikable, M+ = moderately likable, H = highly likable.) Data from Kaplan (1971a).*

*A priori* dispositions merit further study. One interesting question might be: What personality variables are related to a given disposition? Unlike previous work on personality correlates (see the section entitled "Global Dispositions"), it is proposed that personality variables be related to global dispositions identified apart from the subject's impressions of specific stimulus persons. Another question is the generality of laws governing disposition and information integration. Do the same results obtain when nonevaluative impressions are formed? Most tests of the model have employed impressions and dispositions of likableness. However, a growing body of literature indicates that the general model is workable within a variety of other response dimensions (Anderson, 1974a; Hamilton & Huffman, 1971; Kaplan, 1971c).

## GENERALITY OR SPECIFICITY OF DISPOSITIONAL EFFECTS

A central question in personality research is whether personality effects upon behavior are trans-situationally consistent or situationally specific. Some have argued (for example, Bem, 1972; Mischel, 1968) that personality dispositions are limited to given situations, their presence or manifestation being determined by moderator variables in the situation. Others (for example, Alker, 1972) disagree, suggesting that personality exerts a consistent effect across situations.

This question finds an echo in social judgment. The early expectation (for example, Asch, 1946; Gage & Cronbach, 1955) was for high consistency of dispositional effects across stimulus persons, but subsequent empirical results were mixed and inconclusive (Burwen & Campbell, 1957; Gross, 1961; see also reviews by Shrauger & Altrocchi, 1964; Taguiri, 1969). In agreement with the specificity position, the work on *a priori* dispositions suggests several moderator variables which regulate the effect of dispositions. These include veridicality and source prestige factors and amount, redundancy, and consistency of information. Though dispositions are globally characteristic of the individual, their manifestation in judgment is modifiable by situational and stimulus variables (see Kaplan, 1975b, for further discussion).

## CONCLUDING COMMENTS

Much of what we know about individual differences in social judgment can be included in an information-integration approach to judgment. Integration theory (Anderson, 1974a) provides a unified and powerful framework for considering

judge variables. As with any judgment, person-judgment impressions are formed by integrating available information
values with dispositions, allowing for different importance
weights of the two. Individual differences may be found at
several points in the integration process. First, several
personality factors can be shown to affect the weighting of
stimulus components, relative both to one another, and to
pre-existing dispositions. Second, people may differ in the
values they assign to stimulus components. Third, people may
differ in attributing additional characteristics to others
based on known attributes.

Finally, people differ in the pre-existing dispositions
they bring to judgment. Social judgments represent a
weighted balance between the information being processed and
the dispositions, so that dispositional effects may vary with
the stimulus person and the situation. That is, the effects
of dispositions, and therefore the extent of individual differences in response, are parallel for different values of
stimuli. Dispositional effects diminish, however, with
increased amount of nonredundant information and increased
importance of information for the judgment. Dispositions also
affect the weighting of disposition-incongruent information,
so that when discounting occurs in sets of inconsistent
information, individual differences are enhanced.

In social judgment the old generality that behavior is a
function of the person and the environment seems alive and
well. In fact, one can add: *The function appears to be a
weighted average!*

## ACKNOWLEDGMENTS

Preparation of this chapter was facilitated by National
Institute of Mental Health Grant MH23516. The research
reported here was supported by grants from the National
Institute of Mental Health (MH19388) and the National Science
Foundation (GS27290). Robert Ahlering, Marcia Donnerstein,
Steven Gabler, David Hildebrandt, Gwen Kemmerick, Paul Olczak,
and Polly Ann Robertus assisted in the experiments summarized
here, and their able help is gratefully acknowledged. The
comments of Norman Anderson and Manard Stewart on a draft of
this chapter are appreciated.

REFERENCES

Alker, H. A.   Is personality situationally specific or intra-physically consistent?  *Journal of Personality*, 1972, *40*, 1-16.

Altrocchi, J., Shrauger, S., & McLeod, M. A.   Attribution of hostility to self and others by expressors, sensitizers, and repressors.  *Journal of Clinical Psychology*, 1964, *20*, 233.

Anderson, N. H.   Primacy effects in personality impression formation using a generalized order effect paradigm. *Journal of Personality and Social Psychology*, 1965, *2*, 1-9.

Anderson, N. H.   A simple model for information integration. In R. P. Abelson, E. Aronson, W. J. McGuire, T. M. Newcomb, M. J. Rosenberg, & P. H. Tannenbaum (Eds.), *Theories of cognitive consistency:  A sourcebook*.  Chicago:  Rand McNally, 1968.

Anderson, N. H.   Comment on "An analysis-of-variance model for the assessment of configural cue utilization in clinical judgment."  *Psychological Bulletin*, 1969, *72*, 63-65.

Anderson, N. H.   Functional measurement and psychophysical judgment.  *Psychological Review*, 1970, *77*, 153-170.

Anderson, N. H.   Two more tests against change of meaning in adjective combinations.  *Journal of Verbal Learning and Verbal Behavior*, 1971, *10*, 75-85.

Anderson, N. H.   Looking for configurality in clinical judgment.  *Psychological Bulletin*, 1972, *78*, 93-102.

Anderson, N. H.   Functional measurement of social desirability. *Sociometry*, 1973, *36*, 89-98.

Anderson, N. H.   Information integration theory:  A brief survey.  In D. H. Krantz, R. C. Atkinson, R. D. Luce, & P. Suppes (Eds.), *Contemporary developments in mathematical psychology*.  San Francisco:  Freeman, 1974.  (a)

Anderson, N. H.   Algebraic models in perception.  In E. C. Carterette & M. P. Friedman (Eds.), *Handbook of perception* (Vol. 2).  New York:  Academic Press, 1974.  (b)

Anderson, N. H.   Cognitive algebra:  Integration theory applied to social attribution.  In L. Berkowitz (Ed.), *Advances in experimental social psychology* (Vol. 7). New York:  Academic Press, 1974.  (c)

Anderson, N. H., & Jacobson, A.   Effect of stimulus inconsis-tency and discounting instructions in personality impres-sion formation.  *Journal of Personality and Social Psychology*, 1965, *2*, 531-539.

Asch, S. E.   Forming impressions of personality.  *Journal of Abnormal and Social Psychology*, 1946, *41*, 258-290.

Bem, D. J.   Constructing cross-situational consistencies in
    behavior:   Some thoughts on Alker's critique of Mischel.
    *Journal of Personality*, 1972, *40*, 17-26.
Bieri, J., Atkins, A., Briar, S., Leaman, R., Miller, H., &
    Tripodi, T.   *Clinical and social judgment:   The discrimina-
    tion of behavioral information.*   New York:   Wiley, 1966.
Boucher, J., & Osgood, C. E.   The pollyanna hypothesis.
    *Journal of Verbal Learning and Verbal Behavior*, 1969, *8*,
    1-8.
Bruner, J. S., & Taguiri, R.   The perception of people.   In
    G. Lindzey (Ed.), *Handbook of social psychology* (Vol. 2).
    Cambridge, Mass.:   Addison-Wesley, 1954.
Burwen, L. S., & Campbell, D. T.   The generality of attitudes
    toward authority and nonauthority figures.   *Journal of
    Abnormal and Social Psychology*, 1957, *54*, 24-31.
Byrne, D.   *The attraction paradigm.*   New York:   Academic
    Press, 1971.
Carroll, J. D.   Individual differences and multidimensional
    scaling.   In R. N. Shepard, A. K. Romney, & S. Nerlove
    (Eds.), *Multidimensional scaling:   Theory and applications
    in the behavioral sciences* (Vol. 1).   New York:   Seminar
    Press, 1972.
Crockett, W. H.   Cognitive complexity and impression formation.
    In B. A. Maher (Ed.), *Progress in experimental personality
    research* (Vol. 2).   New York:   Academic Press, 1965.
Crockett, W. H., & Meidinger, T.   Authoritarianism and inter-
    personal perception.   *Journal of Abnormal and Social
    Psychology*, 1956, *53*, 378-380.
Cronbach, L. J.   Processes affecting scores on "understanding
    of others" and "assumed similarity."   *Psychological
    Bulletin*, 1955, *52*, 177-193.
Dawes, R. M., & Corrigan, B.   Linear models in decision making.
    *Psychological Bulletin*, 1974, *81*, 95-106.
Dustin, D. S., & Baldwin, P. M.   Redundancy in impression
    formation.   *Journal of Personality and Social Psychology*,
    1966, *3*, 500-506.
Edwards, A. L.   Social desirability and the description of
    others.   *Journal of Abnormal and Social Psychology*, 1959,
    *59*, 434-436.
Ehrlich, H. J., & Lipsey, C.   Affective style as a variable in
    person perception.   *Journal of Personality*, 1969, *37*,
    522-540.
Einhorn, H. J.   Use of nonlinear, noncompensatory models in
    decision making.   *Psychological Bulletin*, 1970, *73*,
    221-230.

Feather, N. T. Valence of outcome and expectation of success in relation to task difficulty and perceived locus of control. *Journal of Personality and Social Psychology*, 1967, *7*, 372–386.

Felipe, A. I. Evaluative versus descriptive consistency in trait inferences. *Journal of Personality and Social Psychology*, 1970, *16*, 627–638.

Gage, N. L., & Cronbach, L. J. Conceptual and methodological problems in interpersonal perception. *Psychological Review*, 1955, *62*, 411–422.

Garskof, B. E., Shapiro, E. G., & Brandstadter, J. Order of emission in continued association as a predictor of individual free recall. *Psychonomic Science*, 1967, *7*, 209–210.

Goldberg, L. R. Simple models or simple processes? Some research on clinical judgments. *American Psychologist*, 1968, *23*, 483–496.

Gollin, E. S. Organizational characteristics of social judgment: A developmental investigation. *Journal of Personality*, 1958, *26*, 139–154.

Griffitt, W. B. Environmental effects on interpersonal affective behavior: Ambient effective temperature and attraction. *Journal of Personality and Social Psychology*, 1970, *15*, 240–244.

Griffitt, W. B., & Veitch, R. Hot and crowded: Influences of population density and temperature on interpersonal affective behavior. *Journal of Personality and Social Psychology*, 1971, *17*, 92–98.

Gross, C. F. Intrajudge consistency in ratings of heterogeneous persons. *Journal of Abnormal and Social Psychology*, 1961, *62*, 605–610.

Halverson, C. F., Jr. Interpersonal perception: Cognitive complexity and trait implication. *Journal of Consulting and Clinical Psychology*, 1970, *34*, 86–90.

Hamilton, D. L. The structure of personality judgments: Comments on Kuusinen's paper and further evidence. *Scandanavian Journal of Psychology*, 1970, *11*, 261–265.

Hamilton, D. L. Implicit personality theories: Dimensions of interpersonal cognition. Symposium paper presented at the annual meeting of the American Psychological Association, Washington D.C., September, 1971.

Hamilton, D. L., & Fallot, R. D. Information salience as a weighting factor in impression formation. *Journal of Personality and Social Psychology*, 1974, *30*, 444–448.

Hamilton, D. L., & Huffman, L. J. Generality of impression formation processes for evaluative and nonevaluative judgments. *Journal of Personality and Social Psychology*, 1971, *20*, 200–207.

Harvey, O. J., Hunt, D. E., & Schroder, H. M. *Conceptual systems and personality organization*. New York: Wiley, 1961.

Hendrick, C., & Costantini, A. F. Effects of varying trait inconsistency and response requirements on the primacy effect in impression formation. *Journal of Personality and Social Psychology*, 1970, *15*, 158-164.

Hoffman, P. J., Slovic, P., & Rorer, L. G. An analysis-of-variance model for the assessment of configural cue utilization in clinical judgment. *Psychological Bulletin*, 1968, *69*, 338-349.

Jackson, P., & Warr, P. Instances and inferences. *British Journal of Psychology*, 1974, *65*, 547-549.

Johnson, M. P., & Ewens, W. L. Power relations and affective style as determinants of confidence in impression formation. *Proceedings, 77th Annual Convention of the American Psychological Awsociation*, 1969, 349-350.

Jones, E. E. Authoritarianism as a determinant of first-impression formation. *Journal of Personality*, 1954, *23*, 107-127.

Jones, E. E., & DeCharms, R. The organizing function of interaction roles in person perception. *Journal of Abnormal and Social Psychology*, 1958, *57*, 155-164.

Jones, E. E., Kanouse, D. E., Kelley, H. H., Nisbett, R. E., Valins, S., & Weiner, B. *Attribution: Perceiving the causes of behavior*. New York: General Learning Press, 1971.

Kaplan, K. J., & Fishbein, M. The source of beliefs, their saliency, and prediction of attitude. *The Journal of Social Psychology*, 1969, *78*, 63-74.

Kaplan, M. F. Repression-sensitization and prediction of self-descriptive behavior: Response vs. situational cue variables. *Journal of Abnormal Psychology*, 1967, *72*, 354-361.

Kaplan, M. F. Differentiation among targets in social perception as a function of response hierarchy. *Psychonomic Science*, 1968, *10*, 227-228. (a)

Kaplan, M. F. Elicitation of information and response biases of repressors, sensitizers, and neutrals in behavior prediction. *Journal of Personality*, 1968, *36*, 84-91. (b)

Kaplan, M. F. Forming impressions of personality: The effect of the initial impression. *Psychonomic Science*, 1970, *18*, 255-256.

Kaplan, M. F. Dispositional effects and weight of information in impression formation. *Journal of Personality and Social Psychology*, 1971, *18*, 279-284. (a)

Kaplan, M. F.    Response hierarchy, reception, and the process of person perception. *Human Relations*, 1971, *24*, 189-199.    (b)

Kaplan, M. F.    The effect of judgmental dispositions in forming impressions of personality. *Canadian Journal of Behavioral Science*, 1971, *3*, 259-267.    (c)

Kaplan, M. F.    The determination of trait redundancy in personality impression formation. *Psychonomic Science*, 1971, *23*, 280-282.    (d)

Kaplan, M. F.    The effect of evaluative dispositions, and amount and credibility of information on forming impressions of personality. *Psychonomic Science*, 1971, *24*, 174-176.    (e)

Kaplan, M. F.    The modifying effect of stimulus information on the consistency of individual differences in impression formation. *Journal of Experimental Research in Personality*, 1972, *6*, 213-219.

Kaplan, M. F.    Stimulus inconsistency and response dispositions in forming judgments of other persons. *Journal of Personality and Social Psychology*, 1973, *25*, 58-64.

Kaplan, M. F.    Context induced shifts in personality trait evaluations:    A comment on the evaluative halo effect and the meaning change interpretations. *Psychological Bulletin*, 1974, *81*, 891-895.

Kaplan, M. F.    Evaluative judgments are based on evaluative information:    Evidence against meaning change in evaluative effects. *Memory and Cognition*, 1975, in press.    (a)

Kaplan, M. F.    Measurement and generality of response dispositions in person perception. *Journal of Personality*, 1975, in press.    (b)

Kaplan, M. F., & Anderson, N. H.    Information integration theory and reinforcement theory as approaches to interpersonal attraction. *Journal of Personality and Social Psychology*, 1973, *25*, 301-312.

Kaplan, M. F., & Major, G.    Will you like me at set-size 3 as much as you might at 6?:    Amount of information and attraction.    Paper presented at the annual meeting of the Psychonomic Society, St. Louis, November, 1973.

Kates, S. L.    First impression formation and authoritarianism. *Human Relations*, 1959, *12*, 277-286.

Kelley, H. H.    The warm-cold variable in first impressions of persons. *Journal of Personality*, 1950, *18*, 431-439.

Kelly, J. S., & Rice, L. E.    Effects of dogmatism and field dependence upon the perception and utilization of discrepant information.    Paper presented at the annual meeting of the Western Psychological Association, Los Angeles, May, 1970.

Koltuv, B. B.  Some characteristics of intrajudge trait inter-correlations. *Psychological Monographs*, 1962, *76*(33, Whole No. 552).

Kuusinen, J.  Factorial invariance of personality ratings. *Scandanavian Journal of Psychology*, 1969, *10*, 33–44.

Lampel, A. K., & Anderson, N. H.  Combining visual and verbal information in an impression-formation task. *Journal of Personality and Social Psychology*, 1968, *9*, 1–6.

Leon, M., Oden, G. C., & Anderson, N. H.  Functional measurement of social values. *Journal of Personality and Social Psychology*, 1973, *27*, 301–310.

Levin, I. P., & Schmidt, C. F.  Differential influence of information in an impression-formation task with binary intermittent responding. *Journal of Experimental Psychology*, 1970, *84*, 374–376.

Manis, M., Gleason, T. C., & Dawes, R. M.  The evaluation of complex social stimuli. *Journal of Personality and Social Psychology*, 1966, *3*, 404–419.

Matcom, A. J.  Impression formation as a function of adjustment. *Psychological Monographs*, 1963, *77*(No. 5, Whole No. 568).

Mayo, C. W., & Crockett, W. H.  Cognitive complexity and primacy-recency effects in impression formation. *Journal of Abnormal and Social Psychology*, 1964, *68*, 335–338.

Miller, A. G.  Effect of attitude similarity-dissimilarity on the utilization of additional stimulus inputs in judgments of interpersonal attraction. *Psychonomic Science*, 1972, *26*, 199–203.

Mischel, W.  *Personality and assessment*.  New York:  Wiley, 1968.

Newcomb, T.  An experiment designed to test the validity of a rating technique. *Journal of Applied Psychology*, 1931, *22*, 279–289.

Nidorf, L. J.  *Individual differences in impression formation*. Unpublished doctoral dissertation, Clark University, 1961.

Osgood, C. E., Suci, G. I., & Tannenbaum, P. H.  *The measurement of meaning*.  Urbana, Illinois:  University of Illinois Press, 1957.

Palmer, J., & Altrocchi, J.  Attribution of hostile intent as unconscious. *Journal of Personality*, 1967, *35*, 164–177.

Passini, F. T., & Norman, W. T.  A universal conception of personality structure? *Journal of Personality and Social Psychology*, 1966, *4*, 44–49.

Peabody, D.  Evaluative and descriptive aspects in personality perception:  A reappraisal. *Journal of Personality and Social Psychology*, 1970, *16*, 639–646.

Pedersen, D. M.  The measurement of individual differences in perceived personality-trait relationships and their relation to certain determinants. *Journal of Social Psychology*, 1965, *65*, 233–258.

Pettigrew, T. F.  The measurement and correlates of category width as a cognitive variable. *Journal of Personality*, 1958, *26*, 532–544.

Richey, M. H., McClelland, L., & Shimkunas, A. M.  Relative influence of positive and negative information in impression formation and persistence. *Journal of Personality and Social Psychology*, 1967, *6*, 322–327.

Rosenberg, S., Nelson, C., & Vivekananthan, P. S.  A multidimensional approach to the structure of personality impressions. *Journal of Personality and Social Psychology*, 1968, *9*, 283–294.

Rosenberg, S., & Olshan, K.  Evaluative and descriptive aspects in personality perception. *Journal of Personality and Social Psychology*, 1970, *16*, 619–626.

Rosenberg, S., & Sedlak, A.  Structural representations of implicit personality theory. In L. Berkowitz (Ed.), *Advances in experimental social psychology* (Vol. 6). New York: Academic Press, 1972.

Rosenthal, R. A.  *Cognitive complexity and the implicit personality theory of the judge.* Unpublished doctoral dissertation, University of Michigan, 1961.

Schmidt, C. F.  Personality impression formation as a function of relatedness of information and length of set. *Journal of Personality and Social Psychology*, 1969, *12*, 6–11.

Schneider, D. J.  Implicit personality theory: A review. *Psychological Bulletin*, 1973, *79*, 294–309.

Scodel, A., & Mussen, P.  Social perceptions of authoritarians and non-authoritarians. *Journal of Abnormal and Social Psychology*, 1953, *48*, 181–184.

Shapiro, D., & Taguiri, R.  Sex differences in inferring personality traits. *The Journal of Psychology*, 1959, *47*, 127–136.

Sherman, R.  Individual differences in perceived trait relationships as a function of dimensional salience. *Multivariate Behavioral Research*, 1972, *7*, 109–129.

Shrauger, S., & Altrocchi, J.  The personality of the perceiver as a factor in person perception. *Psychological Bulletin*, 1964, *62*, 289–308.

Sigall, H., & Aronson, E.  Liking for an evaluator as a function of her physical attractiveness and nature of the evaluations. *Journal of Experimental Social Psychology*, 1969, *5*, 93–100.

Steiner, I. D.   Ethnocentrism and tolerance of trait inconsistency. *Journal of Abnormal and Social Psychology*, 1954, *49*, 349-354.

Steiner, I. D., & Johnson, H. H.   Authoritarianism and "tolerance of trait inconsistency." *Journal of Abnormal and Social Psychology*, 1963, *67*, 388-391.

Steiner, I. D., & Johnson, H. H.   Category width and responses to interpersonal disagreements. *Journal of Personality and Social Psychology*, 1965, *2*, 290-292.

Taguiri, R.   Person perception.   In G. Lindzey & E. Aronson (Eds.), *The handbook of social psychology* (Vol. 3). Reading:  Addison-Wesley, 1969.

Tesser, A.   Differential weighting and directed meaning as explanations of primacy in impression formation. *Psychonomic Science*, 1968, *11*, 299-300.

Thorndike, E. L.   A constant error in psychological ratings. *Journal of Applied Psychology*, 1920, *4*, 25-29.

Ware, R., & Harvey, O. J.   A cognitive determinant of impression formation. *Journal of Personality and Social Psychology*, 1967, *5*, 38-44.

Wiggins, N. L., & Hoffman, P. J.   Three models of clinical judgment. *Journal of Abnormal Psychology*, 1968, *73*, 70-77.

Wyer, R. S., Jr.   Changes in meaning and halo effects in personality impression formation. *Journal of Personality and Social Psychology*, 1974, *29*, 829-835.

# 7. INTEGRATING VERBAL INFORMATION: THE REFERENTIAL-COMMUNICATION PARADIGM[1]

*Melvin Manis and Marjorie B. Platt*
The University of Michigan and Ann Arbor
Veterans Administration Hospital

| | |
|---|---|
| Introduction | 174 |
| Related Work | 175 |
| Information Integration | 175 |
| Empathy | 176 |
| Redundancy and Communication | 177 |
| Theoretical Framework and Examples | 177 |
| Empirical Results: Decoding | 183 |
| Empirical Results: Encoding | 186 |
| Ensemble Size and Communication | 189 |
| Immediate-Response Condition | 190 |
| Delayed-Response Condition | 195 |
| Implication | 196 |
| Concluding Remarks | 197 |
| References | 197 |

[1]All statements are those of the authors and do not necessarily represent the opinions or policy of the Veterans Administration.

## INTRODUCTION

The research described in this chapter derives in part from a simplified model of the communication process. In this model we assume that the communicator (for example, speaker) has an idea or image in his mind that he wants to convey to another person. The material that he hopes to convey is termed the intended referent. Since the intended referent cannot be conveyed *directly*, it must be transmitted in a symbolic form, as a spoken or written message. However, if the speaker constructs his message skillfully and the listener does his job well, an interchange between the two normally enables the listener to *infer* the communicator's intended referent (that is, the information that the communication was meant to convey).

This abbreviated sketch suggests that it may be possible objectively to assess communication accuracy if we can obtain clear-cut indexes of (1) the communicator's intended referent and (2) the recipient's inference. If the recipient's inference is accurate, we can conclude that communication has been successful; if it is inaccurate (that is, if the recipient fails to infer the communicator's intended meaning), we must conclude that there has to some degree been a failure in communication.

Despite the simplicity of this analysis, it is difficult to apply to everyday discourse, for we rarely have an objective indication of what the communicator *intended* to convey, nor do we have a clear-cut record of the recipient's *understanding* of the message he has received. To remedy this situation, a number of investigators (Krauss & Weinheimer, 1964; Lantz & Stefflre, 1964; Rosenberg & Cohen, 1966; Manis & van Rooijen, 1973) have studied communication under relatively controlled experimental conditions. A common approach is to present a speaker with a concrete referent (such as an abstract design or a photograph of a person's face); the speaker's task is to describe this referent in sufficient detail that a listener might be able to identify it when presented with a larger set of similar stimuli. If the listener's decoding of the message is accurate (that is, if he can identify the referent that the speaker was describing), then the experimenter concludes that communication has been successful, for in such a case the speaker will have been demonstrably successful in transmitting the information that he intended (that is, the identity of the target referent).

This chapter describes a program of research that posed the following general question: How is communication accuracy affected when an individual is presented with a *set* of descriptive messages, all based on the same target referent, rather

174

than with just one? In the studies that we undertook, different aspects of this problem were singled out for special attention by focusing, for example, on the *relationship* between the individual messages in a particular set or on the *size* of the message set (the number of individual passages that it included). In essence, then, we sought to explore a number of issues that revolved about the individual's capacity to integrate the information conveyed in freely written descriptive passages.

RELATED WORK

*INFORMATION INTEGRATION*

The study of information integration has been pursued most actively using the impression-formation paradigm (Anderson, 1968; Fishbein & Hunter, 1964; Manis, Gleason, & Dawes, 1966). In the typical study of impression formation, a respondent may be asked to estimate the "likability" of an individual who has been described, say, as "shy, intelligent, and irresponsible." Since the *true* likability of such an individual is not known, most investigators have focused on the relationship between (1) the input information that is available to the judge and (2) the judge's final impression. Although these experiments permit a careful examination of the respondent's implicit rules for integrating diverse inputs, in contrast to the work described in this chapter, they lack a good criterion of "correctness" and hence do not shed much light on the problem of cognitive effectiveness (or accuracy).

Experiments that are designed from the Bayesian viewpoint (Edwards, 1968; Slovic & Lichtenstein, 1971) are less vulnerable to this criticism, since these studies allow the investigator to compare (1) the respondent's subjective certainty concerning a given hypothesis with (2) the certainty that he "should" feel, according to Bayes's theorem. In much of the Bayesian research, however, there is no real question about which one of the competing hypotheses is more likely, given the available evidence. The investigator may, indeed, eliminate the few respondents who favor an incorrect (unreasonable) hypothesis, for in this tradition of research interest has often been focused on determining whether the respondent recognizes the *degree* to which the dominant hypothesis is implied by the available evidence.

175

*EMPATHY*

Another research area that is tangentially related to the present effort is reflected in the studies of empathy (or predictive accuracy) that were particularly popular in the 1950s (Taguiri, 1969). In this work the respondents were normally provided with meaningful information about someone (a filmed interview, perhaps) which they were to use in forming a subjective impression about that person's self-image. To assess the accuracy of these impressions, the usual procedure was to have the respondent attempt to predict the target individual's self-description on a set of structured personality items drawn, say, from the MMPI. By comparing the respondent's *predictions* with the target person's *actual* response to these same items, it was possible to derive what seemed to be a reasonable measure of social sensitivity (or empathy).

Many investigators used procedures of this type to assess the empathic skills of their respondents in the hope that they might uncover the psychological attributes (for example, intelligence, personality traits, and so on) that are associated with individual differences in this domain. Unfortunately, however, following several years of rather intensive effort, this approach lost its appeal for many investigators when it was discovered that most of the empathy measures did not yield a "pure" index of social sensitivity and were, indeed, replete with methodological artifacts that made them virtually uninterpretable (Cronbach, 1955, 1958; Gage & Cronbach, 1955). For example, it was discovered that many respondents had a strong tendency to assume that other people were generally similar to themselves. By predicting that the other would answer personality items in accordance with one's own dispositions, a respondent might fortuitously produce a relatively accurate set of predictions, providing that there was in fact substantial similarity between the self-concept of the predictor and that of the person whose responses he was attempting to predict. Unfortunately, when faced with someone who was unlike himself, this same predictor might prove quite inaccurate, for he would often persevere in his assumption that the other was somewhat similar to himself. Complications of this sort proved manifold and ultimately discouraged many investigators.

Despite the fact that they derive from a substantially different theoretical background, these earlier studies of empathy bear some relationship to the present program of research. In both cases, respondents are provided with socially meaningful information which they attempt to process in order to make some more distal inference that is subsequently scored in terms of correctness (or accuracy). The two

176

research traditions are quite different, however, in the sense
that the empathy researchers were primarily concerned with
individual differences in performance, while the present effort
is mainly focused on the impact that may be produced through
situational variations in the amount and type of input that is
made available to the respondents. Moreover, the problems of
artifact that proved so irksome to the empathy researchers do
not seem relevant in the work that is described below, mainly
because of our emphasis on input variables.

## REDUNDANCY AND COMMUNICATION

### THEORETICAL FRAMEWORK AND EXAMPLES

The first study in our program was designed to explore the
impact of redundancy on referential communication. Consider
a case in which a respondent has been provided with a pair of
verbal descriptions, both based on the same referent (a picture of an actor portraying one of several emotions). The
component descriptions in such a message pair may be closely
related to each other, or they may convey relatively independent information; that is, they may vary in *redundancy*.

In studies of impression formation, redundancy is usually
assessed by having a sample of judges indicate the likelihood
of co-occurrence for various trait pairs (for example, how
likely is it that an *honest* man will also be *friendly*?). This
approach was rejected in the present program because of the
complex and extended descriptive passages that we planned to
use. Instead, the redundancy of each message pair was defined
by the similarity of the choice profiles that were elicited
by the component descriptions when they were presented for
decoding, one at a time (Cronbach & Gleser, 1953).[2] We assumed here that in decoding any single passage, the photographs
that were selected most frequently by the norm group were the
photographs that the *individual* respondent would regard as the

---

[2]Profile similarity was assessed by using the Euclidean

$$D = \sqrt{\sum_{i=1}^{n} (f_{i_1} - f_{i_2})^2}$$

distance measure, (Osgood & Suci, 1952). In this expression
the term $f_{i_1}$ refers to the frequency with which alternative $i$
was chosen in response to description 1. It is important
to note that the $D$ score is an inverse measure of redundancy,
for low $D$ scores reflect similar choice profiles and hence are
indicative of high redundancy.

most "plausible" alternatives, as compared with photographs that were chosen less frequently. A pair of descriptions that elicited a similar pattern of referent choices was thus regarded as redundant, since, in the main, these descriptions implied the same referents. Following a similar rationale, we considered descriptions that led to different response profiles nonredundant.

This approach to the concept of redundancy is closely related to a tradition of research in the area of concept identification (Trabasso & Bower, 1968), in which two or more cues are regarded as redundant if they occur in the same set of stimulus objects. For example, the stimuli in a concept-formation experiment can be arranged such that all the *red* objects are also *square*, in which case these cues (or labels) might be regarded as redundant within the context of the experiment. In such a setting, if a stimulus was described as *red* by one respondent and *square* by another, these descriptions would provide redundant information--that is, the two terms would imply the same referent (or referents) to a naive listener, since a stimulus would be red if and only if it was also square. In a similar vein, we have been exclusively concerned with *referential* redundancy--the extent to which two descriptive passages do (or do not) imply the same referent object(s).

The conceptual definition of redundancy implies, other things being equal, that a redundant pair of messages will contain *less* information than a nonredundant pair. This leads rather directly to the prediction that, in general, nonredundant message sets (message *pairs* in the present case) should produce more accurate communication than redundant pairs. The basis for this prediction can be shown rather clearly if we consider Figure 1.

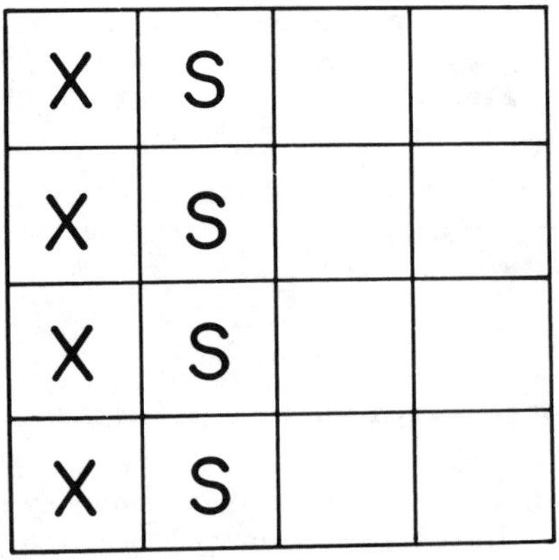

*Fig. 1. A hypothetical problem in referential communication (see text).*

Suppose a respondent (receiver) attempted to locate the position of an unseen target referent, $T$, in a 4 × 4 matrix like the one shown in Figure 1. Assume, moreover, that the only information he had available was an imperfect pair of redundant messages, such as (1) "The $T$ is on the far left" and (2) "The $T$ is in a cell containing an $X$." Since each of these messages refers (ambiguously) to the same four cells, they can be regarded as referentially redundant. In addition, since there are four possible locations that are fully consistent with both messages, we might anticipate that if forced to make a choice, the average respondent would have a 25% chance of selecting the proper cell. By contrast, suppose our receiver was given a nonredundant pair of messages that, considered individually, were just as informative as the passages in the first pair. A nonredundant pair of this type might, for example, include the following descriptions: (1) "The $T$ is on the far left" and (2) "The $T$ is in the topmost row." Note that, as in our earlier example, each individual message is consistent with four potential referents. In this case, however, the two messages imply *different* sets of referents (cells), and hence they are relatively nonredundant. Since there is just one cell that is consistent with both descriptions, this message pair should enable an intelligent respondent to locate the target unerringly.

Manis and van Rooijen (1973) explored the relationship between referential redundancy and communication accuracy. Each respondent was provided with several pairs of written descriptions; the passages in each pair were based on the same referent (a photograph of an actor in an emotional pose). The respondent's task was to read each message pair and to select the photograph that appeared to be the referent for that pair from an array that included 24 emotional poses, all showing the same actor. Some message pairs contained descriptions that were relatively redundant in the sense that when presented individually, they elicited similar response profiles (that is, they were associated with similar referent alternatives); other message pairs were relatively nonredundant. The results indicated that, as predicted, other things being equal, the nonredundant message pairs produced a higher level of performance than the redundant pairs.

In conducting this initial study, it was noted that there was a general tendency for the redundant message pairs to contain descriptions that elicited comparatively high hit rates when presented singly. To counteract the problem that this presented and provide a relatively unbiased assessment of the relationship between redundancy and communicative accuracy, Manis and van Rooijen resorted to statistical correction techniques. One approach involved the development of a "corrected"

179

accuracy measure, to eliminate between–pair differences that
were attributable to the "quality" of the component passages.
This was accomplished by computing, for each pair, the difference between the obtained proportion of correct responses (*raw
accuracy*) and the mean proportion correct elicited by the
individual components (*expected accuracy*).  Subsequent analysis
indicated that there was, as predicted, a significant relationship between the "corrected" accuracy measure and the redundancy of the component descriptions.  Figure 2 presents this
relationship in graphic form.  When the component descriptions

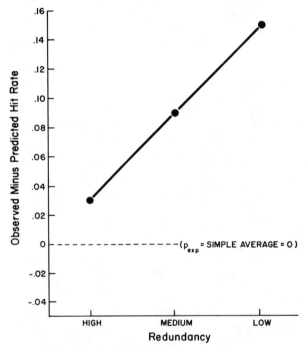

*Fig. 2.  Corrected accuracy scores as a
function of redundancy.*

evoked disparate (nonredundant) choice profiles, resultant
accuracy was substantially higher than the mean validity of
the contributing passages; by contrast, redundant message
pairs yielded accuracy scores that were more closely approximated by the mean of their constituents.  Virtually identical
results were obtained when the impact of the component

validities was controlled by the more traditional partial-correlation procedure.

Many psychologists regard correction procedures (like the one depicted in Figure 2) as less than optimal and prefer to use experimental rather than statistical controls whenever possible. In part, the next experiment that we undertook represented an attempt to replicate this initial finding with an improved methodology to provide firmer experimental control. A second aim of this study was to assess the impact of forgetting on our respondents' ability to decode redundant (versus nonredundant) message pairs.

Redundancy is believed to safeguard communication when messages are transmitted in a "noisy" (distracting) environment. Under these conditions, even if part of a message is forgotten or not received (due to interruption, faulty hearing, and so on), comprehension need not be unduly impaired, for the redundancy of the message may enable a receiver to infer the significance of the parts that are missing. This analysis suggested that redundant message pairs might be relatively resistant to the effects of forgetting and would show relatively stable performance patterns if a respondent was forced to store the information he had received in memory before attempting to decode it. Thus, if the descriptions in a redundant pair do indeed provide information that is repetitious with respect to the appropriateness of various referent alternatives, then it seemed likely that although part of one passage might be forgotten, decoding accuracy might nonetheless be relatively unaffected, since similar choice-relevant information would theoretically be available from the other description (the one that our hypothetical respondent *could* recall). In contrast, given a nonredundant pair, information that was forgotten from one passage was unlikely to be represented in the other. To illustrate this point in more concrete terms, let us consider some examples drawn from the problem represented in Figure 1.

## Example 1:  Partial Forgetting

Assume that our respondent's task is to read the passages that we provide and to use this information to locate an unseen target referent in one of the cells of Figure 1. Let us first suppose that our respondent has received a pair of *redundant* descriptions depicting the target referent as (a) on the far left and (b) in a cell with an $X$. As noted earlier, a redundant message set of this type should yield a 25% hit rate, for there are *four* cells that are fully consistent with these descriptions. Suppose now that with the passage of time, our respondent remembers only a generalized version of the two

181

descriptions and recalls the target as being (a') in the left *half* of the figure and (b') in a cell that includes *either* an *X* or an *S*. In this garbled version of the original message, the information that is recalled is fully consistent with eight different locations, and hence we would anticipate that the target would be correctly located about 12.5% of the time (one out of eight times). Thus, as a result of memory loss, the expected hit rate would decline from 25% to 12.5% under the assumptions that we have outlined.

By contrast to this first example, let us consider a *non-redundant* message pair, such as (a) the target is on the far left, and (b) the target is in the topmost row. In this case the two descriptions contain independent choice-relevant information. Now consider what would happen if, through the vagaries of forgetting, our respondent could again recall only a generalized version of the original input, comparable to the amount that was recalled in our previous illustration. Suppose, for example, he thought that the target was (a') in the left *half* and (b') in the top *half* of the figure. Although each of these descriptions is consistent with eight locations, there are exactly four cells that fit *both* descriptions, and hence we would expect a hit rate of 25% (one out of four), a decline of 75% from the errorless (100%) performance that we would anticipate had these two nonredundant passages been recalled perfectly. Note, by comparison, that in the case of the *redundant* message pair described in the preceding paragraph, a comparable loss of descriptive information was expected to produce a much smaller performance decrement of 12.5%.

## Example 2: Complete Forgetting of One Passage

To conclude this discussion, let us now assume that one of the passages in each of our hypothetical message pairs has been completely forgotten while the other is retained in the generalized form that has been referred to as description (a'): The target is in the left half of the figure. Since this description is consistent with eight different cells, it should yield a hit rate of 12.5% (one out of eight), regardless of the information that had been encoded in the now-forgotten description (b). For the *redundant* message pair, this expected hit rate of 12.5% is exactly the same as had been anticipated when description (b) had been recalled in the generalized version labeled (b') and represents a 12.5% decline from the performance level that would presumably have been observed had both descriptions been perfectly remembered. For the *nonredundant* pair, the 12.5% hit rate represents a decline of 87.5% from the

100% performance that would be expected, given total recall of the original input.

It is important to note that in these examples we have assumed a constant rate of forgetting for the individual descriptions, whether these passages were originally presented in redundant or nonredundant message pairs. For example, our last illustration suggests that forgetting an entire passage may have scant impact on the hit rates elicited by a redundant message pair, while in the case of a nonredundant pair a similar memory loss may produce a substantial decline in performance.

There are two final points that derive from the examples presented above: (1) Other things being equal, as long as *some* information is retained from each of the component descriptions, we would anticipate superior hit rates in the decoding of nonredundant message pairs (see example 1 above). When a component passage is *completely* forgotten, however (as in example 2), then the "structural" considerations that have been emphasized suggest that we should find similar performance levels in the decoding of redundant and nonredundant pairs. (2) Purely structural considerations do *not* lead us to anticipate a "crossover" pattern. Thus, despite the fact that nonredundant message pairs are expected to yield a relatively rapid decline in performance after an extended retention interval, the structural approach does not lead us to anticipate that these messages will ultimately produce decoding performances that are *inferior* to those elicited by redundant message pairs.

## EMPIRICAL RESULTS: DECODING

Starting with this theoretical framework, our next experiment was designed to compare the decoding performance elicited by redundant and nonredundant message pairs, which were to be decoded either immediately or after an interpolated retention interval. Descriptive messages were selected in accordance with a matching scheme which ensured that the passages included in our redundant and nonredundant pairs were perfectly comparable with respect to the quality of their components (that is, when decoded one at a time, the component descriptions that were combined to form redundant pairs yielded hit rates that were *identical* to the hit rates produced by the passages in the nonredundant pairs). The following passage is reasonably representative of the descriptions that were used in this study and in the other experiments discussed in this chapter:

This guy is so cocky, so confident, that there is no mystery, no doubt about it, and since people know this, they don't seem to mind him at all. He is a caricature of the "braggart captain," the know-it-all who stands in the corner doling out advice. The reason he's frowning is that he plays at being cocky. He's kind of a phony, but nobody minds but the kid erasing something off the schoolhouse bricks.

The descriptive passages in each message pair were presented simultaneously for a 30-second interval by means of a tape-controlled slide projector. After this presentation, on some trials the respondents were next exposed to the array of 24 photographs from which the intended referent was to be selected (see Figure 3). There were other message pairs, however, in which, after reading the descriptive passages, the respondents were without warning required to engage in an irrelevant arithmetic task for eight minutes before the referent array was presented and they were permitted to make their choices.

Figure 4 presents the results of this experiment. Note first that when the respondents were permitted to make their choices without delay, the low-redundancy pairs yielded a higher hit rate than the high-redundancy pairs, a result that essentially replicates the pattern shown in Figure 2. Figure 4 also indicates, as anticipated, that during a relatively lengthy (eight minutes) retention interval, performance deteriorated more rapidly for the low-redundant pairs than for the high-redundant pairs.

Although these results generally supported our expectations, we had not anticipated that after the eight-minute retention interval the redundant message pairs would yield significantly better performance than the nonredundant pairs; this finding is inconsistent with the structural approach that provided the major motivation for the experiment. As we have indicated previously, a purely structural approach implies that as more and more is forgotten from the original descriptive passages, one might ultimately reach a point where redundant and nonredundant message pairs would produce comparable hit rates. Purely structural considerations do not, however, imply the crossover pattern shown in Figure 4 unless they are elaborated or modified in some way.

With the new-found wisdom of hindsight, we are now tempted to believe that our earlier theorizing was deficient in failing to take note of the possibility that the component passages of a nonredundant message pair might be forgotten more quickly than the passages in a redundant pair. Thus, after the retention interval, the redundant pairs may have yielded a superior performance level because the individual messages that comprised these pairs were recalled with greater fidelity. This

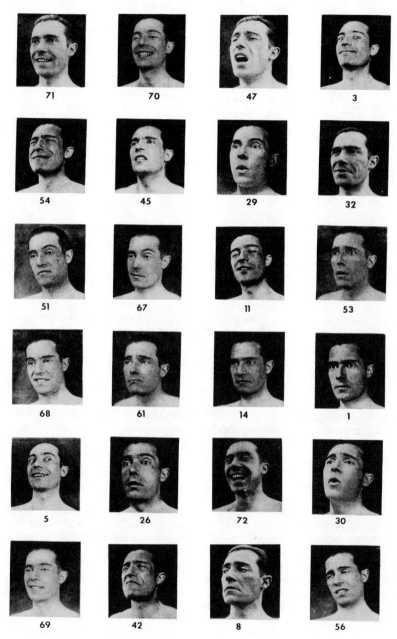

*Fig. 3. Frois-Wittmann photographs from which the respondents made their choices. From Hulin and Katz (1935).*

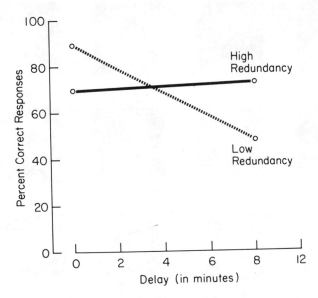

*Fig. 4. Decoding performance as a function of redundancy and delay.*

seems to be a plausible hypothesis if we assume that the descriptions were stored in memory in the form of mental representations, or images. Redundant passages might trigger similar representations and might, as a result, have a relatively lasting impact, like a pair of "repeated trials" in a verbal learning task. The nonredundant message pairs, in contrast, would elicit discrepant images and might thus be forgotten more quickly.

*EMPIRICAL RESULTS: ENCODING*

Although the main thrust of our research program has focused on the respondent's capacity to integrate descriptive information when serving as a decoder, we have also done some work on the encoding process. For example, having shown that nonredundant message pairs lead to more accurate communication than redundant messages if the respondent is permitted to decode the information he has received without delay, we wondered whether the average person would take this fact into account when acting as a communicator. This hypothesis seemed plausible in view of the fact that every individual repeatedly switches between the roles of decoder and encoder; on the other hand, as detailed below, there is some reason to believe that people normally feel more comfortable in handling redundant information.

In our previous work on redundancy, respondents were often asked to indicate how confident they felt that their decoding choices were correct. They generally reported greater confidence when dealing with redundant (rather than nonredundant) message pairs, a pattern that appeared in both the immediate-response and the delayed-response conditions. Kahneman and Tversky (1973) have observed a similar phenomenon; they report that inconsistent (nonredundant) information commonly leads to *subjective uncertainty* when people attempt to integrate psychometric data intuitively in order to predict future behavior (for example, college performance). Tests that provide consistent information will inevitably be highly correlated and can thus be described as measuring the same thing (that is, providing redundant information). Paradoxically, however, despite the individual's confidence when integrating consistent (correlated) test scores, the higher the correlation between the components of a psychometric profile, the lower their multiple correlation with the criterion (assuming comparable validities for the individual tests). Consideration of these facts leads to what Kahneman and Tversky term the *illusion of validity*: The average respondent may, erroneously, have greater confidence in his or her ability to predict some criterion performance when presented with highly correlated (redundant) inputs than when the input scores are relatively independent (low in redundancy) and hence capable of yielding more valid predictions.

A recent study by van Rooijen (1974) provides further evidence that nonredundant information may constitute something of a cognitive dilemma. In a referential-communication task closely resembling the experiments summarized in Figures 2 and 4, van Rooijen found that the average respondent took significantly longer to make his or her choices when decoding nonredundant message pairs than when interpreting redundant message pairs.

If inconsistent (low redundancy) information is normally integrated without much confidence, it might also affect the individual's behavior as a message sender (encoder). That is, since people often take the role of the other during communicative interchanges, they may avoid (inhibit) the encoding of messages that are relatively nonredundant with other information that is available to the person they are addressing so as to maintain the receiver's subjective confidence. Because of our general interest in communication, we decided to explore the merits of this hypothesis, together with the contrasting possibility that people recognize the informational virtues of nonredundancy and take this into account when acting as communicators.

The respondents in this experiment were asked to play the role of message senders. After decoding several sets of descriptive passages, they were presented with a series of six separate items that took the following form: On each item the respondents were presented with a "given" description and were informed of the referent photograph on which it was based. They were then told that since many of the passages were "somewhat vague," readers were sometimes unable to identify the correct target photograph when presented with just this information. Ostensibly to see how well the respondents could supplement the material that was already available, each "given" passage was presented together with two additional descriptions that were based on the same target photograph. Although these additional passages yielded identical hit rates when presented singly, one was referentially redundant with the "given" passage, while the other was not. The respondent's task was to select one of the descriptions from this additional pair such that his choice, when presented together with the "given" passage, would prove most effective in helping a naive reader (decoder) to select the intended target referent.

The results can be summarized succinctly: Our respondents generally felt that a "given" description would be better supplemented by the more redundant of the two additional passages provided. The more redundant description was selected 55% of the time, a result that departed significantly from the 50/50 split that would have been produced had the respondents chosen randomly between the two alternatives.

The results of this experiment thus indicated that when presented with an opportunity to supplement a descriptive passage by choosing between two messages of equal "quality" (that is, messages that produced identical hit rates when presented singly), our respondents were inclined to select *redundant* information in preference to material that was nonredundant. This pattern of results seems congruent with our earlier findings on subjective confidence (see above) and with Kahneman and Tversky's observation that people generally lack confidence when integrating inconsistent information, for the messages that were "sent" in this experiment seemed calculated to reduce the likelihood of such a reaction. The present results also seem closely related to DeSoto's observation (1961) that people normally have a predilection for single orderings and an aversion to discrepant (nonredundant) orderings of the elements in a given set.

## ENSEMBLE SIZE AND COMMUNICATION

The next experiments that we undertook focused on the relationship between communication accuracy and the quantity of verbal information that was available to our respondents. The main purpose of these studies was to explore the performance levels (hit rates) that might be achieved when respondents attempted to decode ensembles composed of several descriptive passages, all based on the same referent photograph.

An intuitive approach to this problem suggests that accuracy will generally improve as people are given more information (more descriptions) on which to base their responses. A similar prediction can readily be derived from a Bayesian point of view, for descriptions that provide limited probabilistic information when considered individually can theoretically be combined to generate overwhelming support for a particular referent choice. Finally, an adaptation of Fishbein and Hunter's additive-integration model (1964) leads to this same expectation if we assume that each description carries with it a certain amount of valid information and that the information contained in different descriptions is somehow combined in a roughly additive fashion.

An alternative approach to the aggregation problem emphasizes the difficulties that may develop due to the respondent's finite cognitive capacity (Fitts & Posner, 1967). If a message set is sufficiently large, it may exceed the respondent's cognitive limits and produce poorer performance than would have been obtained from a smaller set. By dividing his attention among the component descriptions in a large ensemble, the respondent may, for example, impair his ability to process the individual messages effectively. Thus, in contrast to the views outlined in the preceding paragraph, it seemed quite possible that a performance *decrement* might ultimately be obtained if a message ensemble became too large.

Two experiments were performed to test this general hypothesis. In both cases the respondents attempted to decode message sets of varying size. The descriptive passages in these studies were based on the same referent photographs that had been used in our redundancy experiments; the individual passages were presented one at a time, with the exposure duration controlled by a slide projector. After all of the passages in a given message set had been shown, the respondents were presented with a slide showing the 24 referent alternatives (see Figure 3) and were instructed to select the appropriate one. On half the trials (immediate response), subjects were permitted to make their choices immediately after reading the descriptive passages; on the other trials (delayed response) they were required to work on a difficult set of mental-arithmetic problems for two minutes before seeing the slide that showed the various referent-alternatives.

Our two experiments produced very similar results, and hence only the more extensive of the two (the study that explored the widest variation in ensemble sizes) is presented in any detail below. Since both experiments indicated that the various message ensembles produced somewhat different performance patterns in the immediate-response and the delayed-response conditions, these results will be discussed separately.

*IMMEDIATE-RESPONSE CONDITION*

Homogeneous Ensembles

Figure 5 shows the obtained hit rates for *homogeneous* ensembles, which contained either all poor-quality (low-valid) descriptions or all high-quality (high-valid) descriptions.

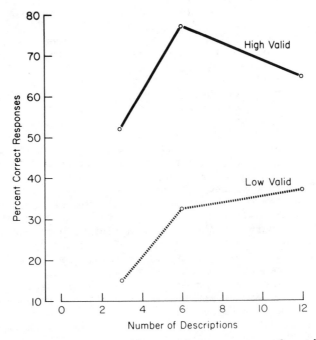

*Fig. 5. Decoding performance as a function of ensemble size; homogeneous message sets.*

The low-valid ensembles included descriptions that yielded hit rates of 10% to 32% when they were decoded one at a time; random guessing would have produced a hit rate of about 4%. These ensembles produced regular performance gains as they were enlarged, a pattern that was consistent with our expectations. We were, however, surprised to find that in the high-valid ensembles, in which the individual passages yielded hit rates of 40% to 64%, there was a relatively *constant* level of performance, regardless of the ensemble size. That is, despite the generally upward trend that Figure 5 depicts, neither of our experiments yielded a significant gain in performance as the high-valid ensembles were enlarged. These results were surprising both in a theoretical sense and in view of the fact that Manis and van Rooijen (1973) had previously observed systematic performance gains in a very similar situation. In this earlier study, however, the component messages in each ensemble were presented simultaneously, on a single page, and were available for a virtually unlimited period of review and study while the respondents decided which one of the referent alternatives constituted the most appropriate choice.

In contrast, the results shown in Figure 5 were obtained in a setting in which the individual descriptions were presented for 15 seconds each and were not available for review when the choice alternatives were finally shown. This suggests that the memory demands in the present situation may have been crucial in the results obtained. It may be, for example, that the high-valid passages contained certain critical phrasings and nuances that were not represented in the abstract, "coded" representations which were often used as a mnemonic aid. Moreover, when a single passage contains enough information to yield a comparatively high hit rate, it may be particularly difficult to generate performance gains by simply enlarging the message set; to be most useful, the added message would have to be carefully coordinated with the information that was already available. This problem is doubtless exacerbated when the individual descriptions must be retained in memory, for the detailed information that might prove most helpful in supplementing a given message (or set of messages) might not be accurately represented in our respondents' coded abstracts, even if these needed details *had* been included in the original (complete) messages. In a homogeneous set of *low*-valid descriptions, on the other hand, there is a better chance that a new message might usefully complement the meager store of information that had been provided in other low-valid passages, even if the available information was represented in a generalized, coded form.

191

## Heterogeneous Ensembles

The preceding section has focused on the effects of set size in homogeneous message ensembles, ensembles that contained either all high-valid or all low-valid passages. We have also collected a fair amount of data using *heterogeneous* ensembles, which included both high-valid and low-valid passages presented in randomly determined sequences. Figure 6 shows the results.

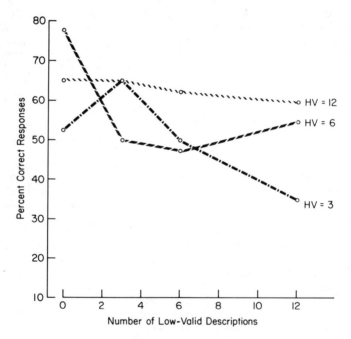

*Fig. 6. Decoding performance as a function of the ensemble composition. The curves labeled HV = 3, 6, and 12 represent message sets that included 3, 6, and 12 high-valid passages, respectively.*

Let us first consider the pattern that was produced when a given "core" of high-valid passages was presented in ensembles that varied in the number of low-valid passages they contained. Note that for ensembles that included a relatively small number of high-valid compor nts (that is, the curves labeled HV = 3 and HV = 6), there was a fairly regular decline in performance as the ensembles included more and more low-valid passages. In contrast to these *descending* performance

192

patterns, Figure 6 suggests that for ensembles with a sizable core of high-valid components (that is, when HV = 12), the introduction of more and more low-valid passages produced relatively little effect.

Perhaps the most interesting feature of these results was the inconstant effect that was produced as more and more low-valid passages were included in different types of ensembles. For homogeneous ensembles that were *devoid* of high-valid passages (Figure 5), the obtained hit rate was directly related to the number of low-valid passages that were available. On the other hand, in heterogeneous ensembles that included a *moderate* number of high-valid descriptions (Figure 6), performance was *inversely* related to the size of the low-valid message set; for heterogeneous ensembles that contained *many* high-valid passages, the obtained hit rates remained relatively constant, despite substantial changes in the number of low-valid components.

Figure 7 summarizes all of these results by showing how the effect that was produced by variations in the number of low-valid descriptions was dependent upon the size of the high-valid core. Data are presented from two experiments that differed only in the exposure time that was available for reading the individual passages and in the number of descriptive passages that were included in the various ensembles; the curve labeled 15-second exposure summarizes the data previously presented in Figures 5 and 6.[3]

The vertical axis in Figure 7 reflects the overall performance patterns (ascending or descending) that were generated by increasing the number of low-valid components. This variable was quantified by computing the sign and magnitude of the linear trends relating (1) the observed hit rates to (2) the number of low-valid passages.[4] Note that in both studies this relationship was initially *positive* (when there were no high-valid passages in the ensemble), then became *negative* (in

---

[3]The experiment that is summarized in the curve labeled 30-second exposure involved message ensembles with zero, one, three, or six high-valid passages and zero, one, three, or six low-valid passages.

[4]More concretely, the variable that is plotted on the vertical axis was derived from a series of $F$ ratios; that is, the variance in the observed hit rates that was linearly related to the number of low-valid descriptions was divided by an appropriate error term. Negative values on this variable represent data sets in which the obtained hit rate was inversely related to the amount of low-valid information; positive values represent a direct relationship between these variables.

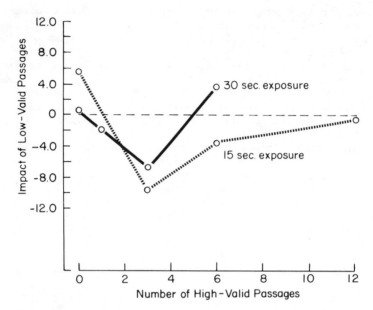

*Fig. 7. The impact of the low-valid passages as influenced by the size of the high-valid message set (see text).*

ensembles that included just a few high-valid descriptions), and ultimately drifted upward into the *zero range*, an indication that in ensembles with a sufficiently large core of high-valid passages, the obtained hit rates were essentially unaffected by the number of low-valid passages included.[5]

These results suggest that if a message ensemble is devoid of high-valid descriptions, the information that is conveyed by the low-valid passages may follow the incremental pattern

---

[5]Some readers may be disturbed that our two experiments yielded somewhat different results for the ensembles that included six high-valid passages (HV = 6). As shown in Figure 7, when the individual passages were each exposed for 15 seconds, these ensembles showed a negative relationship between the observed hit rates and the number of low-valid passages in the different message sets; in contrast, the corresponding relationship is positive (but not significantly so) when the individual passages were exposed for 30 seconds. We assume that these divergent results are due to the fact that the respondents had more time to study and consolidate the individual passages when provided with the longer exposure.

that is implied by an additive model. In contrast, in *hetero-geneous* ensembles the inclusion of more and more low-valid passages does *not* improve communication and, indeed, may inter-fere with the decoder's performance.

In heterogeneous ensembles that included only a modest amount of good (high-valid) information, additions to the low-valid message set significantly impaired performance. This decline may derive from the respondent's limited cognitive capacity, for by including more and more low-valid messages we are probably increasing the likelihood that our respondent will be unable to recall effectively the few high-valid passages with which he has been provided. This should, of course, re-duce the probability that he will select the intended referent. When, on the other hand, the ensemble includes *many* high-valid passages, the fact that one or more of these descriptions may be forgotten as we enlarge the low-valid set is less critical, since our respondent will still have a good chance of retain-ing some high-valid (accurate) information. In brief, the high-valid passages may be interchangeable to a degree and may at times "backstop" one another.

## DELAYED-RESPONSE CONDITION

In both of our experiments, when presented in the delayed-response format, the homogeneous message sets yielded results that were similar to the patterns we had previously observed in the immediate-response condition (see Figure 5). That is, the ensembles that included only low-valid descriptions showed a *direct* relationship between the size of the message set and the observed hit rate, while the high-valid ensembles produced a *constant* performance level, regardless of how many passages were included.

For the heterogeneous message sets, the performance levels were directly related to the number of high-valid passages. This effect was obtained in both of our studies and was, once again, generally consistent with the results in the immediate-response condition.

Unfortunately, the heterogeneous ensembles also yielded some problematic results, for the impact of the low-valid passages proved inconsistent from one study to the next. In the experi-ment in which each passage was exposed for 30 seconds, the hit rates in the delayed-response condition were directly related to the number of low-valid passages. This trend was *not* replicated, however, when the exposure time was shortened to 15 seconds, for in this case the size of the low-valid message set had essentially no impact on the hit rates that were generated by the heterogeneous ensembles. Although it is possible that these conflicting results derive from the different exposure intervals in our two experiments, we prefer to interpret this matter with some caution and feel that the available data do not provide an adequate basis for any confident conclusion.

In summary, then, the delayed-response condition yielded effects that were similar in many ways to the results observed in the immediate-response condition. The major difference between the two appeared in the heterogeneous ensembles. When presented in the immediate-response format, these ensembles yielded a complex but replicable pattern of results in which the impact of the low-valid passages was dependent upon the number of high-valid messages in the set (see Figures 5 and 6). In contrast, when the heterogeneous ensembles were presented in the delayed-response format, the low-valid messages led to inconsistent results that were difficult to interpret with any confidence.

## IMPLICATIONS

At a theoretical level, these experiments seem inconsistent with the implications of a simple additive model and provide at least indirect support for an overload postulate. Most importantly, the results in both of our experiments showed that performance was *impaired* when a message set that contained a small number of high-valid passages was enlarged through the inclusion of more and more low-valid information (see Figures 6 and 7). We suspect that this pattern derives from our respondents' limited processing capacity, for it is possible that by increasing the size of the low-valid message set we simultaneously made it difficult for the respondents to keep track of the few high-valid passages with which they had been provided. It is important to note that reliable overload results were *not* obtained in an earlier study (Manis & van Rooijen, 1973, Exp. II) in which our respondents were provided with a virtually unlimited opportunity to review the input descriptions while choosing from the array of referent photographs. This implies (not surprisingly) that it may be difficult to overload a respondent who is able to reread and study each of the descriptions in a message ensemble until he feels relatively confident about his decoding choice.

Unfortunately, we do not have an adequate explanation for the fact that the overload phenomenon was reliably manifested in the immediate-response condition (in *both* of our present experiments) but not in the delayed-response format. Future experimentation might profitably be addressed to the retention process with special emphasis on the way in which descriptive material is coded, stored, and retrieved when it is presented as part of a larger descriptive message ensemble.

In considering the significance of this research for psychological theorizing at a more general level (that is, beyond the communication domain), it would seem wise to proceed with caution. An important feature of the present studies is that different descriptions of any particular referent tend to be redundant with one another, even if they have been written by different people. That is, they tend to elicit rather similar patterns of response when decoded individually. The message ensembles that were presented to our respondents were, of necessity, assembled within this constraint. We can only speculate about the results that might be obtained in an integration task in which the successive informative inputs were truly independent.

## CONCLUDING REMARKS

The referential-communication paradigm provides an excellent research site for studying the integration of verbal materials. We have been particularly impressed by the fact that this approach enables the investigator to use complex, extended messages in an interesting and relatively well controlled experimental setting.

## REFERENCES

Anderson, N. H.  A simple model for information integration. In R. P. Abelson, E. Aronson, W. J. McGuire, T. M. Newcomb, M. J. Rosenberg, and P. H. Tannenbaum (Eds.), *Theories of cognitive consistency: A sourcebook*.  Chicago: Rand McNally, 1968.

Cronbach, L. J.  Processes affecting scores on "understanding of others" and "assumed similarity."  *Psychological Bulletin*, 1955, *52*, 177-193.

Cronbach, L. J.  Proposals leading to analytic treatment of social perception scores.  In R. Taguiri and L. Petrullo (Eds.), *Person perception and interpersonal behavior*. Stanford, Calif.:  Stanford University Press, 1958.

Cronbach, L. J., & Gleser, G. C.  Assessing similarity between profiles.  *Psychological Bulletin*, 1953, *50*, 456-473.

DeSoto, C. B.  The predilection for single orderings.  *Journal of Abnormal and Social Psychology*, 1961, *62*, 16-23.

Dustin, D. S., & Baldwin, P. M.  Redundancy in impression formation.  *Journal of Personality and Social Psychology*, 1966, *3*, 500-506.

Edwards, W. Conservatism in human information processing. In
B. Kleinmuntz (Ed.), *Formal representation of human judgment*.
New York: Wiley, 1968.

Fishbein, M., & Hunter, R. Summation versus balance in attitude organization and change. *Journal of Abnormal and
Social Psychology*, 1964, *69*, 505-510.

Fitts, P. M., & Posner, M. I. *Human performance*. Monterey,
Calif.: Brooks/Cole, 1967.

Gage, N. L., & Cronbach, L. J. Conceptual and methodological
problems in interpersonal perception. *Psychological Review*,
1955, *62*, 411-422.

Hulin, W. S., & Katz, D. The Frois-Wittmann pictures of facial
expression. *Journal of Experimental Psychology*, 1935, *18*,
482-498.

Kahneman, D., & Tversky, A. On the psychology of prediction.
*Psychological Review*, 1973, *80*, 237-251.

Krauss, R. M., & Weinheimer, S. Changes in reference phrases
as a function of frequency of usage in social interaction:
A preliminary study. *Psychonomic Science*, 1964, *1*, 113-114.

Lantz, D., & Stefflre, V. Language and cognition revisited.
*Journal of Abnormal and Social Psychology*, 1964, *69*,
472-481.

Manis, M., & Armstrong, G. W. Contrast effects in verbal output. *Journal of Experimental Social Psychology*, 1971, *7*,
381-388.

Manis, M., Gleason, T. C., & Dawes, R. M. The evaluation of
complex social stimuli. *Journal of Personality and Social
Psychology*, 1966, *3*, 404-419.

Manis, M., & van Rooijen, L. Integrating the information in
referential messages. In R. L. Solso (Ed.), *Contemporary
issues in cognitive psychology: The Loyola Symposium*.
Washington, D.C.: Winston, 1973.

Osgood, C. E., & Suci, G. J. A measure of relation determined
by both mean difference and profile information. *Psychological Bulletin*, 1952, *49*, 251-262.

Rosenberg, S., & Cohen, B. D. Referential processes of
speakers and listeners. *Psychological Review*, 1966, *73*,
208-231.

Schlosberg, H. The description of facial expressions in terms
of two dimensions. *Journal of Experimental Psychology*,
1952, *44*, 229-237.

Slovic, P., & Lichtenstein, S. Comparison of Bayesian and
regression approaches to the study of information processing
in judgment. *Organizational Behavior and Human Performance*,
1971, *6*, 649-744.

Taguiri, R. Person perception. In G. Lindzey and E. Aronson
(Eds.), *The handbook of social psychology*. (2nd ed.)
Vol. 3. Reading, Mass.: Addison-Wesley, 1969.

Trabasso, T., & Bower, G. H. *Attention in learning: Theory and research*. New York: Wiley, 1968.
Van Rooijen, L. Time processes in interpreting ambiguous descriptions of emotional states. Unpublished doctoral dissertation, The University of Michigan, 1974.

## 8. JUDGMENT AND DECISION PROCESSES IN THE FORMATION AND CHANGE OF SOCIAL ATTITUDES

### Harry S. Upshaw
University of Illinois, Chicago Circle

| | |
|---|---|
| Introduction | 202 |
| An Overview of the System | 204 |
| Phase 1: Processing Information About Alternative Positions on an Issue | 207 |
|   Defining a Set of Alternative Positions | 208 |
|   Evaluating Alternative Positions in Terms of Attributes | 210 |
| Phase 2: Choosing among Alternative Positions | 214 |
|   Predecisional and Postdecisional Judgmental Behavior | 214 |
|   The Actual Process of Choosing Among Alternatives | 217 |
| Phase 3: Describing Oneself on Attitude-Related Variables | 219 |
| Phase 4: Attitude Change and Judgmental Change | 224 |
| Conclusion | 225 |
| References | 225 |

## INTRODUCTION

Throughout the development of the social sciences, the concept of attitude has held a central place, and associated with it have been the concepts of judgment and decision. Over the years several apparently different relationships between attitude, on the one hand, and judgment and decision, on the other, have been the focus of research efforts. In Thurstone's pioneering work (1928) on attitude measurement, judgments and decisions in the form of opinions were the manifest variables from which the latent, hypothetical attitudes could be inferred. Many theorists have followed Thurstone in assuming that judgments and decisions are determined at least in part by logically prior attitudes. Conversely, using the theory of cognitive dissonance, Festinger (1957) argued that many of the behaviors, including some kinds of judgments and decisions, which had been traditionally interpreted as resulting from attitudes in fact preceded and caused the attitudes. More recently, Bem (1967) suggested that attitudes are redundant with many of the behaviors that they are sometimes invoked to explain and that attitudes represent only descriptions of characteristic behaviors. In considering these apparently divergent approaches to the relationship between attitudes and judgments, it is well to bear in mind that two broad classes of judgment and decision are involved in the attitude domain: one that refers to the way in which a person seeks to resolve an issue with respect to an attitude object and another that refers to the way in which a person communicates with others about his attitudes and related matters. The status of attitude as a cause contributing to the latter class seems not to have been disputed. It is the relationship of attitudes to judgments and decisions of the first class that has been controversial.

Although the concepts of attitude and judgment and decision have been closely linked historically, the two fields of study seem not to have developed any real integration. Recent surveys of the attitude literature (McGuire, 1969) and the social-judgment literature (Upshaw, 1974), while documenting some concern for mutual problems, indicate only isolated instances in which the questions of either area reflect the structure of inquiry in the other. Thus, in judgmental research distinctions are not commonly made, for example, among source, message, and recipient characteristics as determinants of judgments, and in attitude research response-scale characteristics and judgmental context are typically not considered. In fact, there is sometimes little assurance that the attitude object is the object of judgment in the response from which a person's attitude is inferred.

202

The present paper starts from the premise that the potential impact across the boundaries of the psychology of attitudes and the psychology of judgment and decision has not been realized because the conceptual issues have not been sufficiently delineated to allow a rigorous cross-application of principles. Remediation could begin in either area. In fact, the present work is addressed to the formulation of an approach to various judgments and decisions that people make in dealing with social issues and social objects. An effort is made to specify certain research questions by which principles of judgment and decision making can be organized coherently for application in what has come to be recognized as the "attitude domain."

In most contexts in which the concept has appeared, attitude has served as a mechanism by which the social psychologist represents the orientations of people toward significant objects in the environment. Most often attitude is conceived as either the cause or the consequence of judgments and decisions affecting the attitude object. In the present work the conception of attitude is that of a hypothetical, latent variable which is issue-specific and object oriented and which guides an individual's attempts to resolve the issue. The essential feature of this concept of attitude is the values that an individual has developed in the past and that he seeks to realize in a particular situation. How he assesses the situation and the action he takes to resolve an issue are largely questions of judgment and decision. The values and goals that underlie and direct his activities in these matters are most likely not primarily judgmental in nature. To understand these features of the system probably requires a much broader time perspective than is common in judgmental research. In fact, much of the individual's cognitive, social, and perceptual developmental history would likely be required to account in a profound way for the values and goals that are engaged by an important social issue. The consequences of that engagement, according to the present scheme, are a series of judgments and decisions which can be accounted for adequately by means of attitude in combination with a set of nonhistorical factors of the sort that judgment and decision theorists are likely to invoke. The intent of the formulation is to incorporate the concept of attitude into a broad system to account for an individual's social judgments and social decisions.

# AN OVERVIEW OF THE SYSTEM

Let us start with an individual who has a system of more or less permanent values that he wishes to implement and a set of momentary needs or desires which imply certain goals he wishes to obtain. During the course of his life, circumstances arise in which he must decide what to believe, how to act, and how to feel about certain states of affairs. These circumstances pose particular issues which the individual seeks to resolve by choosing among a set of alternatives which he must first define. Prior to a choice he presumably searches for information about each alternative, and he integrates the information which he collects both with respect to each one individually and with respect to the set of alternatives as a collective. A particular composite of values and goals is engaged as a consequence of the way in which the person defines the issue. This composite constitutes the person's attitude. A major function of attitude in this formulation is that it is a principal determinant of the person's preference criterion, a rule by which he orders the alternatives that are salient to him according to their acceptability and by which he chooses among the alternatives if it becomes appropriate to do so. An issue, then, is resolved for the person when he discovers a satisfactory strategy for achieving whatever goals and maximizing whatever values have been aroused in the situation.

The issues that cause all of these activities by an individual are for the most part questions that affect others as well. Hence, social pressures may force any given individual toward effectively choosing among alternatives, even though the nonsocial aspects of the situation may not appear to require a decision at that time. One social pressure that should not be discounted is the expectation of other people that the individual discuss "his" position on the issue. Such discussions likely occur with great frequency in everyday life. Furthermore, if one defines "discussions" liberally enough to include a subject's describing his views to an investigator by means of a questionnaire, then they are the stock in trade of much of what is called attitude research. Hence, it must be recognized that participation in research may cause the individual to make judgments and decisions that he may not otherwise have made.

When a person discusses his position on an issue, he may do any of several things. He may, for example, describe his attitude--what values he brings to bear on the issue and how he anticipates their implementation in the situation at hand. He may explain how he defined the issue, or he may describe his preference criterion. He may suggest the implication of

his chosen alternative for the definition and resolution of
other issues, or he may compare himself with other people in
regard to any of these features of his own "attitudinal"
activities. Communication about one's position is undoubtedly
a frequent and important activity which comprises many judgments and decisions involving a host of different referents
and contexts. Because there are so many possible judgments
and decisions normally made in communicating one's resolutions
of social issues, this phase of the system is the point at
which the judgment and decision theorists will likely make
their greatest substantive contributions. Furthermore, this
is the phase in the subject's attitudinal activities in which
investigators typically observe him.

A major purpose served by communication outside the laboratory has come to be called social comparisons. According
to Festinger's analysis (1954), people communicate with others,
especially with their peers, in order to appraise their skills
and to validate their opinions. An intriguing feature of
Festinger's formulation is that the individual is motivated
to influence others to adopt his own tentative views on a
particular matter, and to yield to the attempts of others to
influence him, since either influencing or being influenced
would reduce his uncertainty. This motivation for social
comparison might well be the guiding force in the communication phase of the proposed formulation. It is likely to be
equally important in the final phase of the sytem, which
focuses on attitude change.

In a strict sense, attitude change should be said to occur
only when there has been some alteration in the pattern of
values and goals that an individual brings to bear on a
particular issue. Forces toward attitude change can operate
in conjunction with all of the activities in the system
outlined here. For example, the introduction of an alternative previously unconsidered might suggest the appropriateness
of new values and goals in the situation. New information
about the considered alternatives or changes in the preference
criterion might affect the constellation of values and goals.
Furthermore, it is conceivable that the act of describing to
an audience one's chosen position on an issue might make
salient one's public image, setting into motion forces to
change the underlying attitude. Within the system, therefore,
there are many sources of potential attitude change. In
addition to changes in the underlying attitude, the system
brings into focus a number of other possible changes in a
subject's responses that derive from events at various stages
in the system but that do not literally represent attitude
change. For example, without a change in attitude and its
resultant preference criterion, an individual might embrace

205

a previously rejected alternative or a new alternative when new information suggests that he can best realize his intentions with this alternative. He may gain new information about how his chosen position relates to that of a comparison group and respond by changing the description of his position without any change in the position, in the attitudinal structure, or in the considerations that led to its adoption.

These alternatives to genuine attitude change seem so obvious that it is difficult to believe that the distinctions were not made long ago with regard to each of these aspects of a person's taking a stand on social issues. The fact is, however, that the field has remained with very few explicit distinctions among its dependent variables. This lack of development may be a by-product of a *modus operandi* that has emerged among social psychologists which McGuire (1969) believes responsible for empirical gains despite widespread disagreement over theoretical conceptions:

> . . . in a given experiment on attitude the term can very readily be given an operational definition in terms of observable and scorable responses. Typically the person's attitude regarding an object is operationally defined as a response by which he indicates where he assigns the object of judgment along a dimension of variability [p. 149].

It may be true that an uncritical acceptance of any judgment as an operational definition of the subject's attitude has permitted the accumulation of a large volume of empirical facts. It may also be true that indiscriminant acceptance of operational definitions retarded theoretical development and programmatic research. In the discussion that follows, the point will be made that people make a great many judgments and decisions while coping with social issues. Although related to attitude, they are not all equivalent, and they can be used interchangeably as indexes of attitude only with considerable sacrifice in the precision of the research question. On the other hand, the point will also be made that sometimes a person does encode the same information into more than one judgment. Criteria for recognizing when it is appropriate to interpret multiple judgments as interchangeable indexes will be discussed. For expository purposes the system that has been described here in overview will be detailed in terms of four phases: (1) processing information about alternative positions on an issue; (2) establishing an attitude and a preference order among alternative positions; (3) describing oneself on attitude-related variables; and (4) changing one's positions.

206

PHASE 1:  PROCESSING INFORMATION ABOUT ALTERNATIVE
POSITIONS ON AN ISSUE

Most social issues concern both an object (a person, a
group, a legal statute, and so on) and the question of how
best to react to that object in order to achieve some purpose.
Despite the lack of logic to support the practice, it has
become commonplace in social psychology to interpret the
endorsement of a position as an index of an underlying degree
of affect toward the (attitude) object and to interpret any
change in the endorsement as signifying a change of affect.
This practice may derive from Thurstone's suggestion (1928)
that the nature and extent of a person's affect toward an
object may sometimes be inferred from the opinions endorsed
concerning that object.  Hence, various opinions (positions)
are scaled according to their implicit affect toward the
object, and a subset of the scaled positions are offered to
respondents for endorsement or rejection.  Thurstone invoked
two criteria for the selection of the subset of items presented to respondents.  One was a criterion of ambiguity such
that items were eliminated if there was relatively poor
agreement among judges concerning their affective implications
for the object.  The "irrelevance" criterion eliminated items
for which it was not possible to predict accurately endorsement or rejection from knowledge of their affective-scale
values.  Although the ambiguity criterion has become a
standard feature of what is called the Thurstone scale, the
irrelevance criterion has seldom been employed.  The implications of employing the criterion for interpreting scale
values have been discussed in detail elsewhere (Upshaw, 1968a).
For present purposes it is germane to point out that almost
the only condition in which items would display a high correlation between the probability of endorsement and affective-
scale value would be when the respondent based his acceptance
or rejection upon that scale value.  In other words, unless
the goals of the respondents were to produce favorable or
unfavorable consequences for the object, it is not likely that
a Thurstone scale satisfying the criterion of irrelevance
would be produced.

Thurstone's work in attitude measurement does not, therefore, provide a rationale for the assumption that the position
a person takes on an issue necessarily betrays a general
attitude toward the object on which the issue is focused.
That assumption seems to derive historically from a now
outdated conception of learning whereby certain (affective)
responses are conditioned to the stimulus object and are
released as though by reflex action when the stimulus is
presented.  The fact is that most people are capable of

207

considerable control over their emotions, and they are
capable of designing and carrying through complex sequences of
thought and overt behavior in pursuit of goals. Any analysis
of the judgments and decisions related to attitudes must
recognize these capabilities.

The proposal here is not that the concept of attitude be
abandoned but that it be sharpened. Although granting that
people do acquire positive and negative affect toward objects,
we need not accept the simplistic assumption that people
give vent to their feelings about an object whenever an
opportunity arises. More reasonably, we might expect that a
person's attitude toward an object represents not only his
involvement with that object but also the goals toward which
he strives as he confronts a specific issue. For example, a
faculty member might regard a colleague highly as a fellow
member of the department but believe that he would make a poor
dean, and a mother may love her son but not approve of him as
the President of the United States. The attitude question,
then, is not simply how favorable or unfavorable the subject
is toward the object, but rather how favorable or unfavorable
the subject is toward the object in regard to an issue. A
given object may be the focus of several attitudes, each for
different issues. Attitude, viewed in this way, may explain
much of what occurs when a person takes a stand on an issue,
even though observation of the stand that he takes, in the
absence of knowledge of how he defined the issue, may tell us
little about his attitude.

The first phase of attitude formation under the present
system is the processing of information concerning alternative
positions with respect to issues which engage an attitude.
These alternatives are stimuli in the broadest sense--that is,
in the sense that they can be thought about, talked about, and
acted upon. There are two fundamental research areas within
this phase of the system: how the subject *defines* a set of
alternative positions for a particular issue and how he
appraises these positions. Questions related to the actual
choice among alternative positions are dealt with in a later
phase.

## DEFINING A SET OF ALTERNATIVE POSITIONS

In some instances, both in the laboratory and in the real
world, the set of alternative positions on an issue may be
completely prescribed for the subject, as in a public election.
However, it is not uncommon for alternatives to be more
loosely structured. If we are to understand judgmental and
decisional behavior with respect to attitudes, we must know
the context within which that behavior occurs. It behooves

us, then, to make that context itself an object of study. To do so, we need to isolate the determinants of the act of including any given stimulus in the set of alternatives. What is needed is a theoretical model for predicting the probability that a subject takes into account a particular position in the process of taking a stand on a social issue.

Let us suppose for the present that it is possible to learn whether any particular position was considered as an alternative while arriving at a stand on an issue. The variable of interest has two values, 1 if the stimulus was included in the set of alternatives and 0 if it was not. The task at hand is to specify some predictors of the probability of inclusion.

Offhand, it would appear that there are two major classes of determinants of the probability of inclusion. One is what might be called the appropriateness of the stimulus for the particular issue. The other refers to the circumstances under which the stimulus is made salient to the subject. An otherwise appropriate stimulus may be discounted or even rejected if it is brought to the attention of the subject at an unpropitious time or under certain unfavorable circumstances. Similarly, an otherwise inappropriate stimulus might be seriously considered if it is proposed to the subject by a highly credible source. This second, circumstantial variable most likely functions as a weight to be applied to the appropriateness variable for predicting the probability of inclusion in the set of alternatives. It would appear, then, that we can make reasonable predictions about which alternatives a subject selects for active consideration when he forms a position on an issue. The information that is needed for the analysis is of two sorts, the circumstances under which an eligible position is made salient to the subject and the scale value of that position in terms of appropriateness to the issue at hand.

Before speculating about the determinants of the parameters in the suggested model, we should examine in somewhat more detail what the parameters mean. The appropriateness variable as conceived here is specific to an idiosyncratic issue. This conception does not imply that attitudinal issues are defined capriciously and that they cannot, therefore, be accounted for rigorously. Furthermore, it does not imply any superiority of idiographic approaches to the study of issue defining. Conventional nomothetic approaches are compatible with the conception, provided only that care is taken to specify the nomothetic determinants of the way in which each issue is defined. Probably the most general class of these determinants is the demands arising from the social interaction at the time that an issue is posed. The social context effectively restricts the uniqueness of the definition and may contribute more to the process than does the individual's particular history and personality.

According to this formulation, the subject defines an issue in terms of certain goals that he wishes to achieve. The particular pattern of values and goals that are engaged by an issue constitutes his attitude in that situation. The alternatives that he entertains as ways of resolving the issue are ways of implementing his attitudes. However, as suggested earlier, not all the conceivable ways of resolving the issue, and thereby implementing his attitudes, are included in the set of alternatives. The ones that are excluded are expected to be those which the subject predicts to be less decisive in resolving the issue than are the ones that are included. The expected resolving power of an alternative is its appropriateness.

Aside from appropriateness, the salience of various alternatives needs to be taken into account. Two determinants of salience are likely to be the trustworthiness and expertise of the source of a position. The source need not advocate a position to make it salient; a professor or a news commentator may suggest positions in the context of public informing. With informing as well as advocacy, source credibility would appear to be a major determinant of the salience of the position described. Among other determinants of this weight are any factors that influence the attention value of the communication by which the position is made known.

At the present stage of development of the system, it is probably not productive to attempt to formulate a long list of possible determinants of the appropriateness and the circumstantial variables or to attempt a more specific formulation of the model than already described. What is important is to establish that this is a feasible and important research area. It is acknowledged that the fundamental dependent variable of whether a subject "takes a position into account" is uncomfortably vague in terms of its observational implications. There are, however, precedents for dealing with variables that are no more directly observable than this one. Possible research strategies include designs involving retrospective interviews, computer simulations, and the testing of causal models that assess the elusive dependent variable in terms of its implications rather than its direct effects.

*EVALUATING ALTERNATIVE POSITIONS IN TERMS OF ATTRIBUTES*

When a subject establishes a set of alternatives for a particular issue, he has a certain amount of information about each element in the set. The input of information does not, of course, cease when he first defines the set of alternatives but may even increase. After a set of alternatives is defined, the decision-making phase requires maximum information for a reliable choice. We should expect, then, that the subject is sensitive to, and may even actually search for, information about various attributes of the alternatives that he is considering. As he receives it from diverse sources, he must then integrate all the available information about each alternative. These considerations suggest several research topics relevant to this part of the system--the effect that membership in the set of alternatives has on a subject's sensitivity to information about a position; the simultaneous processing of information about all the members of the set of alternatives and the effects of unequal amounts of information within the set on the search for new information; and the effects of information integration on the redefinition of the set of alternatives and *vice versa*. Indeed, this part of the system touches upon a wide range of problems that have been studied dealing with cognitive processes oriented toward social decisions and social action. Because so much has already been reported on closely related matters, a detailed analysis of the questions in this part of the system will likely reveal that many of these questions have already been answered and that many others are amenable to at least informed speculation.

To illustrate some of the issues involved in this part of the formulation, let us consider the old war-horse of group-dynamics research, the "Johnny Rocco Case." Johnny Rocco is a fictitious juvenile delinquent who has had a history of troubles of every imaginable sort. In the past he has sometimes been treated sternly by adult authorities, and sometimes he has been treated with obvious compassion and leniency. Johnny soon finds his way back into trouble. The question now is how lenient or stern the authorities should be in dealing with his latest infraction. Suppose that the set of alternative positions consists of three elements: (1) Place Johnny in a foster home in which he is likely to receive an abundance of affection and tolerance for his idiosyncrasies; (2) place him in a foster home in which he will be strictly monitored and subject to stern, objective discipline; and (3) send him to the state reform school, where he is likely to receive a rather indifferent treatment by the staff and strong peer-group pressures. Before deciding among these alternatives, the subject can be expected to obtain and integrate information about each. He may discover, for example, how many of the people who served time in the state institution subsequently committed crimes for which they were sentenced to prison. He may learn of the operating costs of the institution, and he may become informed concerning the probability that an inmate of the institution will suffer a serious illness or physical injury during a given year. Presumably, the subject would seek to consolidate considerations such as these into an impression of the institution. At the same time that he is searching for, receiving, and processing information about the institution, the subject is likely to be performing similar tasks in regard to the other alternatives, culminating in an impression of each.

The simultaneity of impression formation for all the members of the set of alternatives is not the only complexity of this part of the formulation. Another concerns the attributes to which the resulting impressions refer. Most of the pioneering research on impression formation (for example, Asch, 1946; Anderson, 1965) dealt with the specific judgment of how much the subject anticipates liking a particular stimulus person. Apparently, the process describing formation of liking judgments can also describe judgment of any number of other attributes, such as the target person's estimated moral worth, or the likelihood that he would become a nuisance if he were encouraged to visit, or the impact that making friends with the stimulus person would be likely to have on the subject's other friendships (see the chapter by Kaplan). Judgments such as these might, in fact, be considered by the subject as components of an impression in terms of anticipated liking. In a similar fashion, the subject, in ordering a set of alternatives according to his preference, must judge the alternatives along many component dimensions. The possible effects of these intervening judgments upon the ultimate preference estimates and upon the choice among alternatives is a research question with interesting implications for information integration generally as well as for the attitude system described here.

In the Johnny Rocco example, it seems likely that during the information-processing stage the subject orders the alternatives according to a number of different attributes—for example, the extent to which the alternative dispositions of the case are likely to result in benefit or harm to society and to Johnny himself. The information that the subject obtains would have to be integrated for each of the alternatives and for each of the judgmental dimensions. Although the current literature (see Kaplan's chapter in this volume) provides what appears to be a basic approach to the phenomenon of information integration, the problem as it appears in the proposed system seems to require more complex models than have yet been proposed in the literature. What is required is a way of determining the composition rules that an individual employs in combining simple attributes into useful concepts. Phrased in this way, the methodological problem appears amenable to solution by means of application of multidimensional-scaling procedures (Carroll & Wish, 1974; Wish & Carroll, 1974).

The integration of available information presumably culminates in an impression of each alternative stimulus in terms of a variety of judgmental dimensions. These impressions refer to the statuses of the stimuli in terms of subjective continua. To communicate with others, and possibly with oneself, the individual must project the stimulus positions from the metric-free subjective continua to response scales. An elegant feature of Anderson's functional measurement (1970) is that it results in both information concerning the composition rules of a complex variable and interval-scale values for compound stimuli in terms of the response dimension. That a method exists for achieving response scaling at the same time that we discover details of the information-integration process should not obscure the fact that more than one psychological operation underlies the data. By separating information integration from the scaling problem, we call attention to the fact that two very different classes of phenomena might be observed during this phase of the attitude system. One class is perceptual-cognitive, and it concerns events that occur at the level of the subjective quantity (see Upshaw, 1969a). The other class concerns effects upon the judgmental scale by which the subject describes his perceptions and cognitions.

The conjoining of a subjective continuum with a response scale has been described as the essence of judgment (Upshaw, 1969a, 1974). According to that conception, judgments are simple linear functions of the subjective representations of their corresponding stimuli, and the slope and intercept of the linear function describe the unit and origin, respectively, of the judgmental scale. Effects at the level of response scale and those at the level of the subjective quantity should not be expected to have the same consequences for the ultimate adoption of an attitudinal position. However, it probably should not be simply assumed, as it has been by some (for example, Stevens, 1958), that response effects are of no consequence. It is, after all, a person's response and not its underlying meaning which is the stimulus for other people. It is possible that people are themselves influenced independently by their own previous judgments and by the information that is encoded in those judgments. Consider a statement that former President Dwight D. Eisenhower made to Walter Cronkite in a televised interview. Cronkite asked Eisenhower whether he had a political philosophy. In response, Eisenhower remarked that as President he always collected a wide range of opinions about an issue and then tended to pick the middle one. At the risk of taking his statement more literally than it was intended, we can imagine that Eisenhower sought to array

policy alternatives from liberal to conservative. A judgment
of a political opinion in terms of liberalism-conservatism
would appear to be highly susceptible to context effects
which, it has been argued elsewhere (Upshaw, 1969a), are most
often scale effects. On the other hand, there is no strong
evidence to suggest that context affects the basic process of
information integration (Anderson, 1974) by which the stimuli
are presumably ordered prior to actual judgment. Hence, the
destiny of the country during the Eisenhower years may have
been importantly affected by the sometimes disparaged scale
effects operating through the President's judgments of
liberalism-conservatism. In any case, it seems desirable to
distinguish between the absolute judgment of alternatives and
the logically prior integration of information about those
alternatives.

## PHASE 2: CHOOSING AMONG ALTERNATIVE POSITIONS

The first phase consists of defining a set of alternatives
and integrating available information about each. These
activities are preparatory to the individual's choice among
the alternatives. It is appropriate, therefore, to distinguish between informing oneself about the impending decision
and the act of deciding. The temporal boundaries of this
second phase cannot be established with precision because
many of the behaviors which are assumed to occur during the
phase are not directly observable. Included among these
behaviors are an implicit rehearsal of the most salient features of the various alternatives, one or more trial applications of a decision rule, and assessment of the consequences
of the tentative and "final" decisions.

In this section two aspects of the second phase will be
discussed separately. The first concerns the judgmental
activities before and after a decision, and the second
concerns the actual process that a person employs in deciding
among alternative positions.

### PREDECISIONAL AND POSTDECISIONAL JUDGMENTAL BEHAVIOR

To separate predecisional and postdecisional judgmental
phenomena, we must know exactly when a decision occurred.
Such knowledge is generally impossible to obtain because
decision making is probably not a discrete event, despite our
tendency to talk about it as if it were. Aronson (1968)
discussed the difficulty of determining introspectively when,
for example, a decision was made to buy a house. Certainly,
he argued, the decision predated the exchange of legal papers.

He suggested that the covert act of deciding may begin at any time after the person has come to believe that he has examined all of the information that is to be available to him.  Janis (1959) and Festinger (1964) emphasized the public commitment to a position as an indicator that a decision has been made. Perhaps what we want to call the "act of deciding" would be better described as a process of increasing commitment to a particular alternative.  The pace of developing commitment probably quickens when the subject judges that he has examined all of the evidence that is to be available to him, and it probably peaks with public disclosure.  If choice is defined in terms of a lower and an upper threshold of commitment, then it is more meaningful to talk about judgmental phenomena that occur early and late in the process than to talk about predecisional and postdecisional effects.  The latter terminology is used here in order to be consistent with the reasonably large amount of literature that has been developed in recent years.

Three theoretical orientations toward social decision making have focused attention upon the impact of deciding among alternatives on the evaluation of those alternatives. Festinger's theory of cognitive dissonance (1957, 1964), Janis and Mann's conflict theory of decision making (1968), and Brehm's theory of psychological reactance (1966, 1972) predict somewhat different phenomena.  Cognitive dissonance, for example, is expected to occur after a decision in proportion to the extent to which the chosen alternative has undesirable aspects and the rejected alternatives have desirable aspects. According to the theory, a person can be expected to evaluate all the alternatives with maximum objectivity before making a decision, but to distort his evaluations postdecisionally so as to bolster his choice, and thereby reduce dissonance.  Hence, the chosen alternative may be re-evaluated as more desirable, the rejected alternatives may be re-evaluated as less desirable, or both of these effects may occur.

Janis and Mann suggested that the preceding cognitive distortions occur only in situations in which the perceived challenge to an individual's present course of action is relatively mild.  When a relatively strong challenge is perceived, the individual reacts rationally, with an objective appraisal of the available alternatives.  Accordingly, the preferred alternative may be re-evaluated as more desirable and the less preferred alternatives as less desirable either before or after a decision if conditions favor defensiveness on the part of the individual.

According to Brehm's theory of psychological reactance, people are motivated to maintain freedom of choice at all times.  When an event occurs that restricts or threatens to restrict a person's freedom, a noxious state occurs which is called reactance. To reduce the arousal level of reactance, the person acts to restore his freedom of choice. One of the more interesting aspects of this theory is that reactance is often self-imposed. In fact, every decision can be expected to instigate reactance because it implies a loss of freedom to choose the rejected alternatives. As the time for commitment to a choice draws nearer, the perceived threat to one's freedom is apparently intensified. Therefore, reactance is expected to increase until the point of commitment and to decrease after the commitment. Consistent with this line of thought, Linder and Crane (1970) and Linder, Wortman, and Brehm (1971) found that subjects evaluate the most preferred and less preferred alternatives more nearly alike as the time of decision approaches. The postcommitment reactance effect of an increasing separation in judged desirability of the chosen and rejected alternatives as a function of time has apparently not been tested explicitly. At least one experiment (Walster, 1964), although conceived and described in other theoretical terms, produced results that are consistent with the reactance hypothesis.

None of the theories considered here has been abundantly supported in its predictions of judgmental distortions in the decision process. However, it does appear to be well established that the judged desirability of alternatives often changes in systematic ways during the period of decision making (for example, Brehm, 1956; Brehm & Cohen, 1959; Brehm, Stires, Sensenig, & Shaban, 1966; Deutsch, Krauss, & Rosenau, 1962; Festinger, 1964; Gerard, Blevins, & Malcolm, 1964; in addition to those studies cited earlier). Unfortunately, the literature on the effects of decision on judged desirability is contradictory. Whether the desirability of the most preferred alternative is increased or decreased, there is a theory to account for it. Furthermore, apparent shifts in both directions have been demonstrated for the most preferred alternatives and for the less preferred alternatives.

The three theories discussed here have in common a principle by which a person's judgments are distorted in order to satisfy a momentary need. Implicitly, all three theories assume that these judgmental distortions occur at the perceptual level, as opposed to the response level, suggesting that the distortions are part of a self-deception intended to save the person from some amount of subsequent cognitive labor. The perceptual or judgmental mechanisms that might mediate these distortions are difficult to imagine. It is possible that the phenomenon under examination is not a perceptual distortion at all but is instead an alteration in the size of the unit of the reference scale that the person employs in judging the alternatives. A reduction in unit size would be manifested by an increased separation of the alternatives, and an increased unit size by a decreased separation. As described in an earlier paper relating judgmental principles to cognitive-consistency phenomena (Upshaw, 1968b), the critical test of a scale interpretation as opposed to a perceptual-distortion interpretation lies in a demonstration that whatever change is observed in regard to the focal stimuli is consistent with a scale-wide effect. The plausibility of a scale-wide effect in the present case is suggested by two considerations. One is the fact that the notion of a decision implies a narrowing of the range of alternatives along a scale of desirability. The second is the demonstrated direct relationship between stimulus range and the size of the judgmental unit (Gravetter & Lockhead, 1973; Upshaw, 1969a, 1969b). Hence, the fundamental fact concerning changes in the evaluation of alternatives during decision making may be a systematic shift in the range of salient alternatives during the process of decision making. This possibility warrants investigation.

## THE ACTUAL PROCESS OF CHOOSING AMONG ALTERNATIVES

It has often been assumed, as in the previous section, that immediately prior to a person's choosing among alternatives he reduces each alternative to a single value on a scale of utility (desirability or preference) and that he chooses the alternative with the highest scale value. This assumption is implicit in the work by Janis and Mann (1968), and it is explicit in a formulation suggested by Upshaw (1964). It is, furthermore, consistent with much current thinking in decision theory. Under this model the critical activities that are involved in actual decision making are those concerned with developing and applying a preference criterion. The individual must pool all of the information that he has acquired concerning properties of the various alternatives, so that he can order the set of alternatives according to his preference for them. Underlying the resulting preference scale is a preference criterion that the individual presumably employs to map stimulus attributes onto preferences. If the composition of that rule were known in an individual case, then a person's choices should be predictable.

A question of fundamental relevance to the preference-criterion model of choice is that of the determinants of the structure of the preference criterion. Obviously related to this question is the way in which the individual has defined the issue at hand. Also related to it are the goals and values which the individual brings to bear upon the resolution

217

of the issue. These goals and values, when directed to an issue, define the person's attitude. Hence, attitude is probably the most important determinant of the precise way in which the person combines stimulus attributes to produce a preference ordering. Because "attitude" is defined here in terms of what the person hopes to accomplish in a particular situation, considerations such as strategies to maximize utility or to minimize regret may be included in the preference criterion. Accordingly, a monotonic relationship is expected between the probability that a given alternative would be chosen and the value of that alternative on the individual's preference scale. In light of this relationship, it is apparent that the key to research on the actual process of choosing among alternative positions is the specification of a person's preference criterion. The three obvious methodological approaches for this purpose are conjoint measurement (Luce & Tukey, 1964; Tversky, 1967), functional measurement (Anderson, 1970; Shanteau & Anderson, 1969), and the linear model (Slovic & Lichtenstein, 1971). Functional measurement and the linear model would be useful for the empirical determination of the composition of the preference criterion, whereas conjoint measurement provides a means of both testing a hypothesized structure and simultaneously providing for the quantification of a structure that is shown to fit.

That methods exist for specifying the composition of preference criteria permits research in which attitudinal variables are related not only to a person's choice among alternatives but also to the rule that he invokes to make his choice. Hence, experiments are possible in which the dependent variable is a vector of weights corresponding to the subject's preference criterion. Furthermore, because the preference criterion is viewed as an immediate and direct consequence of attitude, its quantification provides perhaps the most defensible criterion measure of a person's attitude on an issue.

The model of choice that underlies the discussion so far supposes that the person defines a rule by which he orders all salient alternatives according to his preference for them and that he subsequently chooses that alternative at one extreme of the ordering. This model seems appropriate for those situations in which an attitude is engaged. Thus, when an individual is faced with an important decision which he hopes to resolve in a way that furthers a value of his, the individual can be expected to undertake the considerable effort that is implied by the model. There are likely to be situations, however, in which the individual's stake does not appear high enough to justify that effort. In extreme cases he might make arbitrary decisions based upon little systematic thought or planning.  In other situations it seems likely that people adopt purposeful decision strategies which, nevertheless, do not involve the extensive deliberations that are required under the preference-criterion model.

Tversky (1972) has proposed a theory of choice behavior which may apply in a number of situations and which has important implications when it does apply.  His theory, the elimination-by-aspects (EBA) model, assumes that a person arrives at a choice by first selecting some aspect of the salient alternatives and then eliminating all of the alternatives that do not include the selected aspect.  This process is then continued until a single alternative remains.  Tversky showed that under the EBA model the probability that any particular alternative is chosen depends upon the extent to which the aspects of that alternative are shared by others in the set and the sequence in which aspects are selected for the elimination process.  Hence, the person who employs the EBA model in choosing a position is particularly subject to social influence, both deliberate and unintentional.  The extent to which the EBA model is employed in real life would be interesting to know.  It would also be interesting to know the determinants of the adoption of the EBA model as opposed to the preference-criterion model.  These questions are answerable.


## PHASE 3:  DESCRIBING ONESELF ON ATTITUDE-RELATED VARIABLES

The immediate social situation is obviously a major determinant of much that is involved in social decision making. It provides cues concerning what types of decisions may or should be made under particular circumstances and by whom.  It suggests the propriety of particular goals and the legitimacy of means to attain them.  It also provides the stimulus for an individual to communicate with others about his position on various social issues.  It is to this communication phase that we now turn.

According to Festinger's analysis of social comparisons, people seek communication with others in part to validate their opinions.  By establishing concordance between ourselves and similar others, we reduce uncertainty about whether we have made optimal decisions.  A social-comparisons episode is an encounter in which all participants want to find themselves in harmony with their colleagues and will do almost anything that is required to produce that harmony, including changing their own views and pressuring their colleagues to change theirs.  Any motivation of an individual to validate his opinions through the mechanism of social comparisons certainly

provides the instigation for communication about his way of
defining and dealing with social issues.  Another determinant
of communication is the normative demand which sometimes
exists for a person to express a view on an issue.  In an
extreme example two people who meet might exchange such
pleasantries as "It is a nice day, isn't it?" with no expectation of resolving uncertainty by means of the exchange.  Normative demands for the expression of opinions are also made by
public-opinion pollsters and social-science investigators.

When, for whatever reason, a person communicates his views
on an issue, he engages in a process of encoding information
about some specific referent into a response language.  The
result is a judgment that is jointly determined by the information and by properties of the language.  One approach to
the study of response effects in communication about one's
beliefs, opinions, and attitudes is represented by the work of
Wyer (1973).  According to that formulation, the response that
a person employs to describe his views is, in effect, an
inference that he makes about himself.  The judgment that he
renders is thought to represent a selection from a response
repertoire.  The choice among alternative responses is presumably based upon consideration of conditional subjective
probabilities that each response would be appropriate, given
the individual's belief about himself which he wishes to
encode into his judgment.

The Wyer approach portrays the communicator as a decision
maker who chooses among pre-existing categorical responses.
Another approach, represented by the work of Upshaw (1969a),
portrays the communicator as a measuring device which yields
a quantitative statement about the referent attitude, decision,
and so on.  According to this approach, any judgment reflects
properties of the response scales as well as the informational
content that the individual seeks to communicate.  A number of
possible personality and social determinants of reference-
scale origin and unit have been described (Murdoch, 1969;
Ostrom, 1966; Ostrom & Upshaw, 1968, 1970; Upshaw, 1968b,
1969a, 1970).

It is obviously important in the study of attitude-related
phenomena to distinguish between a person's attitudes, beliefs,
and opinions, on the one hand, and how he describes them, on
the other.  The problem has not often been faced in the literature.  McGuire's observation (1969), noted earlier, that
competing attitude theorists achieve a truce in their conceptual conflict by agreeing to define "attitude" operationally
as a judgment describes a style of research which, unfortunately, has led to a widespread neglect of the multiple determinants of those judgments.  However, it is apparent that
there are judgmental referents besides the communicator's

attitude and that any given judgment conveys information about the subject's judgmental behavior in addition to information about the intended referent.

Methods are needed by which effects due to informational content or to response processes can be separated in the analysis of attitude-related dependent variables. In many published studies the two types of phenomena are hopelessly confounded. A promising approach for this purpose is an adaptation of the logic that underlies the Campbell and Fiske (1959) multitrait-multimethod matrix. With this approach the investigator would provide at least two different response modes in terms of which subjects make equivalent judgments. These response modes are analogous to multiple methods for the measurement of the same trait. The experimental design would also require subjects to render judgments concerning different referents in terms of the same response scales. Effects at the level of the informational content of judgments would be expected on all measures of that content, and effects at the level of scale would be expected on all judgments made in terms of the particular scale.

The approach that is advocated here presupposes equivalent judgments of the same content. Exactly what is meant by that concept should be made clear. The problem is the same as that which has been dealt with by mental-test theorists (for example, Lord & Novick, 1968). Their approach involves hypothesizing a set of "true" scores which exist independent of any metric and which underlie any set of observed scores. An observed score is defined as a linear function of its corresponding true score, with the slope parameter of the linear function referring to the scale unit of the observed scores and the intercept parameter to the scale origin. Two tests that measure the same underlying trait must, according to this formulation, reflect the same true scores, but they may or may not differ in regard to scale parameters and the size of a random-error component that is included in the definition of the observed scores. Tests which meet the requirement of equivalent true scores, but which differ in other components, are called *congeneric* tests. For the problem at hand it is apparent that congeneric scales are required. Methods for determining whether measures function as congeneric scales in a particular set of data are available (Jöreskog, 1971; Lord, 1973). They can be adapted readily to judgments.

If subjects were required to respond in terms of congeneric scales, it would then be possible to separate those effects that are scale-specific from those that are more general and which, therefore, are likely to have their locus in the informational content of the subject's judgments. Confidence

in the separation of these effects would be strengthened by a
supplementary analysis of judgments on a single scale that has
different informational content.  For example, the judgment of
interest in a particular study might be the number of years of
imprisonment that the subject advocates as punishment for a
particular crime, such as rape.  The sentence scale is also
applicable to other crimes, such as embezzlement and fraud.
Any experimental effect upon the parameters of the scale
should be observed for all judgments rendered in terms of the
scale.  It is apparent, therefore, that the confounding of
response effects and those which concern informational content
can be resolved by appropriate experimental designs and attention to the psychometric properties of the dependent variables.

The concept of congeneric scales was described above as a
methodological device for separating substantive and response
effects.  It should be noted that the concept is potentially
useful as a methodological tool for isolating the particular
referent of judgments.  When a person communicates his views
concerning an issue, whether in an experiment or in real life,
the information that he seeks to convey may refer to any number of facets of his thinking and feeling about the issue.
He may, for example, describe some characteristic of the
particular alternative that he has chosen (for example, how
much benefit is expected to accrue to the target object or the
likelihood that any benefit will accrue to the object).  He
may attempt in his response to describe himself relative to
other people based upon the implications of the position he
has adopted (as opposed to rating his chosen position relative
to other alternatives).  He may describe those values which he
sought to implement in selecting a position on the issue--that
is, his attitude.  There are a great variety of potential
dependent variables in attitude-related research which, if
explicitly recognized, might greatly enrich the literature.
In many instances those variables which refer to different
judgmental referents could best be studied by straightforward
adaptations of existing attitude-measurement procedures
(Upshaw, 1968a).  However, in some instances, differentiation
among judgmental referents might best proceed in a fashion
similar to that advocated above for distinguishing between
substantive and response-scale effects.  In such applications
it is expected that any difference in regard to referents
would result in the failure of sets of judgments to meet the
criteria of congeneric scales.

In addition to its methodological usefulness, the concept
of congeneric scales might prove to be of substantive interest.
Psychophysicists have shown that the human judge can fairly
easily conjoin almost any two sets of magnitudes (Jones, 1974;
Stevens, 1974).  Because of this, judgments of any particular

set of stimuli might be rendered in terms of any one of virtually an infinite number of response scales (any pair of which, it might be noted, would presumably function as congeneric scales). The point has been made in psychophysics that a judge can convey the same information in judgments which are superficially quite different. He is often called upon to do precisely that in his social behavior. A trial judge, for example, must often impose a prison sentence or its equivalent fine; the politician calls upon his audience to be liberal, middle-of-the-road, or conservative, and he specifies a public policy that he has judged to be equivalent to the label that he advocates. When a position along one dimension is equated with one along another dimension, either of two logical relationships between the two judgments may prevail. To describe the possibilities, let us again invoke the test-theory model which defines observed judgments in terms of a statistical regression on "true" scores. One relationship underlying judged equivalence might be that the true-score component of one judgment is a determinant of the true score of the second judgment. Hence, the politician who urges voters to demonstrate their conservatism by agreeing to sell national forests to paper mills may have initially decided upon the public policy and subsequently decided that the policy is a conservative one. In that case the policy is a determinant of judged conservatism.

A second relationship that might account for equivalence judgments is the congeneric-scale model, which requires that the two judgments correspond to the same true scores. Hence, the policy advocated by the politician would be viewed as his choice from a set of alternatives which he presumably ordered according to a preference criterion, and his use of the label "conservative" to describe himself would be viewed as a choice from a set of alternative labels that were ordered according to the same preference criterion that was the basis of a choice of policy. Congeneric scales imply what might be called a *parallel-reference-scale* model underlying equivalence judgments as distinguished from an *interdependent-reference-scale* model. Although these two models differ in the processes to which they refer, they cannot always be distinguished in practice. Consideration in terms of the regression of observed judgments on true scores leads to the conclusion that the interdependent-scale model can be distinguished from the parallel-scale model when one of its two judgments has a source of a true-score variance that is not shared by the other. Despite the fact that the two models cannot always be distinguished, they can, nevertheless, be studied rigorously. Just how fruitful that study would be remains to be seen.

PHASE 4:   ATTITUDE CHANGE AND JUDGMENTAL CHANGE

The system that has been described in the preceding pages
is one which calls attention to many facets of a person's
taking a stand on an issue.  By careful specification of
dependent variables, each of these facets can be studied
separately.  The time has come to end the truce that McGuire
(1969) noted whereby competing theorists accept judgments
as operational definitions of attitudes.  It is apparent that
the tradition of equating attitude with virtually any judgment of the attitude object is not one that fosters detailed
analysis of any problem.  It should be recognized that there
are many aspects to the taking of stands on issues that are
not directly and explicitly attitudinal in character.  To
define all of these phenomena as attitudinal prejudges the
nature of permissible theories.

As emphasized here, "attitude change" refers to a change
in the values and goals that an individual pursues in the
resolution of an issue.  It seems inescapable that much of
the data that has been interpreted in the literature as
attitude change is literally not that at all.  There is no
doubt that attitudes do sometimes change.  The social-
comparisons process which was suggested as a determinant of
communication of one's views is likely to be a strong determinant of attitude change.  Presumably, a person who seeks to
validate his beliefs by comparison with similar others must
occasionally fail in the effort.  Since, according to
Festinger's analysis, the participant in social comparisons is
motivated simultaneously to persuade others to his views and
to change his views to accord with those of similar others,
this process may be an important source of true attitude
change.  Another source of attitude change, in line with the
present conception, is the outcome of the decisions that the
person makes in an effort to resolve the issue.  If, in fact,
the alternative that he chose does not effectively resolve the
issue as he anticipated that it would, then he might be motivated to reopen the question and choose another alternative.
A shift in choice might not, of course, reflect a change in
attitude.  It may simply correspond to a reassessment of the
alternatives in terms of the unchanged preference criterion.
However, the actual outcome following an initial choice might
occasion a re-examination of the values that the individual
sought to implement by his decision and thereby produce
genuine attitude change.

CONCLUSION

An effort has been made in this paper to present a systematic approach to a person's taking a position on issues of social concern. The approach emphasizes the many acts of judgment and decision that comprise this type of behavior. Each component act is a potential target of study, as are the relationships among them. Only with the delineation of specific questions relating to judgment and decision will the full resources of the accumulated knowledge in the psychology of judgment and decision be usable in the psychology of social attitudes.

REFERENCES

Anderson, N. H. Averaging versus adding as a stimulus-combination rule in impression formation. *Journal of Experimental Psychology*, 1965, *70*, 394-400.

Anderson, N. H. Functional measurement and psychophysical judgment. *Psychological Review*, 1970, *77*, 153-170.

Anderson, N. H. *Methods for studying information integration.* (Center for Human Information Processing, 43) La Jolla, Calif.: University of California at San Diego, 1974.

Aronson, E. Comment: Time--Past, present, and future. In R. P. Abelson, E. Aronson, W. J. McGuire, T. M. Newcomb, M. J. Rosenberg, and P. H. Tannenbaum (Eds.), *Theories of cognitive consistency: A sourcebook.* Chicago: Rand McNally, 1968.

Asch, S. E. Forming impressions of personality. *Journal of Abnormal and Social Psychology*, 1946, *41*, 258-290.

Bem, D. J. Self-perception: An alternative interpretation of cognitive dissonance phenomena. *Psychological Review*, 1967, *74*, 183-200.

Brehm, J. W. Postdecision changes in the desirability of alternatives. *Journal of Abnormal and Social Psychology*, 1956, *52*, 384-389.

Brehm, J. W. *A theory of psychological reactance.* New York: Academic Press, 1966.

Brehm, J. W. *Responses to loss of freedom: A theory of psychological reactance.* Morristown, N.J.: General Learning Press, 1972.

Brehm, J. W., & Cohen, A. R. Reevaluation of choice alternatives as a function of their number and qualitative similarity. *Journal of Abnormal and Social Psychology*, 1959, *58*, 373-378.

Brehm, J. W., Stires, L. K., Sensenig, J., & Shaban, J. The attractiveness of an eliminated choice alternative. *Journal of Experimental Social Psychology*, 1966, *2*, 301–313.

Campbell, D. T., & Fiske, D. W. Convergent and discriminant validation by the multitrait-multimethod matrix. *Psychological Bulletin*, 1959, *56*, 81–105.

Carroll, J. D., & Wish, M. Models and methods for three-way multidimensional scaling. In R. C. Atkinson, D. H. Krantz, R. D. Luce, and P. Suppes (Eds.), *Contemporary developments in mathematical psychology*. Vol. 2. San Francisco: Freeman, 1974.

Deutsch, M., Krauss, R. M., & Rosenau, N. Dissonance or defensiveness? *Journal of Personality*, 1962, *30*, 16–28.

Festinger, L. A theory of social comparison processes. *Human Relations*, 1954, *7*, 117–140.

Festinger, L. *A theory of cognitive dissonance*. New York: Harper & Row, 1957.

Festinger, L. (Ed.) *Conflict, decision, and dissonance*. Stanford, Calif.: Stanford University Press, 1964.

Gerard, H. B., Blevans, S. A., & Malcolm, T. Self-evaluation and the evaluation of choice alternatives. *Journal of Personality*, 1964, *32*, 395–410.

Gravetter, F., & Lockhead, G. R. Criterial range as a frame of reference for stimulus judgment. *Psychological Review*, 1973, *80*, 203–216.

Janis, I. L. Motivational factors in the resolution of decisional conflicts. In M. R. Jones (Ed.), *Nebraska symposium on motivation*. Vol. 7. Lincoln: University of Nebraska Press, 1959.

Janis, I. L., & Mann, L. A conflict-theory approach to attitude change and decision making. In A. G. Greenwald, T. C. Brock, and T. M. Ostrom (Eds.), *Psychological foundations of attitudes*. New York: Academic Press, 1968.

Jones, F. N. Overview of psychophysical scaling methods. In E. C. Carterette and M. P. Friedman (Eds.), *Handbook of perception*. Vol. 2. *Psychophysical judgment and measurement*. New York: Academic Press, 1974.

Jöreskog, K. G. Statistical analysis of sets of congeneric tests. *Psychometrika*, 1971, *36*, 109–133.

Linder, D. E., & Crane, K. A. Reactance theory analysis of predecisional cognitive processes. *Journal of Personality and Social Psychology*, 1970, *15*, 258–264.

Linder, D. E., Wortman, C. B., & Brehm, J. W. Temporal changes in predecision preferences among choice alternatives. *Journal of Personality and Social Psychology*, 1971, *19*, 282–284.

Lord, F. M. Testing if two measuring procedures measure the same dimension. *Psychological Bulletin*, 1973, *79*, 71–72.

226

Lord, F. M., & Novick, M. R. *Statistical theories of mental test scores*. Reading, Mass.: Addison-Wesley, 1968.

Luce, R. D., & Tukey, J. Simultaneous conjoint measurement: A new type of fundamental measurement. *Journal of Mathematical Psychology*, 1964, *1*, 1-27.

McGuire, W. J. The nature of attitudes and attitude change. In G. Lindzey and E. Aronson (Eds.), *Handbook of social psychology*. (2nd ed.) Reading, Mass.: Addison-Wesley, 1969.

Murdoch, P. Effects of perspective and payment on reference scale formation. *Journal of Experimental Research in Personality*, 1969, *3*, 301-310.

Ostrom, T. M. Perspective as an intervening construct in the judgment of attitude statements. *Journal of Personality and Social Psychology*, 1966, *3*, 135-144.

Ostrom, T. M., & Upshaw, H. S. Psychological perspective and attitude change. In A. G. Greenwald, T. C. Brock, and T. M. Ostrom (Eds.), *Psychological foundations of attitudes*. New York: Academic Press, 1968.

Ostrom, T. M., & Upshaw, H. S. Race differences in the judgment of attitude statements over a thirty-five-year period. *Journal of Personality*, 1970, *38*, 235-248.

Shanteau, J. C., & Anderson, N. H. Test of a conflict model for preference judgment. *Journal of Mathematical Psychology*, 1969, *6*, 312-325.

Slovic, P., & Lichtenstein, S. Comparison of Bayesian and regression approaches to the study of information processing in judgment. *Organizational Behavior and Human Performance*, 1971, *6*, 649-744.

Stevens, S. S. Adaptation level vs. the relativity of judgments. *American Journal of Psychology*, 1958, *71*, 633-646.

Stevens, S. S. Perceptual magnitude and its measurement. In E. C. Carterette and M. P. Friedman (Eds.), *Handbook of perception*. Vol. 2. *Psychophysical judgment and measurement*. New York: Academic Press, 1974.

Thurstone, L. L. Attitudes can be measured. *American Journal of Sociology*, 1928, *33*, 529-554.

Tversky, A. A general theory of polynomial conjoint measurement. *Journal of Mathematical Psychology*, 1967, *4*, 1-20.

Tversky, A. Elimination by aspects: A theory of choice. *Psychological Review*, 1972, *79*, 281-299.

Upshaw, H. S. Opinion change vs. reference scale change in the study of attitudes. Paper presented at the meeting of the American Psychological Association, Los Angeles, September 1964. (Mimeographed)

Upshaw, H. S. Attitude measurement. In H. M. Blalock, Jr., and A. B. Blalock (Eds.), *Methodology in social research*. New York: McGraw-Hill, 1968. (a)

Upshaw, H. S.   Cognitive consistency and the psychology of
    judgment.   In R. P. Abelson, E. Aronson, W. J. McGuire,
    T. M. Newcomb, M. J. Rosenberg, and P. H. Tannenbaum (Eds.),
    *Theories of cognitive consistency: A sourcebook*.   Chicago:
    Rand McNally, 1968.   (b)
Upshaw, H. S.   The personal reference scale:   An approach to
    social judgment.   In L. Berkowitz (Ed.), *Advances in
    experimental social psychology*.   Vol. 4.   New York:
    Academic Press, 1969.   (a)
Upshaw, H. S.   Stimulus range and the judgmental unit.
    *Journal of Experimental Social Psychology*, 1969, *5*, 1–11.
    (b)
Upshaw, H. S.   The effect of unit size on the range of the
    reference scale.   *Journal of Experimental Social Psychology*,
    1970, *6*, 129–139.
Upshaw, H. S.   Personality and social effects in judgment.
    In E. C. Carterette and M. P. Friedman (Eds.), *Handbook of
    perception*.   Vol. 2.   *Psychophysical judgment and measure-
    ment*.   New York:   Academic Press, 1974.
Walster, E.   The temporal sequence of post-decision processes.
    In L. Festinger (Ed.), *Conflict, decision, and dissonance*.
    Stanford, Calif.:   Stanford University Press, 1964.
Wish, M., & Carroll, J. D.   Applications of INDSCAL to studies
    of human perception and judgment.   In E. C. Carterette and
    M. P. Friedman (Eds.), *Handbook of perception*.   Vol. 2.
    *Psychophysical judgment and measurement*.   New York:
    Academic Press, 1974.
Wyer, R. S., Jr.   Category ratings as "subjective expected
    values":   Implications for attitude formation and change.
    *Psychological Review*, 1973, *80*, 446–467.

9.  *THE ROLE OF PROBABILISTIC AND*
    *SYLLOGISTIC REASONING IN*
    *COGNITIVE ORGANIZATION*
    *AND SOCIAL INFERENCE*

*Robert S. Wyer, Jr.*
University of Illinois, Urbana-Champaign

Introduction                                                                    230
The Nature of Cognitions                                                        233
Tests of Subjective-Probability Models of Social Inference                      236
  Inferences of Conjunctive Probabilities                                       237
  Bayes's Theorem                                                               242
  A Probabilistic Description of Syllogistic Inference                          243
Implications of a Syllogistic Model of Cognitive Functioning                    246
  Cognitive Organization                                                        246
  Belief and Opinion Change                                                     249
  Social Evaluation and Impression Formation                                    250
The Contribution of Nonlogical Factors to Inference Phenomena                   255
  Statement of Principles                                                       255
  An Empirical Test                                                             260
  Evaluation                                                                    265
  Implications for Cognitive Organization and Change                            265
Concluding Remarks                                                              266
References                                                                      267

## INTRODUCTION

Research and theory on cognitive organization and social inference have generated a variety of models to describe the manner in which persons put together information in order to draw a conclusion about an object or event. Certain of these hypotheses are based upon the assumption that the processes underlying these inferences are logical (McGuire, 1960). Others take into account the possible role of nonlogical factors in cognitive organization and social inference (Heider, 1958; Abelson & Rosenberg, 1958). Still others (see Anderson, 1971, 1974; Fishbein, 1963) assume that persons apply certain algebraic or arithmetic rules (summation, averaging, or multiplication) in drawing an inference from a given amount of information. Finally, other models pertain to the possibility that people process information in a manner implied by the laws of statistics or probability (see Edwards, 1968).

These various models, and the assumptions underlying them, are not necessarily incompatible. More than one type of rule could be, and undoubtedly is, used by subjects to make inferences about objects on the basis of the information they have available. However, in order to understand the conditions under which different models, or sets of related models, apply, one must acquire a clear conceptual understanding of the underlying cognitive processes implied by these models. Unfortunately, many of us who have been engaged in the development of such models have tended to focus primarily upon the mathematical properties of the formulations we have proposed while ignoring the implications of these models for what subjects are actually doing. (The present writer must share the brunt of this criticism; see Wyer and Goldberg, 1970.)

The tendency noted above has been particularly evident in research on subjective-probability formulations. These models are typically based upon the general assumption that the relations among subjective probabilities (that is, subjective estimates of the likelihood that a statement is true, an event will occur, an object has a particular attribute, and so on) conform to the laws of mathematical probability. Although these laws are related *mathematically*, there is no *a priori* reason to believe that because one equation based upon the laws of mathematical probability describes human inference processes accurately, a second equation will also describe inference processes. In fact, the cognitive processes implied by different relations among subjective probabilities may differ considerably. This point will be elaborated presently.

It may be worthwhile at this point to distinguish between *cognitive organization*, the manner in which previously formed beliefs and attitudes are inter-related and stored in memory, and *social inference*, the process whereby several pieces of *new* information about an object are combined to form a *new* cognition about (or judgment of) this object. Although this latter process is clearly not devoid of the effects of previous experience, in many formulations of social inference these effects are typically assumed to be constant over the objects being judged     (see Anderson, 1965; Kaplan, 1971; Wyer, 1969).

The distinction between cognitive organization and social inference may seem subtle and may often be difficult to demonstrate empirically. However, the distinction is nevertheless important, since there is no *a priori* reason to assume that the principles governing these processes are identical. To give an example, a subject may infer that two hypothetical persons, A and B, like each other, based upon information that each likes a third person, C. However, the same subject may personally know several persons who dislike one another intensely despite their mutual admiration for a third. Moreover, he may experience no cognitive tension whatsoever when made aware of these sets of cognitions. To this extent, cognitive balance principles (Heider, 1958) would be a more appropriate description of social-inference processes than of cognitive organization processes. (For an extensive discussion of this possibility, see Wyer, 1974b.)

What, then, are the criteria to be used in determining the validity of a hypothetical principle of social inference and/or cognitive organization? Suppose the hypothetical principle in question describes cognition C as a function of A and B. Then, if the functional relation among these cognitions is clearly stated, one criterion is of course the extent to which the relation provides an accurate quantitative description of the actual relations among the cognitions involved (A, B, and C). A second, more qualitative criterion is whether information bearing directly upon A and B combines subjectively to affect C in the manner implied by the relation. These criteria are not identical. As Birnbaum (1973) has pointed out, it is often possible to obtain reasonably accurate quantitative predictions based upon an invalid model. On the other hand, information bearing upon A and B may affect C in a way that appears functionally consistent with the model, and yet the actual value of C may be nowhere near that predicted. Thus, the validity of a model may be equivocal without simultaneous tests of both its qualitative and quantitative implications.

The general criteria outlined above can usually be applied quite easily in testing the validity of a hypothetical description of how inferences about unfamiliar objects and events are formed on the basis of new information about them. However, they may be more difficult to apply when evaluating the

validity of a principle hypothesized to govern the organization
of previously formed cognitions. A person's cognitive system
contains a large number of highly inter-related attitudes and
beliefs, not all of which are salient to him at any given time.
Even though a principle may typically be applied by a subject
in organizing his cognitions, any particular set of his cognitions may not appear related in precisely the manner implied
by this principle, simply because the subject has seldom considered the cognitions in relation to one another, and thus
has not recently applied the principle to them. Once these
cognitions do become salient to him, he should of course become
aware of any inconsistencies among them and should reorganize
them in a manner implied by the rule. This reorganization may
take some time to occur. However, if the cognitions involved
are reported by the subject at a later time, their relation
should correspond more closely to that implied by the rule than
they were when reported the first time. If this does not occur,
it would mean either that subjects do not organize their cognitions in any systematic way whatsoever or that the particular
principle postulated to govern their organization is invalid.

The criteria proposed for validating a hypothetical principle of social inference or cognitive organization generally
require that the principle be stated precisely. That is, it
must be able to generate *a priori* point predictions of the
manner in which new information combines to affect judgments
of hypothetical objects and events, or of the inter-relatedness
of previously formed cognitions about familiar objects and
events. It is perhaps for this reason that interest has
developed in subjective-probability models. Since beliefs can
be defined as subjective probabilities, the laws of mathematical probability, if applicable to human information processing,
could be used to generate precise quantitative predictions of
the relations among beliefs and the manner in which information
bearing upon one belief will affect others. Research applying
one or another subjective-probability model has taken many
directions. One path has been exemplified by the use of
Bayes's theorem to describe the manner in which persons revise
their beliefs upon receipt of new information (Ajzen, 1971;
Edwards, 1968; Slovic & Lichtenstein, 1971; Trope, 1974). A
second application has been stimulated by McGuire's model of
syllogistic inference (1960), which theoretically describes
beliefs in the conclusion of a syllogism as a function of
beliefs in the premises of the syllogism. A third and less
focused line of research has simply been stimulated by the
question of whether the laws of mathematical probability do
indeed provide a generally valid description of the relations
among subjective probabilities (Peterson & Beach, 1967; Wyer &
Goldberg, 1970). In fact, rigorous tests of these various

formulations have provided strong support for only one set of
equations based upon the laws of objective probability, namely,
those that appear to describe syllogistic reasoning. This
restriction upon the conditions to which subjective-probability
models apply is not necessarily disappointing, since many
inference tasks with which persons are confronted may well
involve this type of reasoning. However, it emphasizes the
point made previously, that the mathematical relatedness of a
series of hypothetical descriptions of cognitive functioning
does not necessarily imply their psychological relatedness.
Each may imply a quite different underlying cognitive process,
and only certain of these processes may actually occur.

In the pages that follow, some evidence will be provided in
support of these assertions. First, the conceptualization of
beliefs and attitudes that underlies the application of subjective-probability models to social-inference and cognitive-
organization phenomena will be made more explicit. Second,
data will be presented bearing upon the validity of several
hypothetical relations among subjective probabilities. The
implications of one of these relations, a description of syllogistic reasoning, for social-inference and cognitive-
organization processes will then be pursued. Finally, an
approach will be suggested for identifying the role of nonlogical factors in cognitive organization and social inference,
and the way in which the effects of such factors may ultimately
be incorporated into the syllogistic-probabilistic model upon
which this paper focuses will be discussed.

## THE NATURE OF COGNITIONS

Since the conceptual underpinnings of the research and
theory to be discussed in this chapter are elaborated in detail elsewhere (Wyer, 1974b), the reader will be spared an
extensive discussion here. Both beliefs and attitudes are
conceptualized as estimates of the likelihood that an object
is a member of a cognitive category. For example, the belief
statement "Italians are romantic" and the attitude statement
"I like Italians" can both be viewed as statements concerning
the membership of the object "Italians" in a cognitive category
("romantic" in the first case and "persons I like" in the
second). The magnitude of agreement with each statement can
be viewed as an estimate of the likelihood that "Italians"
are indeed members of the category described in the statement
or, alternatively, as an estimate of the likelihood that the
statement itself belongs to the cognitive category "true."
Viewed from this perspective, there is no essential difference
between attitudes and beliefs; both pertain to the membership

of an object (or a statement) in a cognitive category. The only difference lies in the fact that in the case of an attitude, the cognitive category involved has traditionally been denoted "evaluative" by psychologists. Whether the processes underlying the organization of and change in cognitions depend upon the type of categories involved is an empirical question.

This conception of an attitude ignores the affective, or emotional, component typically assumed to underlie overt expressions of liking for an object. However, note that this conception does not preclude the existence of such emotional states. One's emotional reaction to an object may indeed provide him with information that affects his judgments of the object, much as information from external sources affects judgments of the sort we have defined as beliefs. It is unlikely, however, that emotional reactions are the *only* type of information upon which such judgments are based. In any event, we have simply omitted the existence of an internal emotional state from the *definition* of an attitude, so that the presence of such a state, and its effects upon judgments, become matters for empirical investigation.

Evaluative judgments of objects are typically assessed along category scales of magnitude rather than probability. However, this distinction may be of greater methodological than theoretical importance. As we have argued elsewhere (Wyer, 1973a, 1974b), "probability" judgments and "magnitude" judgments may both result from an attempt by subjects to identify the most representative cognitive category to which an object belongs. That is, when required to make a judgment, a subject may first attempt to identify the range of categories available to him for classifying the stimulus object, and may assign some subjective probability to the object's membership in each. His estimate may then be some subjective "expected value" of this distribution of probabilities.

To see this analogy more clearly, suppose a subject is asked to estimate the truth of the statement "Italians are romantic." His estimate can in many instances be viewed as the expected value of the object along a two-category scale with values 0 (not romantic) and 1 (romantic); that is, his judgment can be represented by the expression

$$J_I = P_R(1) + P_{R'}(0) = P_R \; ,$$

where $P_R$ and $P_{R'}$ are subjective probabilities that the object "Italian" belongs to the categories "romantic" and "not romantic," respectively. Similarly, one's belief in the validity of the proposition can be viewed as the expected value of the proposition along a two-category scale with values 0 (false) and 1 (true).

234

When a judge is asked to rate an object along a scale composed of more than two categories, the process of arriving at this rating may be similar. That is, the judge may believe that the object belongs to several scale categories with some probability and may therefore assign the object to the category that he believes is most representative of this set. This category may be an expected value of the underlying distribution of subjective probabilities that the object belongs to each of the categories along the scale he is required to use. Thus, assume that a judge is asked to judge "Italians" along a seven-category scale from -3 (dislike very much) to +3 (like very much). He may believe that Italians belong to several available categories with some probability. Suppose these subjective probabilities are distributed as follows:

| Category: | -3 | -2 | -1 | 0 | 1 | 2 | 3 |
|---|---|---|---|---|---|---|---|
| Subjective probability: | 0 | 0 | .1 | .2 | .3 | .3 | .1 |

His overall judgment, $J_O$, may be the expected value of this subjective distribution, or more specifically,

$$J_O = \Sigma P_{iO} V_i = .1(-1) + .2(0) +$$

$$.3(1) + .1(3) = 1.1,$$

where $P_{iO}$ is the subjective probability that the object belongs to category $i$ and $V_i$ is the numerical value assigned to this category.

Preliminary data have been reported in support of this interpretation (Wyer, 1973a). That is, a subject's rating of a hypothetical person described by one or two adjectives along an 11-category scale of likableness is predicted quite accurately from the expected value of the distribution of his estimates of the frequency with which persons described by this information would belong to each of the available response-scale categories. Moreover, the expected value of this distribution is consistently more accurate a predictor than is either the mode or the median of the distribution.

The proposed interpretation of category ratings has other implications. For example, the dispersion of the subjective distribution underlying a subject's rating may reflect his uncertainty about the validity of this rating. Strong support for this hypothesis has indeed been obtained (Wyer, 1973a). These data provide further evidence for the psychological meaningfulness of the distributions generated by subjects, and more generally for the interpretation of category ratings we have proposed.[1]

If both beliefs and attitudes are interpretable as subjective probabilities, and if it were *generally* true that relations among subjective probabilities obey the laws of mathematical probability, the implications would be profound. Unfortunately, however, the applicability of such laws to human information processing may be quite limited. Let us turn to some data bearing upon the applicability of a few of these laws and evaluate their implications.

## TESTS OF SUBJECTIVE-PROBABILITY MODELS OF SOCIAL INFERENCE

Several different equations can be derived from describing the relations between the mathematical probabilities of occurrence of two events, A and B, and the contingency of one event's occurrence upon the occurrence of the other. For example, if A and B are independent,

$$P_{AB} = P_A P_B, \tag{1a}$$

or, if A and B are not independent,

$$P_{AB} = P_A P_{B/A}. \tag{1b}$$

Moreover,

$$P_{B/A} = \frac{P_B P_{A/B}}{P_B P_{A/B} + (1 - P_B)P_{A/B'}} \tag{2}$$

$$P_B = P_A P_{B/A} + (1 - P_A)P_{B/A'}, \tag{3}$$

where $P_A$ and $P_B$ are the probabilities of A and B, respectively, $P_{AB}$ is the conjunctive probability of A and B, $P_{B/A}$ and $P_{B/A'}$ are the conditional probabilities of B given A and not-A, respectively, and $P_{A/B}$ is the conditional probability of A given B. These equations are mathematical tautologies. However, suppose the components of these equations are not objective probabilities, but rather pertain to subjects' *estimates* of the likelihood of the events described. Then the validity

---

[1]This measure of subjective uncertainty, which appears more valid in an index of stimulus ambiguity than the standard deviation over subjects of the category ratings of the stimulus, has value in predicting the relative influence of information when presented in combination (Hinkle, 1974; Wyer, 1973a) and in predicting the extent to which its interpretation will be affected by its context (Wyer, 1974a).

of each equation is an empirical question.

To obtain an intuitive feel for the inference processes implied by the above equations, suppose that in each case a subject receives information bearing upon each of the component probabilities to the right side of the equation, and then is asked to infer the probability on the left. The inferences to which Eqs. (1a) and (1b) pertain are made infrequently. For example, it is unlikely outside the laboratory that a person is asked to infer the likelihood that two propositions in combination are true (for example, the likelihood that *both* marijuana is harmful *and* that it will be legalized within the next 10 years). Thus, although the integration rule implied by these equations is relatively simple, whether subjects actually employ such a rule when called upon to infer $P_{AB}$ from information bearing upon $P_A$ and $P_B$ is less clear.

Since the inferences to which Eqs. (2) and (3) pertain are more apt to occur in everyday life, these equations are more psychologically interesting. For example, Eq. (2), traditionally known as Bayes's theorem, is typically applied in predicting the extent to which a subject will revise his estimate of the likelihood of A after receiving information that B is definitely true. Equation (3) theoretically describes syllogistic inferences of a "conclusion," B, based upon information bearing upon the validity of two sets of premises, one set of the form "A; if A, then B " and the other of the form "not-A; if not-A, then B."

The situations in which the above equations are apt to apply may differ considerably. Moreover, their applicability may depend upon the particular nature of A and B. Perhaps the best initial strategy in evaluating the validity of the models is to determine their applicability in situations that are as "context free" as possible. This strategy was adopted in the series of studies described below.

## INFERENCES OF CONJUNCTIVE PROBABILITIES

To test the validity of Eq. (1a), subjects received information about the frequency with which persons possessed two hypothetical attributes, each denoted by a letter of the alphabet (for example, A and B). These frequencies were described by the adverbs "usually," "sometimes," or "rarely" to convey high, moderate, and low probabilities of possessing A ($P_A$) and B ($P_B$). Nine pairs of statements, representing all combinations of three levels of $P_A$ and three levels of $P_B$, were presented. From each set of information, subjects estimated the likelihood that a particular person (denoted by first name) had both A and B ($P_{AB}$), had A ($P_A$), and had B ($P_B$). These estimates were made along a 100-point scale from 0 (not at all likely) to 100 (extremely likely), but were divided by 100 prior to analyses to convert them to units of subjective probability.

Incidentally, the reader may have some concern about the implicit assumption underlying the above response transformation, that the scale is equal interval with an origin of 0. If quantitative inaccuracies occur between obtained and predicted estimates based upon Eqs. (1a) and (1b) or any of the other equations theoretically relating subjective probabilities, they might be attributed to the invalidity of this scale assumption and not to the invalidity of the equation. On the other hand, accurate quantitative predictions would indicate both that the response-scale transformation is appropriate *and* that the equation is valid. In fact, the assumption that the response-scale transformation is fairly reasonable is indirectly supported by the good fits of Eq. (3) (compare Wyer, 1970b, 1975b), as we shall see in a later section.

Preliminary analyses indicated that the manipulations of $P_A$ and $P_B$ had their intended effects upon subjects' personal estimates of these probabilities. However, the manipulations had strong interactive effects upon estimates of $P_{AB}$. The form of this interaction, shown in Figure 1, was consistent with the multiplicative inference rule implied by Eq. (1a). However, other aspects of the data call the validity of Eq. (1a) into question. For example, while the effects of experimental variables upon predicted values of $P_{AB}$ (calculated for each subject separately by multiplying his estimates of $P_A$ and $P_B$) bear certain similarities to the effects of these variables upon obtained values, the slope of the curves relating obtained values of $P_{AB}$ to $P_A$ at each level of $P_B$ (Figure 1A) is not a constant multiple of the slope of the corresponding curves relating predicted values to $P_A$ (Figure 1B). Moreover, an accurate quantitative fit of Eq. (1a) cannot be obtained through a simple linear transformation of $P_A P_B$ using slope and intercept parameters that are invariant over information sets.

Another, more qualitative implication of Eq. (1a) is that estimates of $P_{AB}$ should be lower than estimates of both $P_A$ and $P_B$. However, this was not consistently the case. For example, under the six informational conditions in which the manipulated levels of $P_A$ and $P_B$ differed, subjects' estimates of $P_{AB}$ were less than their personal estimates of both $P_A$ and $P_B$ only 17.3% of the time, between these component estimates 69.7% of the time, and greater than both component estimates 13.0% of the time. These proportions did not vary appreciably over the informational conditions involved. Nor did they appear due to the fact that some subjects behaved like "multipliers" while others did not. Only 3 of 27 subjects estimated $P_{AB}$ to be less than both $P_A$ and $P_B$ in more than five of the nine

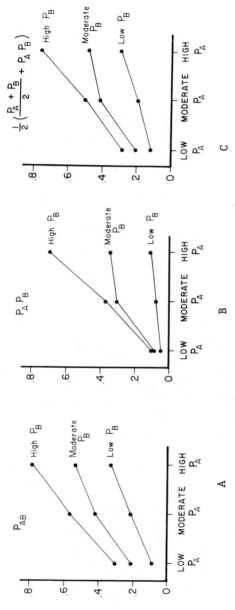

*Fig. 1.* Effects of manipulated levels of $P_A$ and $P_B$ upon $P_{AB}$ *(Part A)*, $P_A P_B$ *(Part B)*, and predicted values of $P_{AB}$ *(Part C) based upon Eq. (4a)*.

informational conditions, and only 8 estimated it to be between $P_A$ and $P_B$ in more than five cases.

The present data suggest that a simple multiplicative rule cannot by itself account for the manner in which subjects arrive at their estimates of conjunctive probabilities. However, a multiplying process may still be involved, at least in part. It was noted somewhat fortuitously that the mean obtained value of $P_{AB}$ typically fell between the product of $P_A$ and $P_B$ and the simple average of these two probabilities. Perhaps subjects are typically uncertain about how to arrive at estimates of the conjunctive, and thus their evaluations represent a compromise between the two alternative rules (multiplicative and averaging). Data support this possibility. Predicted values of $P_{AB}$ based upon the equation

$$P_{AB} = \frac{1}{2} (P_A P_B + \frac{P_A + P_B}{2}) \qquad (4a)$$

are shown in Figure 1C as a function of informational variables. This family of curves is very similar in form to those shown in Figure 1A. Analysis of variance of the difference between estimates $P_{AB}$ and predicted values based upon Eq. (4a) revealed that not only was the overall magnitude of this difference not significant, but its magnitude did not reliably vary over informational conditions (in each case, $F < 1.0$; $p > .25$). A plot of mean obtained values of $P_{AB}$ as a function of mean predicted values, shown in Figure 2C, provides nice visual evidence of the quantitative accuracy of the equation. While Eq. (4a) cannot account for individual instances in which $P_{AB}$ was estimated to be greater than both $P_A$ and $P_B$, its accuracy is nonetheless impressive.

The data described above pertain to inferences based upon independent events. However, a parallel study, in which inferences of $P_{AB}$ were made on the basis of information bearing upon the likelihood of possessing a hypothetical gene $(P_A)$ and the likelihood of possessing an attribute if one possessed the gene $(P_{B/A})$ yielded comparable results. That is, the information had interactive effects of the sort implied by Eq. (1b). However, the quantitative accuracy of this equation was poor (see Figure 2B, Experiment 2), while an expression analogous to Eq. (4a), specifically,

$$P_{AB} = \frac{1}{2} (P_A P_{B/A} + \frac{P_A + P_{B/A}}{2}), \qquad (4b)$$

produced a reasonably accurate fit (see Figure 2C).

The preceding discussion makes salient the need to consider more than one criterion in evaluating the appropriateness of a model of social inference. Although the effects of

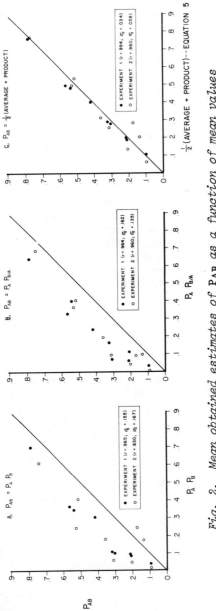

*Fig. 2. Mean obtained estimates of $P_{AB}$ as a function of mean values of $P_AP_B$ (Part A), $P_AP_{B/A}$ (Part B, and predictions based upon Eq. (4a) (when A and B are independent) and Eq. (4b) (when A and B are dependent) (Part C).*

information appeared on the basis of analyses of variance to combine multiplicatively, a multiplicative rule alone was not sufficient to generate accurate quantitative predictions of the manner in which information was used to arrive at estimates of conjunctive probabilities, at least under the conditions investigated in this study.

## BAYES'S THEOREM

A third study was performed, using similar types of stimulus materials, to test the accuracy with which Eq. (2) (Bayes's theorem) is applicable to inference phenomena. Subjects read 27 different sets of information, each of which established a different combination of levels of $P_B$ (high, moderate, and low), $P_{A/B}$, and $P_{A/B'}$. In each case, A was a hypothetical gene and B was a hypothetical attribute. Information was presented in a manner similar to that described previously. (For example, in an instance in which the manipulated levels of $P_B$, $P_{A/B}$, and $P_{A/B'}$ were high, moderate, and low, respectively, this information was of the form "Persons *usually* have attribute B. Persons with attribute B *sometimes* have gene A. Persons without attribute B *rarely* have gene A.") After reading each set of information, subjects estimated the likelihood that a particular hypothetical person had attribute B *if* he had gene A ($P_{B/A}$), and then made estimates corresponding to the other components of Eq. (2).

Analyses of variance of these data yielded significant main effects of each of the three manipulated probabilities but no interactions, indicating that $P_B$, $P_{A/B}$, and $P_{A/B'}$ had independent effects upon estimates of $P_{B/A}$. The standard error of the difference between mean obtained estimates of $P_{B/A}$ and mean predicted estimates based upon Eq. (2) was .203, or over two scale units. Moreover, the correlation between obtained and predicted values was only .607. Estimates of $P_{B/A}$ would appear to be more appropriately predicted from the equation

$$P_{B/A} = k_1 P_B + k_2 P_{A/B} - k_3 P_{A/B},$$

where $k_2 > k_3 > k_1$. It is important to note that this equation predicts effects of informational variables that are generally similar in *direction* to those implied by Bayes's theorem. That is, estimates of $P_{B/A}$ are a positive function of the difference between $P_{A/B}$ and $P_{A/B'}$. However, since $P_{A/B}$ has greater weight than $P_{A/B'}$, this equation, unlike Eq. (2), implies that $P_{B/A}$ may be revised even though $P_{A/B}$ and $P_{A/B'}$ are equal. More generally, it is interesting that $P_{B/A}$ was more strongly inferred from the value of $P_{A/B}$ than from the value of $P_B$. This suggests that subjects infer the likelihood that A implies B primarily from information about the likelihood that

B implies A, and do not give much attention to the uncondition-
al probability that B is true.

Caution should be taken in treating these results as evidence that Bayes's theorem is a *generally* invalid description
of inference processes. As repeatedly stated, the processes
used by subjects in arriving at judgments may vary greatly
over tasks and experimental conditions. However, these data
do suggest that the inference rule used in the situation at
hand is much simpler than that implied by the laws of mathematical probability.

## A PROBABILISTIC DESCRIPTION OF SYLLOGISTIC INFERENCE

Suppose a subject is asked to report his belief in a proposition B. This belief may be based in part upon the strength
of his beliefs that a second proposition, A, is true and that
A, if true, implies B. It may also be based in part upon his
belief that B is true if A is *not* true. Note that these beliefs comprise two logical syllogisms, one of the form [A; if
A, then B; B], and the second of the form [not-A; if not A,
then B; B]. To the extent that the subject reasons logically,
the strength of his belief in the "conclusion" B should be a
function of the combined strengths of his beliefs in the two
sets of premises which, if true, imply B.

The inference process suggested above can theoretically be
described by Eq. (3), where $P_A$ and $P_B$ are the beliefs that A
and B are true, respectively, and $P_{B/A}$ and $P_{B/A'}$ are beliefs
that B is true if A is and is not true, respectively. The
validity of this equation was tested in a situation analogous
to that used in investigating the validity of the other equations described in this section (Wyer, 1975b). Specifically,
subjects received information about the frequency with which
persons possessed a gene A and the frequencies with which persons who did and did not have A possessed an attribute B.
Twenty-seven sets of information, each assumed to reflect a
different combination of levels of $P_A$, $P_{B/A}$, and $P_{B/A'}$, were
presented. From each set of information, subjects estimated
the likelihood that a particular person possessed B ($P_B$), that
he possessed A ($P_A$), that he possessed B *if* he possessed A
($P_{B/A}$), and that he possessed B if he did *not* have A ($P_{B/A'}$).
These judgments were reported along a 0–10 scale and subsequently were divided by 10 to convert them to units of subjective probability.

Equation (3) implies that the effect of information bearing
upon $P_{B/A}$ upon estimates of $P_B$ should be a positive multiplicative function of $P_A$, while the effect of $P_{B/A'}$ upon $P_B$
should be negatively related to the value of $P_A$. As shown in
Figures 3B and 3C, this was indeed the case. Although a barely

243

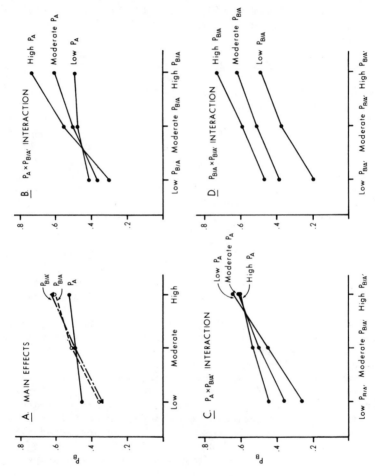

*Fig. 3. Main effects and interactions pertaining to estimates of $P_B$ as a function of experimentally manipulated levels of $P_A$, $P_{B/A}$, and $P_{B/A'}$ (reprinted from Wyer, 1975b).*

significant interaction of $P_{B/A}$ and $P_{B/A}{}'$ occurred (Figure 3D), this interaction appears due to a single deviant point and is too small in magnitude to take seriously pending replication. Thus, these results suggest that information bearing directly upon $P_A$, $P_{B/A}$, and $P_{B/A}{}'$ does indeed combine subjectively to affect judgments in the manner implied by Eq. (3).

To test the quantitative accuracy of Eq. (3), predicted values of $P_B$ were calculated for each subject separately under each of the 27 information conditions. The standard error of the difference between mean obtained and mean predicted values of $P_B$ over these conditions was .047, or less than half a scale unit, without the introduction of *ad hoc* curve-fitting parameters. In addition, the slope and intercept of the best-fitting linear function relating predicted to obtained values of $P_B$ did not differ from their theoretical values of 1 and 0, respectively. Finally, the overall numerical difference between predicted and obtained values was not significantly different from 0 and did not significantly vary over levels of either $P_A$ or $P_{B/A}$. Although the accuracy of the equation would be increased slightly if $P_{B/A}{}'$ were assigned a weight inversely proportional to its scale value, the increase in accuracy obtained by introducing such an *ad hoc* weight would not be sufficient to offset the practical advantage of generating accurate quantitative predictions without introducing empirically determined weighting parameters of unclear psychological significance.

This study provides quite strong support for the validity of Eq. (3) as a description of social-inference processes using the same general type of information, and under similar experimental conditions, in which poor support was obtained for other models patterned after the laws of mathematical probability. It goes without saying, however, that if the applicability of this equation were limited to these quite contrived conditions and informational materials, it would be of little interest. Fortunately, this is not the case. In an earlier study (Wyer, 1970b), stimulus materials consisted of nine different stories, each pertaining to a hypothetical event, A, and its relation to a second event, B. Each story, which was generally interesting for subjects to read, was presented in two parts. The first part contained information implying a low likelihood of occurrence of A $(P_A)$, and established levels of $P_{B/A}$ and $P_{B/A}{}'$ that varied systematically over the nine stories. The second part of the story increased the subjective likelihood of A but contained no additional information bearing directly upon the conditional beliefs. (For example, the first part of one story contained information suggesting that the likelihood of a riot at "State University" $(P_A)$ was low, and also information bearing upon the probabilities that the university president would be fired if there were and were not a riot ($P_{B/A}$ and $P_{B/A'}$); the second part of the story contained information that increased the likelihood that there would be a riot.) The nine stories represented all combinations of three levels of $P_{B/A}$ and three levels of $P_{B/A'}$. After reading each part of a given story, subjects first reported their beliefs corresponding to $P_B$ (in the above example, the likelihood that the university president would be fired), followed by their beliefs corresponding to $P_A$, $P_{B/A}$, and $P_{B/A'}$, each along a scale similar to that used in the experiments described previously. Mean obtained estimates of $P_B$, and changes in $P_B$ after reading the second part of each story, are shown in Figure 4 as a function of predicted values. The standard error of the difference between obtained and predicted values of $P_B$ was .035, and of $\Delta P_B$ (the change in $P_B$ after reading the second part of each story) was .051. As in the first study described, the difference between obtained and predicted values did not vary over levels of $P_A$ and $P_{B/A}$, and varied with the level of $P_{B/A'}$ only after reading the first part of the story. Again, this latter variation, while significant, was small in magnitude.

## IMPLICATIONS OF A SYLLOGISTIC MODEL OF COGNITIVE FUNCTIONING

### COGNITIVE ORGANIZATION

The research described above provides promising support for the applicability of Eq. (3) as a description of syllogistic inferences about hypothetical persons and events. However, this support does not guarantee the validity of the equation in describing the manner in which previously formed cognitions about real persons and objects are actively organized or in describing the effect that one such belief will have upon others. As pointed out earlier, the quantitative accuracy of a model in describing the organization of previously formed cognitions is not in itself an adequate basis for evaluating its validity, as there are theoretical reasons to expect inaccuracies to occur when the cognitions involved have not recently been considered in relation to one another. A better indication of the validity of a hypothetical description of the process used by subjects in actively organizing their beliefs and attitudes is whether the accuracy of this description increases after these cognitions become salient to subjects in temporal contiguity.

By applying this criterion, substantial evidence has accumulated for the validity of Eq. (3) as a principle of cognitive organization. McGuire (1960) found that when subjects

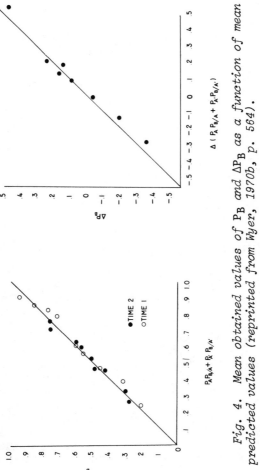

Fig. 4. Mean obtained values of $P_B$ and $\Delta P_B$ as a function of mean predicted values (reprinted from Wyer, 1970b, p. 564).

247

completed a questionnaire containing belief items comprising a
logical syllogism in two sessions a week apart, the responses
to the items appeared to become more logically consistent in
the second session than they were in the first. McGuire labeled this increase in consistency over time the "Socratic
effect."

McGuire's original model did not provide a precise quantitative index of the magnitude of this effect. However, recent
studies in which Eq. (3) has been applied reinforce McGuire's
earlier findings and support his hypothesis concerning why the
effect occurs. For example, Wyer and Goldberg (1970) used the
absolute difference between obtained and predicted estimates
of $P_B$ as an index of the cognitive inconsistency of beliefs
associated with a given pair of propositions A and B, and
found that for each of 10 different pairs of the nature to
which Eq. (3) pertains, the standard error of this difference
over subjects was less in a second session of the experiment
than it was in the first. Although several explanations of
the effect *other* than McGuire's have been suggested, empirical
tests of their validity have failed. Since much of the evidence bearing upon these explanations has been discussed in
detail elsewhere (Wyer, 1974b), it will not be elaborated here.
Let it suffice to say that the effects do not appear to be the
result of tendencies to respond in a socially desirable (that
is, "consistent") manner once subjects become aware that the
items in the questionnaire are related. Nor is the effect
attributable to practice effects or to increased familiarity
with the type of questionnaire administered. Finally, note
that the predictive accuracy of Eq. (3) would necessarily
increase if all probabilities comprising the equation regressed
toward .50 over sessions. However, the evidence that such
regression actually occurs is limited (compare Henninger, 1974;
Rosen & Wyer, 1972), and when it does occur, it does not appear to be of sufficient magnitude to account for the Socratic
effect. The magnitude of the effect also does not appear to
depend upon whether the beliefs being reported are evaluative
("The legalization of marijuana is desirable") or nonevaluative
("The structure of the family will change substantially by the
end of this century"), or upon whether the issue to which the
belief items pertain is considered by subjects to be important
to them (Wyer, 1974c). These latter data provide indirect
support for the hypothesis that simply the awareness of inconsistent cognitions, regardless of the nature or importance of
these cognitions, is sufficient to stimulate cognitive reorganization of the sort postulated by McGuire.

*BELIEF AND OPINION CHANGE*

Although the occurrence of the Socratic effect supports the validity of Eq. (3) as a description of cognitive-organization processes, a number of questions remain to be resolved. One concerns the number and type of related cognitions that must be made salient in order to stimulate cognitive reorganization. A second concerns the amount of time required for cognitive reorganization to take place. These issues gain additional importance when they are considered in the context of theory and research on the immediate and long-range effects of information upon belief and opinion change. For example, suppose a subject receives a persuasive communication bearing directly upon a premise A. According to Eq. (3), this communication may also affect his belief in an unmentioned conclusion B. However, this latter effect may not occur unless the subject's belief in B is salient to him at the time the communication is presented. Moreover, it may take time for the implications of change in his belief in A to filter down to his belief in B. Watts and Holt (1970) found that a communication bearing directly upon beliefs in a premise had more effect upon beliefs in a conclusion when the latter beliefs were assessed 10 minutes after the communication had been received than when they were assessed immediately afterward. However, the optimum time required for this cognitive reorganization to take place is unclear.

The above emphasis upon *discrepancies* from predictions based upon Eq. (3) when applied to the relations among previously formed beliefs should not be construed as an indication that the formulation is completely useless in describing quantitatively the relations among these beliefs or in predicting the magnitude of the effect that change in one belief will have upon others. In an initial test of the equation's accuracy in describing sets of related beliefs about contemporary social issues, Wyer and Goldberg (1970) found that the standard error of the difference between mean predicted and mean obtained values of $P_B$', calculated without the introduction of *ad hoc* curve-fitting parameters, was not much greater than that obtained in studies of the relations among newly formed beliefs. Changes in $P_B$ produced by persuasive communications bearing upon A were less accurately predicted. However, no other contemporary formulation of cognitive organization has been demonstrated to provide as accurate predictions in a comparable situation.

In a more recent study, Wyer (1975a) constructed sets of three propositions, A, B, and C, such that B was both the conclusion of one syllogism of which A was a premise and the premise of a second syllogism of which A was the conclusion.

(For example, in one case, A, B, and C were the propositions "People unconsciously imitate the behavior of persons they see on television," "Watching television causes people to behave more violently," and "Television programs showing unnecessary violence should be banned," respectively.) Subjects were asked to write essays either favoring B or opposing B after receiving information that other college students typically favored or opposed this proposition. All four combinations of essay position and others' position were run. The two social-influence procedures (essay writing and information about others' opinions) had independent effects upon beliefs in B and, to a lesser degree, upon beliefs in C. However, they had interactive effects upon beliefs in A, effects that were not clearly predictable from existing formulations of belief and opinion change. (Specifically, writing essays about B affected beliefs that A was true only when subjects were told that other persons agreed with B.) Nevertheless, the difference between predicted and obtained values of $P_B$, based upon beliefs about A, did not vary significantly over experimental conditions, suggesting that the different effects of influence techniques upon $P_A$ and $P_B$ could be adequately accounted for in terms of the model (specifically, in terms of the effects these influence techniques have upon $P_{B/A}$ and $P_{B/A'}$ as well as upon $P_A$ and $P_B$).

## SOCIAL EVALUATION AND IMPRESSION FORMATION

Although the preceding discussion has focused upon the relations among beliefs, the proposed model can also be applied to evaluative judgments. Suppose a subject receives information about an attribute of a person O and is then asked, based upon this information, to estimate his liking for O. The process underlying this inference can theoretically be described by the equation

$$P_L = P_X P_{L/X} + (1 - P_X)P_{L/X'}, \qquad (5)$$

where $P_L$ is the subjective probability that O is likable, $P_X$ is the belief that O possesses attribute X, and $P_{L/X}$ and $P_{L/X'}$ are conditional beliefs that O is likable if he does and does not have X. The psychological process underlying such an inference may be similar to that assumed to underlie Eq. (3); that is, the judgment that one likes O, or that O is likable, may be the result of a logical inference based in part upon beliefs in the premises of a logical syllogism [O has X; if a person has X, he is likable; O is likable] and in part upon beliefs in the premises of the syllogism [O does not have X; if a person does not have X, he is likable; O is likable]. Note that such an inference would be very similar to that

250

assumed by Jones and Gerard (1967) and others in their conceptualization of an attitude (for example, 0 is "good") as a
conclusion drawn from combining a belief (0 has X) and a value
(X is "good"). Presumably, information that affects the likelihood that 0 has X $(P_\chi)$ should affect beliefs that 0 is likable in a manner implied by this equation.

Although the above analysis is straightforward, some problems arise in providing a rigorous quantitative test of this
equation, even under conditions in which 0 is a hypothetical
person. Personality attributes are believed to be highly
inter-related, as is evident from research on the nature of
"implicit personality theories" (Schneider, 1973). Thus, for
example, information that 0 is *warm* may also affect beliefs
that he has several other attributes in addition to *warm*, and
these beliefs may also be related to the belief that 0 is likable. Though all of these effects should theoretically be
predictable from this general formulation, it may take time for
them to occur. Some indirect evidence for this hypothesis has
been obtained (Wyer, 1973b). Specifically, subjects' beliefs
that they would like a hypothetical person $(P_L)$ after reading
each of two paragraphs describing behavior related to a particular one of his attributes (X) were predicted quite accurately
on the basis of their beliefs associated with X. However,
predictions of $P_L$ based upon beliefs associated with two unmentioned attributes were less accurate. Nevertheless, these
latter discrepancies from prediction were orderly, and of the
sort one might expect if the information presented had not had
time to filter down to the beliefs about unmentioned attributes
of the person described.

Equation (5) has also been applied in actual social-
interaction situations of the sort to which cognitive-balance
theory and similarity-attraction theory (Byrne, 1971) are
relevant (Wyer, 1972). These latter formulations predict that
a person's (P's) attraction to another (0) should be affected
positively by information that 0 is similar to him. In an
investigation of this prediction, each subject (P) estimated
the probability that he would like another (0) both before and
after receiving bogus feedback that 0 believed they were similar or dissimilar to each other with respect to an attribute X.
Changes in P's beliefs that he would like 0, and also his beliefs that 0 would like him, were predicted. Although the
accuracy of these predictions was not as high as that obtained
in other studies applying the general model under consideration, no other existing formulation of cognitive functioning
has done a better job of generating accurate quantitative
descriptions of social-evaluation processes in an actual

social-interaction situation.[2]

## Predictions of Judgments along Category Scales of Magnitude

The conditions of the preceding study were more realistic than those constructed in many studies of impression formation (for example, Anderson, 1962, 1965, 1967; Wyer, 1969, 1970a, 1975c) in which subjects make judgments of a person based upon a list of personality adjectives. However, probabilistic judgments may still seem to have little relevance to research on interpersonal-attraction and social-inference processes, in which "magnitude" judgments are typically made (for example, judgments of likableness). However, suppose, as hypothesized, that a category rating of an object $(E_O)$ is an expected value of an underlying distribution of subjective probabilities that the object belongs to each of the categories comprising the scale; that is,

$$E_O = \Sigma P_{iO} V_i,$$

where $P_{iO}$ is the belief that O belongs to category $i$ and $V_i$ is the numerical value assigned to this category. Suppose further that the belief that O belongs to category $i$ is represented by an extension of Eq. (5); that is,

$$P_i = P_X P_{iO/X} + (1 - P_X) P_{iO/X'}, \qquad (6)$$

where $P_X$ is again the belief that O has X and $P_{iO/X}$ and $P_{iO/X'}$ are the conditional beliefs that O is in $i$ given that he does and does not have X. Then, substituting the second equation into the first and simplifying,

$$E_O = P_X \Sigma P_{iO/X} V_i + (1 - P_X) \Sigma P_{iO/X'} V_i$$

$$= P_X E_{O/X} + (1 - P_X) E_{O/X}, \qquad (7)$$

where $E_{O/X}$ and $E_{O/X'}$ are "conditional evaluations" of O along the category scale, given that O does and does not have X, respectively. If this equation is valid, a quantitative description is provided of the relation between beliefs about an object $(P_X)$ and "attitudes" toward the object $(E_O)$.

---

[2]Congruity theory, which also does not require *ad hoc* curve-fitting parameters to generate quantitative predictions of attitude change, could be applied under conditions similar to those considered here. This formulation typically generates very poor quantitative predictions of attitude change in other domains (see Wyer's 1974b reanalysis of data collected by Osgood and Tannenbaum, 1955).

Preliminary support has been obtained for the validity of this equation (Wyer, 1973a). That is, evaluations of a hypothetical person along with 21-category scale of likableness, based upon paragraphs describing an attribute of this person (X), were predicted to within one scale unit from estimates of the likelihood that the person possessed X and conditional evaluations of persons who do and do not possess the attribute. This accuracy was not an artifact of the similarity between $E_O$ and the conditionals.

Category judgments along a scale of likableness are often assumed to reflect attitudes toward the object. Thus, if Eq. (7) is valid and is applicable in less contrived situations than the ones constructed in the above study, it could be of substantial value in predicting the effect of change in beliefs about an object $(P_X)$ upon attitudes toward the object $(E_O)$. The object does not, of course, need to be a person. For example, the model could theoretically be applied in predicting the effect of change in one's belief that Republican administrations have inflationary economic policies $(P_X)$ upon his attitude toward Republican administrations $(E_O)$.

## Combined Effects of Information upon Social Evaluation

In each of the situations described above, the information presented about the object to be evaluated pertained primarily to a single attribute. When information about several different attributes is presented simultaneously, the process of arriving at estimates of the likelihood that a person is theoretically a member of any given scale category $i$ is theoretically the same as that described by Eq. (6) except that in this case the components of the predictor do not pertain to a single attribute but rather to a configuration of attributes. That is, there is a subjective distribution of probabilities that the object described by the configuration of attributes belongs to each of the scale categories, and the actual rating of the person is an expected value of this subjective distribution; that is,

$$E_O = P_C E_{O/C} + (1 - P_C)E_{O/C'},$$

where $C$ is not one attribute but a collective of attributes.

The above comments have implications for the extent to which evaluative judgments of an object described by several pieces of information can be predicted from the judgments of objects described by each component piece of information when considered separately. Most approaches assume that the collective evaluation is an algebraic function of the component evaluations. According to the formulation proposed here, this would be the case only under conditions in which the subjective distribution of probabilities that a person described by several attributes belongs to each scale category can be predicted from information about the subjective distributions of probabilities that a person described by each attribute separately belongs to each category. In general, this cannot be done. To see this intuitively, consider two attributes, A and B. Presumably there is a subjective distribution of objects described by each attribute along the category scale. Some of the objects in the distribution of those described by A are likely to also be in the distribution of those described by B; that is, some objects may possess both A and B in combination. However, there is no *a priori* means of predicting either the number of such objects, or the shape of the distribution of such objects along the scale, on the basis of knowledge of the component distributions alone. Thus, there is no way of predicting the collective evaluation from the component evaluations without making some simplifying assumptions. However, certain assumptions, although obviously invalid in detail, have been demonstrated to generate reasonably accurate quantitative predictions of the evaluations of persons described by two adjectives from knowledge of the subjective distributions associated with the components (Wyer, 1973a).

Aside from its implications that *any* model that generates predictions of collective evaluations from component ratings is, at best, an approximation, the preceding analysis suggests a quite different *process* of information integration from that typically assumed by more traditional algebraic formulations of information integration, a process that is neither summative nor averaging. Rather, the process is somewhat akin to that of concept identification; that is, the subject uses the information presented him to circumscribe the range of possible categories to which an object can belong, and his judgment represents the category he believes is most representative of this set, based upon the information available to him. As more information is presented, the range of alternative categories to which the object belongs, and the distribution of probabilities associated with membership in the categories, may change, and these changes may lead to a revised estimate of which category is most representative. Critical tests of these alternative conceptualizations of information integration, and the conditions under which they apply, remain to be made. It should be noted, however, that the conceptualization proposed here can in principle account for many of the phenomena typically observed in impression-formation research (Wyer, 1973a, 1974b).

## THE CONTRIBUTION OF NONLOGICAL FACTORS TO INFERENCE PHENOMENA

The support for Eq. (3) and its derivatives in a variety of domains suggests that syllogistic reasoning plays an important role in social inference and cognitive organization. However, other, nonlogical factors undoubtedly also contribute to these inferences (for a review of research on such factors, see Johnson, 1972). It is conceivable that general principles can be developed that will enable one to identify and assess the contributions of both logical and nonlogical factors to inferences. In the remaining section of this chapter, we will propose such a set of principles that appear upon initial test to have considerable generality, and thus that may represent an initial step toward the attainment of this objective.

### STATEMENT OF PRINCIPLES

Consider two classes of objects, X and Y (for example, "businessmen" and "conservatives"). There are eight different conclusions one might draw concerning the relation between membership in one of these categories and membership in the second. These conclusions would have the form $X$ is $Y$ ("Businessmen are conservatives"), $X$ is $Y'$ ("Businessmen are not conservatives"), $X'$ is $Y$, $X'$ is $Y'$, $Y$ is $X$, $Y$ is $X'$, $Y'$ is $X$, and $Y'$ is $X'$. Suppose a subject receives information bearing upon X and Y and then is asked to judge the validity of these eight alternative conclusions. How might he proceed?

In the situation described above, a subject may first identify the conclusion he believes is most likely to follow from the information presented. This conclusion and its logical contradictory may then be used as "anchors," or standards of comparison, for judging the validity of other possible conclusions. For example, if $X$ is $Y$ is judged the most likely to be valid of the eight possible conclusions, this conclusion and its contradictory, $X$ is $Y'$ ("Businessmen are not conservatives"), would serve as comparative standards for judging the validity of the other possible conclusions concerning X and Y; those conclusions compared to $X$ is $Y$ would be judged as relatively valid, and those compared to $X$ is $Y'$ would be judged as relatively low in validity. For convenience, denote the most and least likely conclusions to follow from the information as positive and negative anchors (A+ and A-) respectively.

The question now becomes how to determine which alternative conclusions are compared to each anchor. At least two factors may be considered by a subject: the logical equivalence of the relations specified in the conclusion to that specified in the anchor, and whether the conclusion contains identical elements to that in either the anchor or its logical equivalent

ROBERT S. WYER, JR.

(Woodworth & Sells, 1935). For example, suppose the positive anchor is $X$ *is* $Y$. The statements $X$ *is* $Y$ and $Y'$ *is* $X'$ are logically equivalent to this anchor, and the statements with identical elements to these are $Y$ *is* $X$ and $X'$ *is* $Y'$. Moreover, the statements $X$ *is* $Y'$ and $Y$ *is* $X'$ are logically equivalent to the negative anchor, and the statements $Y'$ *is* $X$ and $X'$ *is* $Y$ contain elements identical to these. If this reasoning is correct, then the first four statements would be judged as similar in validity to A+ (and thus as relatively valid), while the other four would be judged as similar in validity to A- (and thus as relatively invalid). Judgments of the validity of each conclusion in the first set should therefore be greater than the validity of each conclusion in the second. To formalize the reasoning outlined above:

*Principle 1: Inferences based upon a set of one or more pieces of information will be made by first identifying the conclusion most likely to be valid, based upon this information. This conclusion and its logical contradictory will serve as positive and negative anchors (A+ and A-) relative to which the validity of other conclusions will be compared.*

*Principle 2: A conclusion will be judged by a person as similar in validity to an anchor if it is identical to the anchor, is logically equivalent to the anchor, or contains elements identical to those described in either the anchor or its logical equivalent.*

Let $P_{ij}$ represent the estimate of the validity of the conclusion $i$ *is* $j$. Then, suppose that the conclusion judged most likely to follow from the information presented is $X$ *is* $Y$. Then, from Principle 1 it follows that $X$ *is* $Y$ and $X$ *is* $Y'$ will serve as the positive and negative anchors, respectively, and from Principle 2 it follows that the four judgments $P_{XY}$, $P_{YX}$, $P_{X'Y'}$, and $P_{Y'X'}$ will each be greater than $P_{XY'}$, $P_{Y'X}$, $P_{X'Y}$, and $P_{YX'}$, or, more generally,

$$P_{XY} + P_{YX} + P_{X'Y'} + P_{Y'X'} >$$
$$P_{XY'} + P_{Y'X} + P_{X'Y} + P_{YX'} \qquad (8)$$

Now, consider possible criteria subjects use to distinguish between the validity of the conclusions within each set differentiated on the basis of Principle 2. Note that each set of four judgments compared in Eq. (8) pertains to statements that vary along three orthogonal dimensions: Similarity to the anchor in *logical meaning*, similarity in *content* (whether the statements contain the same or different elements), and similarity in *form* (whether the subject and predicate categories

are the same or different). The relations among these statements can be clarified by tabulating them as shown in Table 1.
This table shows that similarities to the anchor in form, content, and logical meaning are independent characteristics of
the statements being judged. It seems reasonable to suppose
that a statement's similarity to an anchor in each respect may
contribute to judgments that the statement is similar to the
anchor in validity.

*Principle 3: A conclusion will be judged as similar in
validity to an anchor (A+ or A-) to the extent it is similar
to the anchor in content, form, and logical meaning.*

Principle 3 does not specify the relative magnitudes of the
contributions of the three factors described. However, suppose
that a subject judges a conclusion as similar in validity to
an anchor if it is similar to the anchor in logical meaning.
To this extent, if *X is Y* serves as A+, he should judge both
*X is Y* and *Y' is X'* as more similar in validity to A+, and thus
as more probably valid, than *Y is X* or *X' is Y'*; that is,

$$P_{XY} + P_{Y'X'} > P_{X'Y'} + P_{YX}.$$

On the other hand, he should judge both *X is Y'* and *Y is X'* as
more similar in validity to A-, and thus as less probably
valid, than *X' is Y* or *Y' is X*; that is,

$$P_{XY'} + P_{YX'} < P_{Y'X} + P_{X'Y}.$$

An overall indication of the extent to which subjects use this
criterion can therefore be reflected by combining these two
inequalities:

$$P_{XY} + P_{Y'X'} + P_{Y'X} + P_{X'Y} >$$
$$P_{X'Y'} + P_{YX} + P_{XY'} + P_{YX'}. \qquad (9)$$

Now suppose that a subject judges a conclusion as similar
in validity to an anchor on the basis of its similarity to the
anchor in *content*. To this extent, he should judge *X is Y* and
*Y is X* to be more similar in validity to A+, and thus as more
valid, than *X' is Y'* and *Y' is X'*, and should judge *X is Y'*
and *Y' is X* more similar in validity to A-, and thus as less
valid, than *X' is Y* and *Y is X'*. The tendency to use this
criterion is reflected by the inequality

$$P_{XY} + P_{YX} + P_{X'Y} + P_{YX'} >$$
$$P_{X'Y'} + P_{Y'X'} + P_{XY'} + P_{Y'X}. \qquad (10)$$

TABLE 1
*Tabulation of Eight Sentence Types as a Function of the Anchor to Which They are Compared and Similarity in Form and Content to These Anchors*

|  | Statements compared to A+ | | Statements compared to A- | |
|---|---|---|---|---|
|  | Similar in form | Dissimilar in form | Similar in form | Dissimilar in form |
| Similar in content | X *is* Y (similar to A+ in form, content, and logical meaning) | Y *is* X (similar to A+ in content only) | X *is* Y' (similar to A- in form, content, and logical meaning) | Y' *is* X (similar to A- in content only) |
| Dissimilar in content | X' *is* Y' (similar to A+ in form only) | Y' *is* X' (similar to A+ in logical meaning only) | X' *is* Y (similar to A- in form only) | Y *is* X' (similar to A- in logical meaning only) |

Finally, suppose the subject uses similarity in form to an anchor as a basis for judging the validity of a conclusion. To this extent, he should judge $X$ *is* $Y$ and $X'$ *is* $Y'$ as more similar in validity to A+, or as more valid, than $Y$ *is* $X$ and $Y'$ *is* $X'$, and should judge $X$ *is* $Y'$ and $X'$ *is* $Y$ as more similar in validity to A-, or as less valid, than $Y$ *is* $X'$ and $Y'$ *is* $X$. Therefore, to the extent he uses this criterion,

$$P_{XY} + P_{X'Y'} + P_{Y'X} + P_{YX'} >$$
$$P_{YX} + P_{Y'X'} + P_{XY'} + P_{X'Y}. \tag{11}$$

If the preceding analysis is sound, its implications are both conceptually and methodologically important. Note that the four comparisons described by Eqs. (8)-(11) are orthogonal. Thus, estimates of the validity of any given conclusion can be described as an additive function of the independent contribution of the four factors to which these equations pertain.

Finally, note from Table 1 that within each set of four conclusions compared to a particular anchor, one is identical to the anchor, and thus is similar to it with respect to all three characteristics specified in Principle 3, while the others are similar to the anchor in one and only one of these respects. Thus, if the relative contributions to inferences of form, content, and logical similarity can be inferred from the relative magnitudes of the inequalities specified in Eqs. (9)-(11), and if Principle 2 is valid, the rank order of judgments of the eight alternative conclusions about the relations between membership in X and membership in Y can be predicted. For example, suppose that similarity to an anchor in content contributes most to judgments of a conclusion's validity, followed by similarity in form and then similarity in logical meaning. Then, among the conclusions compared to A+,

$$P_{XY} > P_{YX} > P_{X'Y} > P_{Y'X'},$$

and among those compared to A-,

$$P_{XY'} < P_{Y'X} < P_{X'Y} < P_{YX'}.$$

Since each of the four judgments in the first set should be greater than each of those in the second (Principle 2),

$$P_{XY} > P_{YX} > P_{X'Y'} > P_{Y'X'} >$$
$$P_{YX'} > P_{X'Y} > P_{Y'X} > P_{XY'}. \tag{12}$$

To provide a more concrete example of the implications of Principles 1-3, suppose that a subject believes that the conclusion most likely to be drawn from information presented him

is "Businessmen are conservatives." Then he will use this conclusion and its contradictory, "Businessmen are not conservatives," as positive and negative anchors, respectively. It
follows from Principle 2 that he will believe the conclusions
"Businessmen are conservatives," "Conservatives are businessmen," "Nonbusinessmen are not conservatives," and "Nonconservatives are not businessmen" to be more valid than the conclusions "Conservatives are not businessmen," "Nonbusinessmen are
conservatives," "Nonconservatives are businessmen," and "Businessmen are not conservatives." Finally, if the comparisons
defined by Eqs. (9)-(11) reveal that within each set of four
conclusions, similarity to an anchor in content contributes
most to judgments that the conclusions are similar to the
anchor in validity, followed by similarity in form and then by
similarity in logical meaning, estimates that the eight conclusions are valid should decrease with the ordinal position
in which they are listed above. (Other rank orderings would
of course be predicted on the basis of different assumptions
about the relative contributions of the three factors.)

To apply Principles 1-3 in an actual situation, one must of
course be able to identify the conclusion a person believes
is most likely to follow from the information presented him.
The difficulty of this task may vary with the complexity of
the information presented. In the initial tests of the applicability of these principles and their generalizability over
stimulus domains (that is, types of categories denoted X and Y
in our examples), the information presented consisted of either
a single sentence which was identical to one of the eight conclusions, two sentences which if true logically implied the
validity of one of these conclusions, or two sentences which
if true did not have a logically valid conclusion. In the
first two instances, it seems reasonable to expect the conclusion that is identical to the statement conveyed in the stimulus information, or the one that logically follows from the
information, to serve as A+. In the third case, however, the
nature of the positive anchor is less clear. However, even in
this instance, certain conclusions can be drawn concerning the
sets of conclusions judged most and least likely to be valid,
based upon the information presented. We will reconsider this
possibility shortly.

*AN EMPIRICAL TEST*

## Procedure and Stimulus Materials

Introductory psychology students, untrained in formal logic,
inferred the likelihood that each of eight different conclusions was valid based upon stimulus information consisting of

one or two sentences.  Four stimulus domains were considered.
Stimulus items in each domain pertained to three groups of
objects, A, B, and C.  The four single-stimulus items in each
domain were of the form $A$ $is$ $B$, $A$ $is$ $B'$, $A'$ $is$ $B$, and $A'$ $is$ $B'$.
The eight conclusions to be evaluated on the basis of these
stimuli were of the form $A$ $is$ $B$, $A$ $is$ $B'$, $A'$ $is$ $B$, $A'$ $is$ $B'$,
$B$ $is$ $A$, $B$ $is$ $A'$, $B'$ $is$ $A$, and $B'$ $is$ $A'$.  Sixteen pairs of
stimulus items in each domain were formed by combining each of
the four stimulus items described above with each of four
statements that were similar in form but pertained to membership or nonmembership in groups B and C.  The eight response
items were identical to those used in obtaining judgments of
single items with the substitution of elements C and C' for B
and B', respectively.

In one of the four stimulus domains considered, the groups
described were abstract; A, B, and C were simply denoted
"members of A," "members of B," and "members of C," respectively.  In the other three domains, the groups were familiar
to subjects.  Specifically, in one domain the three groups
were "collies," "dogs," and "animals"; in a second, "businessmen," "conservatives," and "Republicans"; and in the third,
"women's liberationists," "apathetic persons," and "trouble-
makers."

## Inferences Based upon Single Statements

In analyzing judgments based upon single stimulus items,
these judgments, defined in units of subjective probability,
were first labeled to conform to the notation in Table 1 and
Eqs. (8)-(12) by letting X represent the subject of the stimulus item (A or A') and letting Y represent the predicate of
this item (B or B').  Thus, in all cases, $X$ $is$ $Y$ is the conclusion assumed to function as A+.

$P_{XY}$ was greater than any other judgment at all 16 combinations of stimulus-item type and domain, while $P_{XY'}$ was less
than any other judgment in 15 of 16 cases.  These data support
the assumption that the conclusion identical to the stimulus
item and its contradictory function as positive and negative
anchors, respectively.  Moreover, not only was the mean judgment of conclusions presumably compared to A+ consistently
greater than the mean judgment of items compared to A- (mean
difference = .398), but the two sets of judgments were virtually nonoverlapping; in only two of 256 possible instances
(16 instances for each of four stimulus items in each of four
domains) was the judgment of a conclusion hypothetically compared to A- greater than the judgment of one of the four conclusions hypothetically compared to A+.  Thus, Principle 2 was
also supported.  Moreover, the magnitude of the difference

between the two sets of judgments compared on the basis of Eq. (8) was not significantly contingent upon either the stimulus domain or the type of stimulus item from which inferences were drawn.

The contributions of the three informational characteristics postulated to affect inferences on the basis of Principle 3 were estimated by subtracting the mean of the judgments to the right of each inequality in Eqs. (9)-(11) from the mean of the judgments to the left of this inequality. The contributions of all three characteristics were statistically significant and independent of stimulus domain; similarity to the anchor in content contributed most (.126), while logical similarity (.096) and form similarity (.088) contributed about equally. Further analyses revealed that similarity to the positive anchor typically had more effect than did similarity to the negative anchor. Moreover, the effects of similarity in form, content, and logical meaning were somewhat greater when the subject of the stimulus item was positive (A or B) than when it was negative (not-A or not-B).

## Inferences Based upon Pairs of Statements with Logically Valid Conclusions

Of the 16 different pairs of stimuli upon which judgments were based, eight had logically valid conclusions. Averaged over stimulus domains, the conclusion that followed logically from the stimulus pair was judged more probably valid than any other conclusion in all eight cases, while the logical contradictory of this conclusion was judged less probably valid than any other in seven of eight cases. These data justified the assumption that the logically implied conclusion and its contradictory function as A+ and A-, respectively.

To apply Principles 2 and 3, the subject and predicate of the logically valid conclusion were relabeled X and Y, respectively, so that in all cases, $X$ $is$ $Y$ was the conclusion assumed to function as A+. Based upon this notation, the overall magnitude of the inequality implied by Principle 2 (Eq. [8]) was large (.339) and significant. Moreover, in not one of 512 possible instances (16 instances for each of eight stimulus pairs in each of four domains) was the mean judgment of a conclusion hypothetically compared to A+ less than the mean judgment of a conclusion hypothetically compared to A-.

The effects of similarity to anchors in content (.052), form (.057), and logical meaning (.035) were also significant, and, as in the case of single-item inferences, the magnitudes of these contributions did not differ significantly over stimulus domains. However, they did depend to some extent upon the type of anchor to which comparisons were made.

262

Specifically, logical similarity to a positive anchor contributed more than did logical similarity to a negative anchor, as in the case of single-item inferences. In addition, the contributions of form and content similarity were both greater when the anchor to which conclusions were compared had a positive predicate (.080 and .078) than when the anchor had a negative predicate (.023 and .044).

## Inferences Based upon Pairs of Statements without Logically Valid Conclusions

When the two stimulus items do not generate a logically valid conclusion, there is no *a priori* basis for predicting the conclusion that subjects judge to be most likely to follow from the information. However, a means of circumscribing the set of conclusions that are most apt to serve as positive anchors is suggested by Chapman and Chapman's hypothesis (1959) that "errors" in syllogistic reasoning may result from invalid transformations of a premise to one that, in combination with the other, *will* generate a valid conclusion. For example, suppose information is presented that *X is Z* and *Y is Z*. Although this information does not yield a logically valid conclusion, the second premise might be transformed to one that is similar to it in content as defined in this paper (specifically, to *Z is Y*); this transformed premise, in combination with the first, would yield the logically valid conclusion *X is Y*. Alternatively, the first premise might be transformed to one that is similar in content (to *Z is X*); this premise, in combination with the second, would imply *Y is X*. Although only transformations of this type were considered by Chapman and Chapman, others are possible by applying criteria of form and logical similarity. However, it turns out that no matter what transformation(s) a subject is assumed to make in order to generate a logically valid conclusion, this conclusion will be one of the four to which the left side of Eq. (8) pertains. Consequently, even if subjects vary randomly in the particular transformation or pair of transformations they make in order to generate a valid conclusion, they should *all* judge each of the four conclusions to the left of the inequality in Eq. (8) to be more valid than each of the four conclusions to the right of this inequality! This is true regardless of the nature of the statements contained in the information, provided a transformation on the basis of criteria specified in Principle 3 enables a logically valid conclusion to be drawn.

Data pertaining to inferences based upon the eight pairs of statements without logically valid conclusions (for example, *A is B*, *B' is C*, and so on) are consistent with this hypothesis. In analyzing these data, it was arbitrarily decided to

transform the second item in each stimulus pair to a statement
that was similar to it in form. This transformation, which
invariably enables a logically valid conclusion to be drawn
(denoted $X$ *is* $Y$), allowed the two sets of four conclusions distinguished on the basis of Eq. (8) to be identified. Analyses
failed to reveal any consistency in the conclusion judged most
likely to be valid based upon the information presented. However, the conclusion judged most likely to be valid was invariably one of the four predicted. Moreover, of 512 possible
paired comparisons between judgments to the left of the inequality in Eq. (8) and judgments to the right of this inequality, all but one was in the direction implied by this equation.

## Predictions of Relative Magnitude of Inferences

Pooled over inferences based upon single items and inferences based upon pairs of items with logically related conclusions, similarity to anchor in content contributed most to
inferences (.089), followed by similarity in form (.072) and
then similarity in logical meaning (.065). Although there
were some contingencies in the relative contributions in the
two sets of data, it was of interest to determine how well a
single rank ordering, based upon the assumption of these relative contributions, could predict the actual rank order of
subjects' judgments of conclusions under the conditions of this
study.

The predicted rank ordering of judgments, based upon the
relative contributions of content, form, and logical equivalence described above, is given by Eq. (12). This equation
predicts the direction of 28 different paired comparisons
between judgments based upon a given set of stimulus items.
The number of times that the actual difference between each
pair of judgments based upon a single stimulus item was in the
same direction as the predicted difference was determined for
each of the 16 combinations of stimulus item and stimulus domain. Actual differences were in the direction implied by Eq.
(12) in 406 of 448 instances (90.6%). If comparisons involving
$P_{XY}$ (judgments of items identical to the stimulus item) and
$P_{XY'}$ (judgments of the contradictory of the stimulus item) are
eliminated from consideration, the equation predicts correctly
in 199 cases of 240 (82.9%).

In the case of inferences based upon stimulus pairs with
logically valid conclusions, 28 different comparisons were
available for each of 32 different sets of stimulus items
(eight sets in each of four domains). Differences between
pairs of judgments based upon Eq. (12) were in the predicted
direction in 776 of these 896 cases (88%). When comparisons
involving judgments of the two assumed anchors were omitted

from consideration, predictions were still accurate in 384 of 480 instances (80%). Considering only comparisons among judgments within each set of four distinguished on the basis of Principle 2, predictions were accurate in 277 of 384 cases (72%).

## EVALUATION

The preliminary data described above provide promising support for the principles hypothesized to govern inferences of class membership and demonstrate their potential value in predicting inferences based both upon single statements and upon pairs of statements. The applicability of these principles does not appear to depend substantially upon the specific objects to which these items pertain. Although the contributions of inference criteria sometimes depend upon the positivity of the elements comprising the stimulus items, these contingencies also generalize over stimulus domains. This does not imply that the type of objects described in stimulus items has no effect whatsoever upon inferences; however, these effects may occur relatively independently of the processes implied by Principles 1-3. Moreover, although subjects' inferences of the validity of alternative conclusions may be biased in the direction of their *a priori* beliefs that these conclusions are valid (Janis & Frick, 1943), this bias was not strong enough to affect the predictive accuracy of Principles 1-3 in this study. Although these principles may need to be refined in order to take into account certain contingencies in the effects of similarity factors identified in the research described above, it is noteworthy that the relative magnitude of inferences can be predicted with between 80% and 90% accuracy on the basis of a single rank ordering (Eq. [12]) that does *not* take these contingencies into account.

## IMPLICATIONS FOR COGNITIVE ORGANIZATION AND CHANGE

If Principles 1-3 apply to cognitive organization processes as well as social inference processes, they have interesting implications for McGuire's syllogistic model of cognitive functioning and for the extension of it described earlier in this paper. Specifically, these principles can potentially be used to predict the effects of information bearing directly upon premises of a syllogism, not only upon beliefs in conclusions that logically follow from these premises, but also upon other conclusions that do not logically follow. For example, suppose A and B, as defined in Eq. (3), are the propositions "Businessmen oppose aid to underdeveloped countries" and "Businessmen are isolationists," respectively. A persuasive communication designed to increase beliefs in A should (assuming that $P_{B/A} > P_{B/A'}$) also affect beliefs in B in a manner described by Eq. (3). However, if Principles 1-3 are valid, the communication should also increase the beliefs "Isolationists are businessmen," "Nonbusinessmen are not isolationists," and "Nonisolationists are not businessmen." Moreover, if the rank order implied by Eq. (12) is generalizable to this domain, the relative magnitudes of these effects should also be predictable.

Principle 3 also has implications for the Socratic effect. It was noted that if the beliefs comprising Eq. (3) are made salient to a subject in temporal contiguity, the subject should perform cognitive work to reduce any inconsistencies among them. However, suppose B is of the form $X$ *is* $Y$ (that is, "Businessmen are isolationists"). Then, this cognitive reorganization might also affect beliefs in propositions that are *not* logically tied to those comprising Eq. (3). Alternatively, suppose a subject becomes aware of beliefs that $X$ *is* $Z$, that $Z$ *is* $Y'$, and that $X$ *is* $Y$. If syllogistic reasoning plays a role in cognitive organization, the subject should change one or more of these beliefs in the direction of greater logical consistency. However, if beliefs that $X$ *is* $Y$ are related to beliefs that $Y$ *is* $X$, that $X'$ *is* $Y'$, and that $Y'$ *is* $X'$, an increase in the salience of one of these latter three cognitions along with beliefs in the premises might *also* produce a Socratic effect. Moreover, the relative magnitude of such an effect may vary with the extent to which the "conclusion" is believed to follow from $X$ *is* $Z$ and $Z$ *is* $Y'$, and therefore may be predictable if the relative contributions to inferences of form similarity, content similarity, and logical similarity are known.

CONCLUDING REMARKS

This paper has summarized the support for a subjective-probability formulation of social inference and cognitive organization and has shown its theoretical and empirical implications in a wide variety of situations in which syllogistic reasoning may play a role. The writer has also attempted to show the manner in which the contributions of nonlogical factors to cognitive functioning could potentially be incorporated into this approach. More generally, however, caution has been stressed in concluding that a single formulation of cognitive processes applies equally well in all situations and in all content domains, because the processes actually used by subjects in drawing inferences are apt to vary considerably over these situations and domains, and may depend upon the type of information, new or old, upon which these inferences are based. Unfortunately, in this paper the writer has failed to practice what he has preached. That is, comparative tests of alternative formulations have not been performed, and the conditions in which the proposed model is apt to apply have not been effectively circumscribed. However, this is clearly the direction that future research should take.

## ACKNOWLEDGMENTS

This paper and the research reported in it were supported by National Science Foundation Grants GS-2291, GS-29241, and SOC 73-05684.

## REFERENCES

Abelson, R. P., & Rosenberg, M. J. Symbolic psycho-logic: A model of attitudinal cognition. *Behavioral Science*, 1958, *3*, 1-13.

Ajzen, I. Attribution of dispositions to an actor: Effects of perceived decision freedom and behavioral utilities. *Journal of Personality and Social Psychology*, 1971, *18*, 144-156.

Anderson, N. H. Application of an additive model to impression formation. *Science*, 1962, *138*, 817-818.

Anderson, N. H. Averaging versus adding as a stimulus combination rule in impression formation. *Journal of Experimental Psychology*, 1965, *70*, 394-400.

Anderson, N. H. Averaging model analysis of set size effects in impression formation. *Journal of Experimental Psychology*, 1967, *75*, 158-165.

Anderson, N. H. Integration theory and attitude change. *Psychological Review*, 1971, *78*, 171-206.

Anderson, N. H. Cognitive algebra: Integration theory applied to social attribution. In L. Berkowitz (Ed.), *Advances in experimental social psychology*. Vol. 7. New York: Academic Press, 1974.

Birnbaum, M. H. The devil rides again: Correlation as an index of fit. *Psychological Bulletin*, 1973, *79*, 239-242.

Byrne, D. *The attraction paradigm*. New York: Academic Press, 1971.

Chapman, L. J., & Chapman, J. P. Atmosphere effect reexamined. *Journal of Experimental Psychology*, 1959, *58*, 220-226.

Edwards, W.  Conservatism in human information processing.  In B. Kleinmuntz (Ed.), *Formal representation of human judgment*.  New York:  Wiley, 1968.

Fishbein, M.  An investigation of the relationships between beliefs about an object and attitudes toward that object. *Human Relations*, 1963, *16*, 233-239.

Heider, F.  *The psychology of interpersonal relations*.  New York:  Wiley, 1958.

Henninger, M.  An information processing approach to the "Socratic effect."  Unpublished master's thesis, University of Illinois, 1974.

Hinkle, R.  The role of subjective uncertainty in information integration.  Unpublished master's thesis, University of Illinois, 1974.

Janis, I., & Frick, F.  The relationship between attitudes toward conclusions and errors in judging the logical validity of syllogisms.  *Journal of Experimental Psychology*, 1943, *33*, 73-77.

Johnson, D. M.  *Systematic introduction to the psychology of thinking*.  New York:  Harper & Row, 1972.

Jones, E. E., & Gerard, H. B.  *Foundations of social psychology*.  New York:  Wiley, 1967.

Kaplan, M. F.  Dispositional effects and the weight of information in impression formation.  *Journal of Personality and Social Psychology*, 1971, *18*, 279-284.

McGuire, W. J.  A syllogistic analysis of cognitive relationships.  In M. J. Rosenberg, C. I. Hovland, W. J. McGuire, R. P. Abelson, & J. W. Brehm (Eds.), *Attitude organization and change*.  New Haven, Conn.:  Yale University Press, 1960.

Osgood, C. E., & Tannenbaum, P. H.  The principle of congruity in the prediction of attitude change.  *Psychological Review*, 1955, *62*, 42-55.

Peterson, C. R., & Beach, L. R.  Man as an intuitive statistician.  *Psychological Bulletin*, 1967, *68*, 29-46.

Rosen, N. A., & Wyer, R. S.  Some further evidence for the "Socratic effect" using a subjective probability model of cognitive organization.  *Journal of Personality and Social Psychology*, 1972, *24*, 420-424.

Schneider, D. J.  Implicit personality theory:  A review. *Psychological Bulletin*, 1973, *79*, 294-309.

Slovic, P., & Lichtenstein, S.  Comparison of Bayesian and regression approaches to the study of information processing in judgment.  *Organizational Behavior and Human Performance*, 1971, *6*, 649-744.

Trope, Y.  Inferential processes in the forced compliance situation:  A Bayesian analysis.  *Journal of Experimental Social Psychology*, 1974, *10*, 1-16.

Watts, W. A., & Holt, L. E.   Logical relationships among beliefs and timing as factors in persuasion. *Journal of
Personality and Social Psychology*, 1970, *16*, 571-582.

Woodworth, R. S., & Sells, S. B.   An atmosphere effect in formal syllogistic reasoning. *Journal of Experimental
Psychology*, 1935, *18*, 451-460.

Wyer, R. S.   A quantitative comparison of three models of
impression formation. *Journal of Experimental Research in
Personality*, 1969, *4*, 29-41.

Wyer, R. S.   Information redundancy, inconsistency, and novelty
and their role in impression formation. *Journal of Experimental Social Psychology*, 1970, *6*, 111-127.   (a)

Wyer, R. S.   The quantitative prediction of belief and opinion
change:  A further test of a subjective probability model.
*Journal of Personality and Social Psychology*, 1970, *16*,
559-571.   (b)

Wyer, R. S.   Test of a subjective probability model of social
evaluation processes. *Journal of Personality and Social
Psychology*, 1972, *22*, 279-286.

Wyer, R. S.   Category ratings as "subjective expected values":
Implications for attitude formation and change. *Psychological Review*, 1973, *80*, 446-467.   (a)

Wyer, R. S.   Further test of a subjective probability model of
social inference processes. *Journal of Research in Personality*, 1973, *7*, 237-253.   (b)

Wyer, R. S.   Changes in meaning and halo effects in personality
impression formation. *Journal of Personality and Social
Psychology*, 1974, *29*, 829-835.   (a)

Wyer, R. S.   *Cognitive organization and change:  An information-processing approach.*  Potomac, Md.:   Erlbaum, 1974.
(b)

Wyer, R. S.   Some implications of the "Socratic effect" for
alternative models of cognitive consistency. *Journal of
Personality*, 1974, *42*, 399-419.   (c)

Wyer, R. S.   Direct and indirect effects of essay writing and
information about other persons' opinions upon beliefs in
logically related propositions. *Journal of Personality and
Social Psychology*, 1975, *31*, 55-63.   (a)

Wyer, R. S.   Functional measurement analysis of a subjective
probability model of cognitive functioning. *Journal of
Personality and Social Psychology*, 1975, *31*, 94-100.   (b)

Wyer, R. S.   Some informational determinants of one's own
liking for a person and beliefs that others will like this
person. *Journal of Personality and Social Psychology*,
1975, in press.   (c)

Wyer, R. S., & Goldberg, L.   A probabilistic analysis of the
relationships between beliefs and attitudes. *Psychological
Review*, 1970, *77*, 100-120.

## 10. SOCIAL JUDGMENT THEORY

*Kenneth R. Hammond and Thomas R. Stewart*
University of Colorado
*Berndt Brehmer*                    *Derick O. Steinmann*
University of Umeå          Metropolitan Life Insurance Company

Why is Judgment Required?                                              272
Basic Concepts                                                        272
  Relationships: The Fundamental Units of Cognition          272
  Principle of Parallel Concepts                             274
  Distinction between Surface and Depth                      275
  Objectives of Social Judgment Theory                       276
Quantitative Method                                                   277
  Analysis of the Cognitive System of an Individual          277
  Description of the Regression Analysis Approach            277
  Extensions of the Method: Interactive Computer Graphics    285
  Extensions of the Method: Analysis of the Relation
    between Cognitive Systems                       287
  Application of Theory and Quantitative Method to Empirical
    Research: Generalization over Cases             290
Discussion of Unique Contributions in Four Cases                      291
  The Single-System Case                                     292
  The Double-System Case                                     293
  The Triple-System Case                                     295
  The *N*-System Case                                        304
Summary                                                               305
References                                                            307

## WHY IS JUDGMENT REQUIRED?

Knowledge of the environment is difficult to acquire because of causal ambiguity--because of the probabilistic, entangled relations among environmental variables. Tolman and Brunswik called attention to the critical role of causal ambiguity in their article "The Organism and the Causal Texture of the Environment" (1935), in which they emphasized the fact that the organism in its normal intercourse with its environment must cope with *numerous, interdependent, multiformal relations* among variables which are *partly relevant* and *partly irrelevant* to its purpose, which carry only a *limited amount of dependability*, and which are *organized in a variety of ways*. The problem for the organism, therefore, is to know its environment under these complex circumstances. In the effort to do so, the organism brings a variety of processes (generally labeled *cognitive*), such as perception, learning, and thinking, to bear on the problem of reducing causal ambiguity. As a part of this effort, human beings often attempt to manipulate variables (by experiments, for example) and sometimes succeed-- in such a manner as to eliminate ambiguity. But when the variables in question *cannot* be manipulated, human beings must use their cognitive resources unaided by manipulation or experiment. They must do the best they can by passive rather than active means to arrive at a conclusion regarding a state of affairs clouded by causal ambiguity. They must, in short, exercise their judgment. Human judgment is a cognitive activity of last resort.

It may seem odd to remind the readers of this volume of the circumstances which require human judgment, yet it is essential that we do so, for it is precisely these circumstances which are so often omitted from studies of human judgment. If we are to understand how human beings cope with judgment tasks, however, not only must such ambiguity be present in the conditions under which human judgment is studied, but causal ambiguity must itself be represented within the framework of a theory of human judgment (Brunswik, 1952, 1956; Hammond, 1955).

## BASIC CONCEPTS

### *RELATIONSHIPS: THE FUNDAMENTAL UNITS OF COGNITION*

The fundamental concept ordinarily employed to describe an environmental "input" to the organism is the stimulus. That concept is rejected here. Although both Tolman and Brunswik used this term, they did not make a complete conceptual commitment to it; both argued that the objects and events

272

apprehended by an organism do more--and less--than "impinge" upon it. Not only does the organism cognitively act on the "input," but the perceived object carries implications for *other objects*. That is why Tolman's position was labeled an S-S theory (that is, a "sign-significate" theory) and con- trasted to an S-R (stimulus-response) theory by competing theoreticians of his time. And that is why Brunswik used the word "cue" to refer to various dimensions of the perceived world. Both these terms, "sign-significate" (or as Tolman also put it, "sign-Gestalt") and "cue," have in common the notion that the raw materials of perception point outward from the organism toward various aspects of the person's ecological surroundings. And whereas "sign-significate" and "cue" point *outward* from the organism to the environment, the concept of stimulus points *inward*. It is for this reason that S-R the- ories in general do not include concepts relating to the en- vironment and that S-R judgment theories, in particular, do not include concepts referring to the properties of judgment tasks (see, for example, Anderson, 1971).

Because "cues" and "sign-significates" point outward, they involve a relation between two variables--proximal and distal, the given and the inferred. Choice of that relation as the fundamental unit of cognition has profound consequences, of course, and it was this choice that eventually led Tolman to introduce the concept of the "cognitive map" in 1948; he ar- gued that cognition involves a subjective representation of the interrelations of goal paths in the organism's environment. Brunswik went further; he demanded a more detailed analysis of the *environment* and a less detailed analysis of the *organism*. Thus, for example, he remarked:

Both organism and environment will have to be seen as systems, each with properties of its own. . . . Each has surface and depth, or overt and covert regions. . . . It follows that, much as psychology must be concerned with the texture of the organism or of its nervous properties and investigate them in depth, it must also be concerned with the texture of the environ- ment [1957, p. 5].

Brunswik's admonition to psychologists to "be concerned with the texture of the environment" gives clear direction to the student of human judgment; his first step must be to learn about and to understand the texture (and by that we mean the causal ambiguity) of the relationships among variables in the tasks which require human judgment. (The methodological corollary is that such ambiguity among relations must be re- presented in the judgment tasks used to study human judgment.)

273

## PRINCIPLE OF PARALLEL CONCEPTS

As can be seen in the above quotation, Brunswik indicated that organismic and environmental systems should be described in symmetrical terms. That symmetry is represented in what Brunswik called the "lens model" of behavior indicated in Figure 1. (Space does not permit more than a cursory reference to the conceptual implications of the lens model; the best of several original sources is Brunswik's "The Conceptual Framework of Psychology," 1952; a secondary source which presents part of what is contained in several original articles is Hammond's *The Psychology of Egon Brunswik*, 1966.)

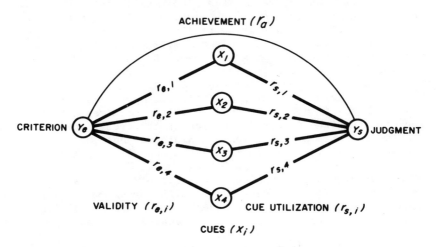

*Fig. 1. Brunswik's lens model.*

As Brunswik describes the lens model, it becomes clear that he employs a principle of parallel concepts, for each concept on one side is paralleled by a similar concept on the other. Thus, cues on the task, or ecological, side vary in *ecological validity*, and on the organismic side there is variation in *cue utilization* by the subject. And just as the relations between cues and distal variables on the ecological side may assume various (linear, curvilinear) *forms*, according to the principle of parallel concepts, the relations between cues and judgments may also assume various function forms on the organismic side. The investigator has similar interests with regard to both sets of variables: to what extent ecological validities are matched by cue utilization and to what extent ecological function forms are matched by subjective function forms. Social judgment theorists are also concerned with the extent to which the principles of organization that control the task system are reflected in the principles of organization that control the cognitive system of the subject.

It is the principle of parallel concepts, therefore, that produces the symmetrical relation between the descriptive terms applied to the organismic system and to the environmental system, and it is this principle that is responsible for the fact that Social Judgment Theory (SJT) includes a set of concepts which apply to task systems as well as person systems.

## DISTINCTION BETWEEN SURFACE AND DEPTH

This distinction is essential to SJT. It derives from the proximal-distal separation in perception theory and thus refers to the separation between what is given and what is inferred. *Surface* data are (given) cues to (inferred) *depth* conditions in the judgment task. By virtue of the principle of parallel concepts, this distinction also applies to organismic judgment systems (see Figure 1). Separation of surface and depth is critical to any theory of judgment (or inference), for it raises the question of the properties of the region that intervenes between them. Because of the importance of this region, we have named it the *zone of ambiguity*.

### The Zone of Ambiguity

The region between depth and surface variables in a given judgment task involves the relations between cause (depth) and effect (surface). Because a single effect may be produced by several causes, as well as because multiple effects may be produced by a single cause, there is ambiguity from cause to effect and effect to cause. Because causes may be related, and because effects are interrelated  the network of task relations can be said to be entangled. Moreover, causal ambiguity is produced because (1) surface data are less than perfectly related to depth variables, (2) functional relations between surface and depth variables may assume a variety of forms (linear, curvilinear), and (3) the relations between surface and depth may be organized (or combined) according to a variety of principles (for example, additivity or pattern). These circumstances give more specific meaning to the term "causal texture," or causal ambiguity.

In short, causal ambiguity within the zone of ambiguity is the source of the human judgment problem, as well as a source of the misunderstandings and disputes that occur when judgments differ. As we shall see below, social judgment theorists direct themselves to reducing causal ambiguity in judgment tasks

and in judgment policies by *externalizing* the properties of
the zone of ambiguity in both systems.

## OBJECTIVES OF SOCIAL JUDGMENT THEORY

So far, we have set forth our assumptions about the environmental circumstances that create the need for human judgment.
In addition, we have indicated the major concepts which SJT
employs in the effort to understand the judgment process that
must cope with these circumstances. The reader will have observed that these assumptions and concepts differ in fundamental ways from those offered by other theorists; he should also
know that our research objectives differ rather markedly from
those of other judgment theorists.

1. SJT is intended to be life relevant; that objective is
a direct legacy from Brunswik.
2. SJT is not a law-seeking theory. It is not aimed at
finding the laws of human judgment; rather, it is intended to
be descriptive.
3. Social judgment theorists are interested in creating
cognitive aids for human judgment--particularly for those persons who must exercise their judgment in the effort to formulate social policy and who will ordinarily find themselves
embroiled in bitter dispute as they do so. Social judgment
theorists intend not only to understand human judgment but to
create and develop ways of improving it.

These objectives have led us to study disputes arising from
differing judgments, and this research has in turn led us to
invent a cognitive aid for persons involved in such disputes.
More specifically, the theory described above, together with
the results of empirical research, indicated that in order to
be effective, a cognitive aid for persons exercising their
judgment should be capable of *displaying pictorially* the
weights, function forms, and uncertainty in persons' judgment
policies as well as in judgment tasks. Without such displays,
persons involved in dispute, or interpersonal learning, can do
little besides exchange incomplete, inaccurate information
about their judgment policies; verbal explanations of their
introspections regarding their judgment processes are their
only recourse. Social judgment theorists, on the other hand,
can now offer persons the use of interactive computer graphics
terminals which will display for them pictorial representations
of their judgment policies, as well as the properties of task
systems. These procedures have been developed from the quantitative method employed by social judgment theorists, a topic
to which we now turn.

QUANTITATIVE METHOD

*ANALYSIS OF THE COGNITIVE SYSTEM OF AN INDIVIDUAL*

The analysis of an individual's cognitive system proceeds in four steps:

1. *Identification of the judgment problem.* The substantive and formal properties of the judgment problem are identified.
2. *Exercise of judgment.* The individual makes judgments about a representative set of cases of the judgment problem.
3. *Analysis of judgment.* The individual's judgments are analyzed to determine the components of his cognitive system.
4. *Display of results.* The results of the analysis are displayed graphically to the individual (ordinarily by inter-active computer graphics techniques).

*DESCRIPTION OF THE REGRESSION ANALYSIS APPROACH*

Identification of the Judgment Problem

This step consists of three parts: (1) defining the judg-ment to be made, (2) identifying the information (cues) on which the judgment is based, and (3) discovering the formal properties (for example, intercorrelations, distributions, and ranges) of the set of cue variables in the task. The proce-dures used in this critical step vary according to the type of judgment problem and the purpose of the analysis. A full-scale study involving extensive data gathering and multivariate analysis could be conducted, or a simple guided interview de-signed to elicit cue variables from the individual might suf-fice. Since methods used in this step are highly situation (and investigator) specific, we shall not attempt to describe them further here. This step is critical for the analysis, however, since the validity of all that follows depends on the proper identification of the judgment problem at this step. It is particularly important that all major cues are identi-fied, since it is unlikely that the omission of a cue at this stage will be detected in later analysis. (But see Stenson, 1974, who shows that certain parameters of the judgment pro-cess can be ascertained even though the cues are not identi-fied.)

Exercise of Judgment

A judgment task is generated that consists of a number of cases representing the judgment problem. Each case consists of a profile representing a different combination or mix of

277

values on the several cues. The individual indicates his judgments by rating several profiles on a numerical scale.

The judgment task may be conducted by pencil-and-paper procedures or by an interactive computer terminal, but the cue information must be presented unambiguously. All possible perceptual confusion must be eliminated from the display so that the task will be wholly judgmental in nature (unless, of course, the investigator is interested in studying the effects of perceptual ambiguity).

The formal properties of the judgment task (for example, distributions and interrelations) should correspond to the properties of the environment that gave rise to the problem. The correspondence of the judgment tasks to the environment (representativeness) is essential if the results of the analysis of the judgment task are to be generalizable.

## Analysis of Judgment

The judgment data are analyzed in terms of multiple regression statistics. The values of the cues are the independent variables in the analysis, and the individual's judgments constitute the dependent variable. The linear model that is fitted by this technique is

$$y_{ij} = \sum_{k=1}^{m} b_{ik} x_{jk} + c_i + e_{ij}, \tag{1}$$

where $y_{ij}$ is the judgment of individual $i$ for profile $j$, $m$ is the number of cues, $b_{ik}$ is the raw score regression weight for individual $i$ on cue $k$, $x_{jk}$ is the value of cue $k$ on profile $j$, $c_i$ is the constant term for individual $i$, and $e_{ij}$ is the residual error from the model of individual $i$ for profile $j$.

### Cognitive Control and Consistency

Hammond and Summers (1972) distinguished between knowledge and cognitive control. But recent research (to be described below) has shown that cognitive control must also be distinguished from cognitive consistency. "Control" refers to the similarity between an individual's judgments and predictions based on a specific model; "consistency" refers to the similarity between repeated judgments of identical profiles.

This distinction can be clarified by noting that when a person makes numerous repeated judgments of the same profile, they will be distributed about their mean, $\overline{Y}_j$, and the variation of those judgments about $\overline{Y}_j$ is due to the individual's *inconsistency*. If the predicted judgments of profile $j$ based

278

on two models (A and B) are $\hat{Y}_{Aj}$ and $\hat{Y}_{Bj}$, then the variation of the repeated judgments about $\hat{Y}_{Aj}$ indicates the individual's *control with respect to model A* on the $j$th profile. The variation of the judgments about $\hat{Y}_{Bj}$ indicates the individual's *control with respect to model B* on the $j$th profile. Since the variance about the mean is always less than the variance around any other point, consistency is the upper bound for control with respect to any model. Note that when the predictions from a model coincide with the mean of the distributions of judgments (for example, if $\overline{Y}_j = \hat{Y}_{Aj}$), control (with respect to that model) is then equal to consistency. Otherwise, control will be lower than consistency.

## Measures of Control and Consistency

Control is measured by estimating the variation of judgments of a set of profiles about predictions produced by a model. The multiple correlation ($R$) provides a measure of control because it measures the correspondence between an individual's judgments and predictions from a specific model.

Consistency is measured by estimating the variation of repeated judgments about their mean. In order to help select the best estimate of this variation, a test for lack of fit of the specific model under consideration should be performed (see, for example, Draper & Smith, 1966, pp. 26-31). This test helps the investigator decide whether the model he is using accounts for all of the consistent variation in the individual's judgment. If there is no evidence of lack of fit of the model, then the $R$ provides a measure of *consistency* as well as *control*. If there is evidence of lack of fit, then $R$ measures only the correspondence between a person's judgments and predictions generated by the model--that is, control with respect to the model used by the investigator. A measure of consistency can then be obtained as follows.

First, a measure of pure error is computed:

$$s_e^2 = \frac{\sum\limits_{i=1}^{p} \frac{1}{2}(y_{ij} - y_{ij}')^2}{p},$$

where $s_e^2$ is the estimate of pure error in the individual's judgments, $y_{ij}$ and $y_{ij}'$ are two judgments made by individual $i$ based on profile $j$ on two different occasions, and $p$ is the total number of repeated profiles.

279

This pure error measure is the variance of the differences between the repeated judgments on each profile and their mean. (For a formula that applies when judgments are repeated more than once, see Draper & Smith, 1966, p. 29.) It will be large if there tends to be a large difference between judgments of the same profile made at different times, and it will be small if judgments made at different times are very similar. The pure error measure can be regarded as an indication of the inconsistency in an individual's judgments.

The pure error measure is then used to compute consistency as follows:

$$\text{Consistency} = \sqrt{\frac{\text{consistent variation}}{\text{total variation}}} =$$

$$\sqrt{\frac{s_y^2 - s_e^2}{s_y^2}} = R_c,$$

where $s_y^2$ is the variance of an individual's judgments. This measure, which we shall call $R_c$, is similar to the intraclass correlation which can be considered an estimate of the upper bound for control with respect to any polynomial regression model (see Winer, 1971, pp. 389–391).

$R_c$ is proposed as a measure of consistency of an individual's judgment here for the first time. Its properties when used in the context of the study of human judgment are unknown. It will be influenced by the variation in the cues, the cue intercorrelations, the number of repeated profiles, and other task properties. The exact nature of these effects remains a topic for future research.

*Nonlinear Models*

The linear regression model has been applied to a variety of judgment problems and has proved useful in many cases (see Slovic & Lichtenstein, 1973, for a review). Moreover, the conceptual simplicity and descriptive power of the linear model make it an important tool for social judgment theorists. (See Dawes & Corrigan, 1974, for an important discussion of the use of the linear model in decision making.)

The analysis is not limited to the linear model, however, for although a linear model is used for the initial fit, it is critically evaluated by the following criteria before being accepted as a representation of a cognitive system:

1. Is the linear representation *useful*? This depends on the purpose of the analysis--task learning, interpersonal learning, or conflict resolution.

2. Is there evidence of significant *bias* from the test for lack of fit of the model? If the repeated judgments necessary for the lack-of-fit test are not available, then a low $R$ signals possible danger in accepting the linear model (although a low $R$ in itself does not mean that the linear model must necessarily be rejected, just as a high $R$ does not mean that the linear model must necessarily be accepted).

3. Is nonlinear variation *shared* among individuals? This is determined by computing correlations among the residuals $(e_{ij})$ for a number of individuals. (These correlations are the $C$ coefficients in the lens model equation to be discussed below.) A high correlation between the residuals for two individuals suggests that the residuals contain reliable judgmental variation which might be identified by a nonlinear model.

If any of the above conditions exists, nonlinear models of judgment must be investigated. A nonlinear (additive) model that has been found useful in several studies is the polynomial model formed by adding squared terms to Eq. (1),

$$y_{ij} = \sum_{k=1}^{m} (b_{ik}x_{jk} + b_{i(k + m)}x_{jk}^2) +$$

$$c_i + e_{ij}, \tag{2}$$

where $b_{i(k + m)}$ is the regression weight for the square of the value of cue $k$. This model is additive because the contribution of any cue is independent of the values of the other cues, yet it will represent the nonlinear (U- and inverted U-shaped) function forms or any cue–judgment function that can be approximated by some portion of a parabola.

A problem encountered in using Eq. (2) is that the weight and function form components are combined. For clarity of description of the judgment system (later) in Step 4, weight and function form should be separated. This separation can be accomplished by algebraic manipulation of Eq. (2).

We begin by defining a function of $x_{jk}$ which is the sum of the linear and nonlinear terms involving $x_{jk}$ in Eq. (2):

$$f_k(x_{jk}) = (b_{ik}x_{jk} + b_{i(k + m)}x_{jk}^2).$$

We further define $f_{k_{\max}}$ as the maximum value of $f_k$ over the range of cue $k$, $f_{k_{\min}}$ as the minimum value of $f_k$ over the range of cue $k$, $y_{\max}$ as the maximum allowable judgment, and $y_{\min}$ as the minimum allowable judgment:

$$g_k = \frac{y_{max} - y_{min}}{f_{k_{max}} - f_{k_{min}}}$$

$$h_k = y_{min} - g_k f_{k_{min}}$$

$$f_k^*(x_{jk}) = g_k f_k(x_{jk}) + h_k$$

Thus, $f_k^*$ will range from $y_{min}$ to $y_{max}$. If $f*$'s are formed in this way for all cues, then Eq. (2) can be rewritten as

$$y_{ij} = \sum_{k=1}^{m} {}^{1/}g_k f_k^*(x_{jk}) - \sum_{k=1}^{m} h_k + c_i + e_{ij}$$

$$= \sum_{k=1}^{m} w_k f_k^*(x_{jk}) + c_i^* + e_{ij}, \tag{3}$$

where

$$w_k = {}^{1/}g_k$$

and

$$c_i^* = c_i - \sum_{k=1}^{m} h_k.$$

This equation separates weight ($w_k$) from function form ($f_k^*$) so that there will be one weight for each cue and the cue weights are applied to function forms all having common ranges.

Equation (3) represents only one of the possible methods for separating weight from function form. An alternative would be to rescale the $f_k$ by standardizing to obtain $f_k^*$ with zero mean and unit variance and then to calculate $w_k$ based on the standardized $f_k^*$. All methods for separating weight and function form would result in algebraically equivalent models when applied to a given sample because they could all be derived from Eq. (2). The selection among several algebraically equivalent models must be made on the basis of the usefulness and clarity of the representation provided by each model.

The method used to derive Eq. (3) (called the "range" method) is useful because whenever the range of each cue is known (as is often the case), the method is independent of any particular sample of cue values. This is true because no sample cue values are involved in the computation of $f_k^*$ or $w_k$. Independence of the sample of cue values is important because identical forms of Eq. (2) derived from two different samples of cue profiles will yield identical forms of Eq. (3). This would not necessarily occur with the standardization method, however. The property of independence is particularly critical for subject-controlled revision of weights and function forms (see below). When an individual is revising weights and function forms, he is, in effect, specifying the form of Eq. (3), which must, in turn, be translated into the form of Eq. (2) for application to a set of profiles. The judgment resulting from the application of specified weights and function forms to a particular profile should not depend on which other profiles happen to occur in the sample, which would be the case with the standardization method.

Although the range method has the advantage of being independent of a particular sample, it has the disadvantage of being dependent on the known ranges of the cues. This is not a serious disadvantage if the ranges accurately reflect the relative dispersions of the cues; however, if the ranges of one or more cues are determined by a few extreme cases, the weights obtained may be invalid or misleading. In such cases, an alternate method may be preferred even though the independence property might have to be relinguished.

The exploration of higher-order regression models need not be limited to the model including squared terms or to the additive model. Rules which are nonadditive with respect to the cues may be examined. For example, Einhorn (1970) describes procedures for analyzing conjunctive and disjunctive noncompensatory models. A variety of nonlinear models that are nonadditive with respect to the cues can be investigated with the use of multiple regression analysis. It is important, however, that such examination be guided by theory and reasonable hypotheses about the judgment problem and that all models be cross-validated. Slovic and Lichtenstein (1973) discuss attempts to investigate nonlinear judgmental models within the regression framework.

Finally, it should be noted that there is a growing recognition on the part of all judgment researchers that many *different* models will frequently provide equally high predictability of a subject's judgments (Goldberg, 1971). In fact, the case which sharply differentiates the predictability of different models is something of a rarity. This embarrassment of riches leads to an important difference between social judgment theorists and other investigators interested in modeling the judgment process. The difference is that social judgment theorists consider the analysis of the cognitive system to be a step in a process designed to aid the individual rather than a competition among models. The social judgment theorist should therefore select the model which is most *useful as a cognitive aid* for helping an individual learn, or for managing conflict, say, even if the most accurate

model accounts for somewhat less variance than some simpler
model. But if the simpler model misleads because, for example,
it does not account for judgmental variation which is crucial
for clarifying reasons for conflict, then the simpler model
must, of course, be rejected. As a result of this perspective,
the social judgment theorist places less emphasis on mathematical precision in cognitive modeling and more emphasis on empirically demonstrating the usefulness of a given model with
regard to a given problem, as noted above (see also Hoffman,
1960).

## Display of Results

The weights and function forms obtained from the analysis
of judgment are presented to the individual immediately following his judgments by means of computer graphics displays.
An example of a pictorial display of weights and function
forms generated by a computer program is presented in Figure 2.
In many applications it is necessary to compare two or more
systems (an individual's cognitive system and a task system,
or the cognitive systems of two or more individuals). A com-
puter-generated pictorial display comparing two systems is
shown in Figure 3.

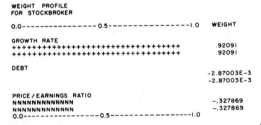

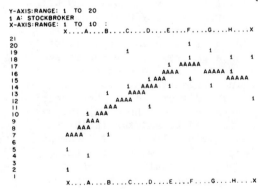

*Fig. 2. An example of a
computer graphics display of
weights and function forms.*

A: SMITH
B: JONES

WEIGHT  PROFILE

0.0----------------------0.5 ----------------1.0     WEIGHT

WAGES
AAAAAAAAAAAAAAAAAAAAAAAAAAAAAAAAAAA          .740226
BBBBBBBB                                     .195698

PRICES
AAA                                          -7.80695E-2
BBBBBBBBBBBBBBBBBBBBBBBBBBBBBBBBBBBBBBBB     -.887725

UNEMPLOYMENT
                                             5.93882E-3
BBBBBBB                                       -.167995
0.0 ----------------0.5----------------1.0

*Fig. 3.   A computer graphics display comparing two systems.*

*EXTENSIONS OF THE METHOD:   INTERACTIVE COMPUTER GRAPHICS*

The steps described above have been used with success in
numerous studies of cognitive process and will continue to be
important in future work.   The availability of interactive
computer graphics devices, however, provides flexibility and
power for the analysis of cognitive systems far beyond what
has been previously available.   Some of the most promising new
procedures are (1) subject-controlled revision of weights and
function forms, (2) use of hierarchical judgment models, and
(3) multimethod, multistage analyses.   All of these are now
being investigated; each will be briefly described below.

Subject-Controlled Revision of Weights and Function Forms
(at the Computer Console)

If the individual wishes to change the weights and function
forms in his judgment policy, he can do so by use of a light
pen or by entering new weights and function forms directly from
the keyboard.   The computer can generate judgments consistent
with the model newly specified by the individual and display
to him these new judgments made in response to a set of profiles.   The individual can then review the judgments which were
derived from the weights and function forms he specified and
can revise his judgment policy (for example, his weights and/or
function forms) again if he is not satisfied with the new judgments.   Thus, the computer provides the individual with

285

complete control over his cognitive system during the exercise of his judgment. The development of this procedure as an aid for the person exercising his judgment illustrates clearly the sharp difference in research aims between social judgment theorists and other judgment researchers who focus their efforts on the search for the correct model of judgment processes.

## Hierarchical Judgment Models

In many cases the cues for a judgment may in fact be judgments themselves. Many, if not most, judgment problems can be described by a single set of cues and judgments only when the researcher demands that the subject limit his cognitive activity in this way. In fact, many, perhaps most, judgment problems must be structured as multilevel hierarchical systems if any sense is to be made from their analysis (a point made quite early by Hammond, Hursch, & Todd, 1964). Under certain conditions, such hierarchical problems can be divided into numerous simple judgment problems, each of which can be analyzed separately. The use of interactive computing makes possible the structuring of the hierarchical problem, the analyses of the subproblems, and the recombining of the subproblems into the hierarchical system. Thus, highly complex judgment problems can be studied by dividing them into manageable subproblems by means of interactive computer graphics. (See Smith, 1973, for a description of this process.)

## Multimethod Analyses

The exploration of an individual's complete cognitive system requires more than the traditional analysis of a *single* judgment task. Moreover, when cues are highly intercorrelated, as they will be in representative judgment tasks, the results of the single task analysis are ambiguous because the weights cannot be strictly interpreted (Darlington, 1968), and as a result, the description of the cognitive system can be misleading. To cope with this problem, *several* tasks are employed in order to provide a multistage analysis of the judgment process. The tasks are constructed in order to remove the ambiguity that results from the use of a single task. Two ways of deriving such tasks are described here.

### *Predicting Each Cue from the Others*

Each cue in turn is considered a judgment to be made from the other cues. The analysis of the resulting tasks will clarify the individual's organization of the cues and the intersubstitutability properties which will permit one cue or set of cues to be substituted for another.

## Successive Omission

Each cue in turn is omitted from the judgment problem so that the individual is forced to make his judgment based on a subset of the original cues.  This method further explores the intersubstitutability properties of the cues and also permits determination of the unique contribution of each cue.  (See Brunswik, 1956, pp. 24, 25, 57, 63, for a discussion of "successive omission.")

Numerous variations on these methods are possible.  For example, a cue could be restricted in range rather than being completely omitted.  Other methods, such as those utilizing confidence judgments or cue-consistency judgments may also prove useful.  Discussion of the analysis of such multimethod data is beyond the scope of this paper.  For a useful example, see Hammond, Kern, Crow, Githens, Groesbeck, Gyr, and Saunders (1959, pp. 526-539), who made use of naturally occurring variations in cue distributions to ascertain cue weights of physicians' ratings of medical students.

The multimethod procedure for the exploration of a cognitive system can be accomplished by use of computer graphics procedures, and, indeed, these procedures appear to be the only feasible ones by which to pursue this problem, for the flexibility of this technology makes it possible to formulate and analyze a variety of tasks according to the demands of a particular problem.  This procedure has not yet been widely used by social judgment theorists, but as the methods become more thoroughly developed and tested, its use will increase.  And although this complex procedure seems a far cry from the simple 50-minute, one-shot experiments currently employed to study human judgment, it seems unlikely that there will be an easy escape from detailed, multimethod, multistage analyses if judgment theorists wish to come to grips with the full range of human judgment.

## EXTENSIONS OF THE METHOD:  ANALYSIS OF THE RELATION BETWEEN COGNITIVE SYSTEMS

### The Lens Model Equation

The models describing two or more cognitive systems provide a basis for analyzing the relation between the systems.  The original lens model equation for analyzing the relation between two systems was proposed by Hursch, Hammond, and Hursch (1964) and modified by Tucker (1964).  Additional formulations have

been developed by Castellan (1972) for dealing with multiple
judgments and multiple criteria, Stewart (1974) for separating
the effects of different types of variation, and Lindell (1974)
for analyzing the components of accuracy as measured by the
sum of squared differences between raw scores. The formulation of Tucker (1964) has been the most widely used by social
judgment theorists and will be discussed here.

The Tucker formulation is

$$r_a = GR_1R_2 + C \sqrt{1 - R_1^2} \sqrt{1 - R_2^2}, \tag{4}$$

where $r_a$ is the correlation between two variables $Y_1$ and $Y_2$
(the variables may be two individuals' judgments—agreement—
or an individual's judgment and an environmental criterion—
achievement); $G$ is the correlation between the components of $Y_1$
and $Y_2$ that are predicted from a linear regression on the cues;
$R_1$ and $R_2$ are the linear multiple correlations between the cues
and $Y_1$ and $Y_2$, respectively; and $C$ is the correlation between
the residuals from the linear regressions of $Y_1$ and $Y_2$.

The indices $R$, $G$, and $C$ can be interpreted as follows:

1. $R$ is a measure of the fit of a specific model. If it is
a model of the environment, then $R$ represents the maximum predictability possible (assuming the correct model). If it is
a model of an individual's cognitive system, then $R$ can be considered a measure of cognitive control with respect to that
particular model (Hammond & Summers, 1972). In most studies
to date, $R$ refers to the fit of a linear multiple regression
model; however, the lens model equation is equally appropriate
if the model includes nonlinear functions of the cues (see
Stewart, 1974).

2. $G$ is the correlation between predictions based on two
models. In a learning situation in which one model represents
an individual and the other represents a task, $G$ is the a-
chievement that would result if both the person model and the
task model were executed with perfect control. If both models
are of individuals, then $G$ is the agreement that would result
from the perfectly consistent application of both models.
Since $G$ and $R$ are statistically independent, they provide a
means of separating the effects of differences in models from
the effects of the control exercised over the application of
those models.

In a task-learning situation, $G$ can be considered a measure
of *knowledge* about the task because $G$ measures the correspondence between the model of the person's cognitive system and
the model of the task system. If we ignore the second term
on the right of Eq. (4), we have

$$r_a = GR_1R_2, \tag{5}$$

or

$$\text{Performance} = \text{knowledge} \times$$

$$\text{cognitive control} \times \text{task control.}$$

This equation indicates that maximum performance is realized
only when knowledge and control are maximized.

3. $C$ measures the relation between the components of $Y_1$ and
$Y_2$ that is not accounted for by the regression analysis. If
the regression analysis is based on a linear model, then a high
$C$ value indicates that there is consistent nonlinear variation
that is shared by the two systems. The presence of a high $C$
value indicates the need for an examination of the original
regression and possible inclusion of nonlinear terms in the
model.

A low $C$ value does not necessarily indicate the absence of
consistent nonlinear variation; it only indicates the absence
of *shared* nonlinear variation. Either system may separately
contain consistent nonlinear components even when $C$ is low.

For more detailed discussions of properties of the lens
model equation, see Castellan (1973) and Stewart (1974).

## Cluster Analysis

In the case in which the cognitive systems of a group of
individuals have been analyzed, there are usually subgroups
within the group who have similar judgmental systems. The
discovery of such subgroups will simplify the description of
the cognitive systems of the group and will identify factions
within the group that are likely to conflict. Cluster analysis
is used to classify members of a group into subgroups that are
similar with respect to their judgments.

Any clustering procedure requires measures of distance or
similarity between objects to be clustered and uses some algo-
rithm to cluster objects once the distances have been computed.
We will briefly discuss two types of distance measures that
can be used to cluster people with similar cognitive systems;
no attempt will be made to discuss the numerous clustering
algorithms that are available. (See Naylor & Wherry, 1965;
Wherry & Naylor, 1966, for discussions of clustering individuals based on judgments.)

### *Similarity between Judgments*

The correlation between the judgments made by two individuals over the same set of cases can be used as a measure of
similarity between individuals. This measure has the advantage
that no models of the cognitive system are needed, and,

289

therefore, errors in the analysis of each individual's cognitive system will not affect the clustering. It has the disadvantage that the unreliability in the individual's judgments will affect the clustering, and therefore it will be possible for two people who have similar cognitive systems to be placed in different clusters simply because both persons are inconsistent.

*Similarity between Models*

The correlation between two cognitive systems executed with perfect consistency (*G* from the lens model equation) can also be used in cluster analysis. This measure eliminates unreliability from the clustering but may produce poor clusters if the analysis of cognitive systems has not been carried out properly (if, for example, the wrong cues or an inappropriate model has been used).

In most applications the second method is preferred because it takes advantage of the judgment analysis. The first method should be used only when one is unable to perform an analysis of judgment or has reason to distrust the results of such an analysis.

We hope that some misconceptions concerning the use of the above quantitative method will be corrected as a result of the above discussion. For example:

1. *Misconception*: SJT is tied to the linear regression model. *Fact*: Linear regression is only the starting point for the analysis.

2. *Misconception*: The method of SJT involves observation of an individual's judgment on one occasion by a single method. *Fact*: A multimethod approach is advocated.

3. *Misconception*: Social judgment theorists offer their models as psychological laws—that is, as isomorphic representations of the process underlying judgment. *Fact*: Models are sought as useful aids to individuals and groups who must exercise their judgment.

4. *Misconception*: The goal of social judgment theorists is to increase the accuracy of judgments. *Fact*: Increased accuracy is only one goal pursued in the effort to aid individuals and groups.

*APPLICATION OF THEORY AND QUANTITATIVE METHOD TO EMPIRICAL RESEARCH: GENERALIZATION OVER CASES*

In keeping with their premises and research aims, social judgment theorists insist upon seeking generality over conditions (rather than generality over persons) as a test of the utility of the theory. They have, therefore, extended their research to four cases which, in their view, encompass the major types of circumstances in which human judgment is employed.

Before the results obtained in each of the four cases are discussed, the importance of testing over conditions needs to be emphasized. For example, conventional judgment theorists typically test their cognitive models under *one* set of task conditions (orthogonal arrangement of task dimensions) while varying task content, whereas social judgment theorists argue that the test for generality should be made over tasks with several *different* formal properties (for example, various intercorrelations among task dimensions) irrespective of content. Failure to include different formal task properties results in the test being one of reliability of results within tasks rather than validity of results over tasks. Testing over tasks with different substantive properties is, therefore, hardly a test of the generality of the model, inasmuch as the identical formal properties of the task can be expected to evoke from the subject the identical method of integrating the data. Since judgment tasks outside the laboratory obviously differ widely in their formal properties, any model which possesses only *substantive* generality is a model of highly restricted generality, and thus of little theoretical or practical interest. Most important, this procedure restricts itself to a case ordinarily not found outside the laboratory, the case involving *independent* task dimensions; it is a *peculiar* case which omits causal entanglement, and thus omits the circumstances which gave rise to the judgment problem in the first place. (See Hammond & Stewart, 1974, for a detailed treatment of this point.)

More important, because of their indifference toward generality over conditions, conventional judgment theorists seldom cross-validate over the variety of sharply different conditions in which human judgment takes place; virtually all their studies involve (1) a person who exercises his judgment in isolation from others with regard to (2) a situation in which the task conditions are unknown to him. In contrast, social judgment theorists insist on testing the utility of SJT across widely differing circumstances, as will be shown below.

DISCUSSION OF UNIQUE CONTRIBUTIONS IN FOUR CASES

Social Judgment Theory distinguishes among four types of judgment situations. These are the single-system case, the double-system case, the triple-system case, and the $N$-system case. Space does not permit discussion of the research carried out within each case; therefore, only the unique contribution that SJT has made to each case will be mentioned.

291

## THE SINGLE-SYSTEM CASE

This is the case ordinarily studied by judgment theorists (see, for example, Anderson, 1971; Edwards, 1968; Kelley, 1973). In this case the judgment processes of the person making the judgment are the only phenomena of interest. No task information other than the value of the cues (or "stimuli") and possibly their interrelations is considered by the researcher.

### Unique Contribution: Separating Knowledge from Cognitive Control

The separation of knowledge and cognitive control (see the above section on quantitative method) has led to a new view of the competence of human judgment and to a shift in theory. Initially the concept of cognitive control was made equivalent to consistency (Hammond & Summers, 1972). That is, the random error in the subject's judgment system provided a measure of his *control* over, and thus his *consistency* in applying, his judgment policy. It is now clear that these terms should be separated, conceptually and mathematically (see above), due to the results of several recent studies.

These studies began with an effort to train two undergraduates to *exercise control* over their judgment processes in what were presumed to be a variety of highly complex tasks—tasks which involved differential weights and various function forms. For example, a simple judgment policy is one which requires only that the subject assign equal weights to, say, three cues, use the information from all three cues in terms of a positive linear function, and employ an additive organizational principle. A more difficult task would require the subject to assign differential weights to the cues and to employ different function forms (for example, a positive linear function form for cue 1, a negative linear function form for cue 2, and a U-shaped function form for cue 3).

The results from an initial study were surprising. The two students were able to exercise effectively various judgment policies over a wide range of tasks which had been presumed to be beyond their capacity. Gillis, Gritz, and Stewart (1975) found the same results with normal controls, and also found that methadone addicts and chronic schizophrenics (under medication) performed nearly as well. Steinmann's study (1974) of college students confirmed the results Gillis and his colleagues obtained with normal subjects. Further work by Weichselbaum (1975) confirmed their results with normals as well as with methadone addicts. In short, studies carried out by different investigators in different laboratories over a

292

variety of subject populations have provided a clear result: Under the proper conditions, human beings can exercise control over their judgment processes with respect to far more complex relations than had been suspected.

To grasp the significance of these findings, one must remember that although the layman expects human judgment to have almost unlimited capacity, judgment researchers have stressed the limitations of human judgment again and again (for a recent example, see Tversky & Kahneman, 1974). The finding that human subjects *can* execute a judgment policy that requires them to organize information drawn from dimensions that vary widely in function form and in weights is, therefore, an important one. Whether human subjects in fact *execute* judgment policies of the complexity indicated above outside the laboratory is another question.

## THE DOUBLE-SYSTEM CASE

In this case (see Figure 1), one person makes judgments about one task system; in addition, task outcomes are *known* (in contrast to the single-system case, in which task outcomes are *unknown*), and, as a result, task structure is known. Moreover, the second task system might be a second *person* about which judgments are to be made. The immediate question raised by the double-system case is the accuracy of judgments, as well as the circumstances which enhance or impair it. In addition, the rate at which one learns to improve his judgment is an important matter. It is in this area that SJT has made a unique contribution.

### Unique Contribution: Providing Cognitive Feedback by Means of Interactive Computer Graphics

The traditional S-R approach to these problems is based on the provision of the correct answer after each trial. How else can people learn other than by observing task outcomes? Unfortunately, social judgment theorists who studied what during the 1960s was called "multiple-cue probability learning" accepted all too readily the traditional notion that learning is dependent upon receiving outcome feedback. A wholly fortuitous discovery by Newton (1965), however, that subjects might well be able to improve their performance without outcome feedback led Todd and Hammond (1965) to investigate an alternative type of feedback. They showed that if subjects were given feedback of a cognitive nature (that is, information about the properties of task systems and their judgment systems), they could rapidly improve their performance without outcome feedback (that is, without being told the correct answer after each trial). Moreover, they found that providing outcome feedback in addition to cognitive feedback did not improve accuracy. Indeed, Hammond, Summers, and Deane (1973) later showed that adding outcome feedback could result in the *impairment* of performance. These preliminary results, obtained from experimental situations involving only the crudest of equipment and materials, led to the search for an appropriate means for displaying (1) the properties of task systems, (2) the properties of cognitive systems of persons, and (3) the degree of match between them. Procedures involving interactive computer graphics techniques (mentioned above) were developed for this purpose and are now in use (see Hammond, 1971; Stewart & Carter, 1973; Hammond & Brehmer, 1973).

These procedures allow the subject not only to see the properties of his own judgment policy (the weights attached to cues, function forms employed, and the control with which he is executing his policy), but also to *compare* his policy with that of another person (or with the properties of the task to be dealt with if these are known; see Figure 3). Thus, interactive computer graphics techniques permit the human subject not only to see a representation of the "cognitive map" that Tolman (1948) spoke of, but to compare it with the causal texture of environmental (or task) systems Brunswik (1956) argued should be investigated in depth. Moreover, cognitive maps of several persons (or task systems) can be compared. Such cognitive material is, of course, appropriate to a cognitive theory intended to be free of stimulus-response concepts. Furthermore, as Lindell (1974) has shown, cognitive feedback enhances learning in those difficult judgment tasks in which task variables are intercorrelated and differential weights are involved.

This contribution by SJT--the development of a *cognitive aid*--has important practical applications, for it is now clear that it is no longer necessary to try to learn how to improve one's judgment by means of outcome feedback (indeed, if the task is complex and involves uncertainty, it will *never* be learned by means of outcome feedback), nor is it necessary to try to learn what the properties of another person's judgment policy are by interrogation on one person's part and introspection on the other's. Persons exercising their judgment can discover, immediately and in pictorial form (by means of computer graphics), the properties of their own judgmental system, as well as the properties of another person's judgmental system, and *change* those properties, if they desire, with complete control. That capability carries considerable significance for judgment situations in which more than one policy maker is involved and in which interpersonal conflict and interpersonal learning become significant phenomena, a point

294

to be developed below. Learning with cognitive aids (in the form of other persons) is a more representative learning situation than the outcome feedback paradigm used in traditional learning studies. Our cognitive aids are only a superior version of what actually takes place when people learn, which they do on the basis of feedforward from other people and feedback from other people, rather than in terms of outcomes following specific judgments.

## THE TRIPLE-SYSTEM CASE

There are two reasons for studying the case involving *two* persons and a task. First, as mentioned earlier, good methodology requires variations over different conditions; second, interpersonal conflict arising from different judgments and interpersonal learning were two highly important topics untouched by judgment theorists and, indeed, hardly investigated by anyone. Investigation of these problem areas is therefore a unique contribution made by social judgment theorists.

### Unique Contribution: Uncovering Cognitive Sources of Interpersonal Conflict

Social Judgment Theory differs sharply from all other approaches to the study of conflict because if focuses only on *cognitive* differences between persons who arrive at conflicting judgments, whereas all other approaches focus only on *differential gain* as the source of conflict; the latter approach has always dominated the field of conflict research. Strangely enough, neither psychologists nor others entertained the possibility that the properties of judgment processes may themselves produce conflict. The basis for the cognitive point of view was set forth by Hammond (1965) and elaborated by Hammond and Brehmer (1973).

The studies carried out by Brehmer and others (to be reported below) support the theory that cognitive differences in themselves are capable of producing conflict; they clearly show that it is unnecessary to appeal to motivational explanations in all cases of conflict. Indeed, it is clear that conflict can readily be increased, diminished, or eliminated by changes in task properties alone.

### The Research Paradigm

The problem in extending SJT to engage this topic was, first, to create circumstances under which it would be possible to observe the interaction between persons whose judgments differ and, second, to discover whether the concepts of SJT in

general, and the parameters of the lens model equation in particular, would provide new and useful information regarding the
interaction.

Experiments within the SJT research paradigm for the triple-
system case simulate a situation in which two persons make inductive inferences from uncertain information (cues). They
use the cues differently, however, to arrive at their judg-
ments--that is, they have different judgment policies. Differences in judgment policy can be created in the laboratory by
*training* the persons to use the information differently, but it
is also possible to *select* persons whose differences stem from
differences in preexperimental experience. The training procedure has the advantage of allowing the investigator to create
precisely whatever differences in judgment policy are required
for the experiment; the selection procedure, on the other hand,
allows the investigator to study socially induced rather than
laboratory-induced differences. The findings so far, however,
indicate that the same results are obtained regardless of
whether training or selection is used (Hammond & Brehmer, 1973;
Helenius, 1973; Rappoport, 1969).

The research focuses upon the changes in judgments that occur as the two persons interact with each other and with the
task. Agreement and conflict are defined objectively in terms
of the actual differences between the judgments made by the
subjects for each problem rather than in terms of subjective
factors (for example, in terms of whether the persons feel that
they are in conflict or not). The experiments are conducted
in two stages: a *training stage*, in which the subjects are
trained to have different policies, and a *conflict stage*, in
which the subjects are brought together in pairs to work on a
set of problems. The problems in the conflict stage usually
differ somewhat from the problems in the training stage, but
the persons are not informed of this or of the fact that they
have been differently trained. On each trial in the conflict
stage, the subjects (1) study a set of cues, (2) make individual judgments from these cues which (3) they announce to each
other, and if their judgments differ, (4) they discuss the
case, until (5) they can reach a joint judgment, agreeable to
both of them, after which (6) the correct answer for the problem is given. The relation between the individual judgments
mentioned in (2) defines the amount of conflict and is thus the
primary dependent variable.

## Interpersonal Conflict Arising from Differences in Judgment

A first important question is whether it is possible to produce disagreement by means of the research paradigm described
above, and if it is possible, whether persons resolve their

judgmental differences as they interact with each other and with the task. The results of roughly 30 studies (including studies carried out in 12 different countries) show, first, that it is indeed possible to produce disagreement and, second, that the disagreement is not resolved (Hammond & Brehmer, 1973).

## Analysis of Conflict in Terms of the Lens Model Equation

The above-mentioned results lead to the question of why conflict is not resolved. The question can be answered through an examination of a measure of conflict based on the lens model equation. This measure expresses the effects of *two* sources of conflict: *systematic* as well as *nonsystematic* differences in judgment policy. Equation (4) disentangles the effects of these two sources. Recall that

$$r_a = GR_1R_2,$$

where $r_a$ is the correlation between the judgments made by Subject 1 and those made by Subject 2 and the other terms are interpreted as in the quantitative discussion above.

In this equation, $r_a$ is a measure of the amount of agreement between the judgments of Subject 1 and Subject 2, $G$ indicates the extent to which the two judgment policies are similar with respect to their systematic aspects, and $R_1$ and $R_2$ indicate the consistency of each of the judgment policies and thus provide a measure of the nonsystematic differences in judgments.[1] As can be seen from the equation, perfect agreement ($r_a = 1.00$) can be reached only if the subjects are identical in the systematic aspects of their judgment policies ($G = 1.00$) *and* if their policies are executed with perfect consistency ($R_1 = R_2 = 1.00$). Thus, the two possible sources of disagreement, *differences* in judgment policy ($G < 1.00$) and *inconsistency* ($R_1$ and for $R_2 < 1.00$) in execution of policies, can be measured. This distinction shows that the mere observation that persons differ

---

[1]In the following discussion, $R$ is used as a measure of consistency for two reasons: (1) The term "consistency" was used exclusively in the original literature cited here. (2) In the studies discussed, the mean of a set of repeated judgments would coincide with the predictions based on the model, and therefore $R$ is a valid measure of consistency. The training procedure resulted in subjects' using an additive policy, and the conflict procedure did not elicit a different type of model; only weights and function forms changed during conflict, with the organizing principle remaining unchanged. Consistency and control are thus identical.

in their judgments does not allow the inference that there are
fundamental differences between judgment policies.  The two
persons may lack perfect consistency, and thus their differences may be caused by inconsistent execution.  The question,
then, is whether subjects fail to reduce their conflict because
they are unable to reduce the systematic differences between
their policies or because they are unable to execute their
judgments with perfect consistency.

## Results

The results of a series of analyses of sources of conflict
show that the relative importance of the two sources of policy
conflict *changes* as the subjects interact with each other and
the task.  At the beginning of the interaction, most of the
conflict is caused by the systematic differences in policy,
but these differences are rapidly reduced.  At the same time,
however, the consistency of the subjects' policies decreases
so that at the end of a 20-trial conflict period, lack of consistency rather than systematic differences in policy is the
main obstacle to agreement.

## Replications

Some typical results are shown in Figure 4.  These results
have been replicated over subject conditions, such as nation-
ality (Brehmer, Azuma, Hammond, Kostron, and Varonos, 1970)
and sex (Hammond & Brehmer, 1973), and task variables, both
with respect to *content* (Hammond & Brehmer, 1973) and with
respect to *formal characteristics*, such as task predictability
(Brehmer, 1973c, 1974c), the distribution of the validities of
cues (Brehmer, 1974c), and the forms of the functions relating
cues to criterion (Brehmer & Hammond, 1973; Brehmer & Kostron,
1973).  The results obtained when the subjects have been
selected because of their  preexperimental differences are similar to those obtained when the subjects have been trained to
have different policies (Rappoport & Summers, 1973).

## Changes in Cue Dependencies:  Negative Consequences of Good Intentions

Subjects decrease their dependency on the cues used initially at a faster rate than they increase their dependency on
the cues used by the other person (see, for example, Brehmer,
1972).  This necessarily leads to a drop in consistency since
$R_1$, which defines consistency, is related to the sum of the
individual cue-judgment correlations which define the subjects'
dependency on the individual cues.  And a decrease in $R$ means

298

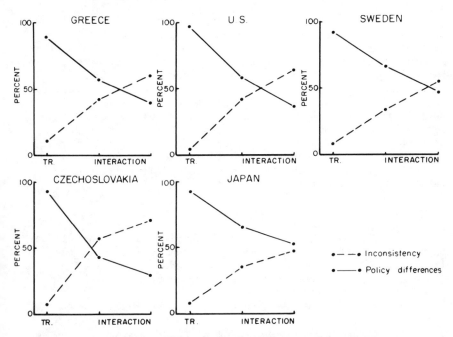

Fig. 4. *The relative contributions (percent) of policy differences (sums of differences in beta weights divided by 2) and inconsistency* $[1 - (R^2_{s_1} + R^2_{s_2})/2]$ *to disagreement as a function of blocks of trials for the five-nation study.*

a decrease in $r_a$ and thus a decrease in agreement, despite good intentions.

A study by Brehmer (1972) in which both subjects were trained to have *identical* judgment policies illustrates clearly the role of change and inconsistency. As the subjects tried to increase their judgmental accuracy in the conflict stage, they began to change; inconsistency developed (their $R$'s decreased), and the subjects began to disagree ($r_a$ decreased), yet their judgment policies remained virtually identical throughout the experiment (as shown by high $G$ values). Thus, inconsistency will not only prevent subjects from reaching agreement but may also *introduce* disagreement where no prior disagreement existed. As this study indicates, however, disagreement may be *false*, since the judgment policies remained virtually identical.

## Behavioral Validation of the Meaning of Inconsistency

The first part of the hypothesis, that inconsistency leads to a lack of understanding, has gained support from two studies (Brehmer, 1974d, 1975) which show that subjects ask each other more questions when their policies are more inconsistent, thus indicating that inconsistency does indeed lead to lack of understanding and that inconsistency is not a mathematical fiction. (Whether inconsistency leads to distrust has still to be investigated.) A different type of behavioral validation has been carried out by Gillis (1975). He found that the phenothiazines commonly used as therapeutic agents in psychiatric hospitals have a deleterious effect on consistency. In short, inconsistency has been systematically related to behavioral observations.

## Conflict Reduction or Task Adaptation?

The results of a series of studies using these conditions support the latter alternative: Only the subject with the incorrect policy shows any appreciable change in policy (Brehmer & Kostron, 1973; Brehmer, 1975; see also Brehmer & Garpebring, 1974).

These results show the important contribution of task characteristics to conflict arising from different judgments and support the value of analyzing conflict in terms of *three* systems rather than restricting the analysis to person characteristics, as is typical of an organism-centered psychology.

## Effects of the Characteristics of the Task on Conflict

We turn now to an examination of the effects of formal characteristics of the task on conflict.

### *Task Consistency*

If judgment policies in a conflict situation are affected by the characteristics of the task in the same way that they are in policy formation, these results lead to the prediction that subjects will develop less consistent policies in conflict tasks of high uncertainty, and, therefore, there will be less agreement under these conditions than when the task is highly predictable. This hypothesis has been confirmed repeatedly (Brehmer, 1973c, 1974b, 1974d, 1975).

300

## Ecological Validities of Cues

When the tasks contain only linear relations, the distribution of the validities of the cues affects the consistency ($R$) but not the similarity ($G$) of policies. In this case, the policies tend to be more consistent when the subjects have to use only one cue than when they have to use multiple cues (Brehmer, 1975). However, both policy similarity and consistency are affected when the tasks contain both linear *and* nonlinear cues (Brehmer & Kostron, 1973). In the latter case, both policy similarity and consistency tend to be higher when the subjects have to use only one cue. These results are presumably due to the difficulties inherent in the use of nonlinear function forms (see Brehmer, 1971a, 1971b, 1973b, 1973c).

## Task Function Forms

Nonlinear function forms lead to lower consistency, presumably because nonlinear functions are harder to execute (see Brehmer, 1971b). The degree of policy similarity ($G$) is not affected by the function forms, however (Brehmer & Hammond, 1973; Brehmer & Kostron, 1973).

## Cue Intercorrelations

Task characteristics also introduce certain constraints on the relation among agreement, judgmental accuracy, and policy similarity. For example, if the cues are positively intercorrelated, the subjects will reach a high level of agreement despite differences in policy. In addition, the intercorrelation between the cues will allow a subject who uses a cue that is in itself of no validity to reach a high level of judgmental accuracy, since the correlation between the cues will ensure that judgments become correlated with one another. When the cues are orthogonal, on the other hand, differences in policy will be directly reflected in disagreement, and dependency on nonvalid cues will lead to a lack of judgmental accuracy. In short, positive cue intercorrelations will lead to *agreement in fact*, despite *disagreement in principle*; they will also lead to judgmental accuracy, despite a faulty policy. This means that when the cues are intercorrelated, there will be less need for the subjects to change their policies, and this, in turn, leads to the hypothesis that the subjects will reach a lower degree of policy similarity when the cues are intercorrelated than when they are orthogonal. This hypothesis was supported in two experiments (Brehmer, 1974b).

These results, then, show that both the level of agreement
and the relative contributions from the two sources of agreement vary in a predictable way with the nature of the task.

*Summary*

First, our results show that conflict arising from different
judgments is not resolved even under the benign conditions pre-
vailing in these experiments. Conflict can indeed be caused
by purely cognitive factors; the commonsense notion that disagreement always involves motivational differences is incorrect.
Second, our results show that conflict does not persist
because the subjects are determined to maintain the systematic
differences between their policies; on the contrary, in these
studies systematic differences between policies are usually
rapidly reduced. But conflict persists, and it persists because of a lack of consistency. The lack of consistency, in
turn, stems from the manner in which the subjects change their
policies.
Third, the results illustrate the importance of task variables in conflict. The task is important, first, because it
is the general focus of cognitive activity in the situation,
second, because of its effects on the structure of the judgment
policies of the participants and thus on agreement, and, third,
because of the constraints it places on agreement, judgmental
accuracy, and policy differences.

## Interpersonal Learning (IPL)

Space permits only a brief summary of the rationale and
results of the studies of interpersonal learning carried out
by social judgment theorists. Research in this area is divided
into two categories: IPL *from* the other and IPL *about* the
other. Each is discussed in turn.

*Interpersonal Learning from the Other*

The research paradigm used in the triple-system case to
study interpersonal conflict lends itself very readily to the
study of IPL from the other because the investigator can specify the properties of the cognitive systems of both learners
as well as the task to be learned.

*Task Variables and Interpersonal Learning*

A series of studies has investigated the effects of task
variables, such as task predictability (Brehmer, 1973b, 1974a,
1974b), function form (Brehmer, 1973a, 1973b; Earle, 1973;

Hammond, 1972), the distribution of validities of the cues
(Brehmer, 1973a, 1973b, 1974a, 1974b), and cue intercorrelations (Brehmer, 1974a). The results of these studies show that
the effects of these variables are similar to those obtained in
the individual learning studies, except that the learning of
nonlinear relations in the task is more rapid in interpersonal
learning than in individual learning. Thus, the results show
(1) that subjects tend to have less optimal judgment policies
when the task predictability is low than when it is high and
(2) that although nonlinear functions are learned more rapidly
in interpersonal learning than in individual learning, performance is nevertheless less optimal for tasks with nonlinear
relations than for tasks with linear relations.

*The Effects of the Characteristics of the Cognitive Systems of
the Learner and the Other*

A stable result in interpersonal learning studies (as well
as those concerning conflict) is this: If one subject is
trained to use a nonlinear relation and the other subject is
trained to use a linear one, and if the interpersonal training
task requires the subjects to use *both* the nonlinear cue and
the linear cue to the same extent, the nonlinearly trained
subject gives up his dependency on his trained cue faster than
the linearly trained subject. The nonlinearly trained subject
also learns to use the cue of the other faster than the linearly trained subject (Brehmer, 1969, 1971a, 1973a, 1973b;
Hammond, 1972; Brehmer & Hammond, 1973). Gillis (1975), Gritz
(1975), and Zachariadis and Varonos (1975) have replicated
these results in studies of the differential effects of psychoactive drugs on interpersonal learning.

*Interpersonal Learning about the Other*

The research paradigm used in the triple-system case also
facilitates the study of this type of IPL; we describe one
study (Mumpower & Hammond, 1974) which illustrates its use.
This study was conducted by training two persons to have widely
different judgment policies, as in the conflict studies described above. In the first case, pairs made judgments about
a two-cue judgment task in which the two cues were highly
intercorrelated. Each member of a pair was then asked to predict the judgments the other would make in 10 additional trials.
In the case in which subjects bring widely differing judgment policies to the joint task and the cues are highly intercorrelated in the joint task, subjects assume their judgment
policies are highly similar because their judgments are similar. Unrestricted discussion does not lead them to detect the

303

fact that their judgment policies are very different; they do not realize that their agreement is *false*, that they are agreeing in fact while disagreeing in principle. In short, they do not learn accurately about each other because the characteristics of the task impede such learning. As soon as the task variables are disentangled (that is, are uncorrelated) by the experimenter, the subjects rapidly learn that they have different judgment policies; assumed similarity decreases, actual similarity remains the same, but predictive accuracy increases. Counterbalancing of conditions shows that the effect is produced entirely by task characteristics—that is, by causal texture.

In sum, SJT has been applied effectively and productively to the study of interpersonal conflict produced by cognitive differences. It has also been successfully applied to two types of interpersonal learning, topics which have not previously been studied in a systematic way. Uncovering the cognitive sources of conflict and the cognitive barriers to interpersonal learning carries large implications for policy formation.

## THE N-*SYSTEM CASE*

This case includes the situation in which a number of persons are studied, regardless of whether the properties of the task system are known. If a number of persons exercise their judgment, policy factions can be detected by means of cluster analysis. As indicated in the quantitative section, this procedure will not only provide information about which persons are arriving at similar judgments but also indicate the characteristics of the disparate policies. Thus, the cognitive bases of conflict within the group are indicated.

## Unique Contribution: Application of Social Judgment Theory to Social Policy Formation

The unique contribution of SJT has been to bring the theory, quantitative procedures, results of research, and technological innovations (externalization of judgment policies by means of interactive computer graphics) to bear on social policy formation outside the laboratory.

Several applications of SJT to social policy show that SJT is indeed life-relevant, that the methodology and the cognitive aids produced by it are appropriate to a wide variety of judgmental problems and demonstrate that although judgment theory is not law seeking *per se*, the empirical regularities observed in the laboratory are also observed outside the laboratory. Such empirical regularities include the following general conclusions: (1) People do not describe accurately and completely their judgmental policies, (2) people are often inconsistent in applying their judgmental policies, (3) only a small number of cues are used, (4) it is difficult to learn another person's policy simply by observing his judgments or by listening to his explanations of them, (5) the cognitive aids described above can reduce conflict and increase learning, and (6) linear, additive organizational principles are often adequate to describe judgment processes.

Examples of the applications include: citizen participation in planning (Stewart & Gelberd, 1972); determining policies about community goals (Steinmann & Stewart, 1973); and modeling physicians' judgments (Stewart, Joyce, & Lindell, 1975). Stewart, West, Hammond, and Kreith (1975) describe the usefulness of SJT for technology assessment; Flack and Summers (1971) illustrate its application to water resource planning; Brady and Rappoport (1973) detail its relevance to policy about nuclear safeguards; and Smith (1973) provides a hierarchical model of the complex judgments of an investment analyst. Also, Balke, Hammond, and Meyer (1973) show its application to labor-management negotiations; Steinmann, Smith, Jurdem, and Hammond (1975) deal with public-land-acquisition policy; and Adelman, Stewart, and Hammond (1975) apply SJT to corporate policy formation.

## SUMMARY

The theory, methodology, and research findings described above are unconventional; they are not yet described in textbooks. But there appears to be a growing recognition on the part of conventional psychology that it must change its research approach. The recent presidential address (Jenkins, 1974) to the Division of Experimental Psychology of the American Psychological Association provides an example; Jenkins warned his colleagues that "a whole theory of an experiment can be elaborated without contributing in an important way to the science because the situation is *artificial and nonrepresentative* [italics ours]" (p. 794). In addition to this surprising statement of agreement with Brunswik (1943) and social judgment theorists who have been making precisely that point for at least a decade (Hammond, 1955, 1965, 1966), Jenkins advocated that research should be life-relevant; he urged his colleagues to "[relate their] laboratory problems to the ecologically valid [Brunswik's term!] problems of everyday life" (p. 794).

This striking departure from conventional methodology included no acknowledgment that Brunswik had called for a "fundamental, all-inclusive shift in our methodological ideology" as early as 1943 (p. 261; see also Hammond, 1966, p. 23; Hammond & Stewart, 1974) and that until 1955 he continued to carry out empirical research and to write articles and books in which he seriously and responsibly considered the many implications of the change Jenkins advocated (something Jenkins failed to do). Perhaps social judgment theorists should be heartened and their convictions strengthened by what appears to be an independent discovery of their methodological position. But it remains to be seen whether conventional psychologists will relinquish "artificial and nonrepresentative" research designs or whether the need for representative design will have to be independently rediscovered periodically.

One might ask what social judgment theorists (who do not have to be convinced of the necessity for an "all-inclusive shift in methodological ideology" and who try to cope with the hard problems associated with that shift) intend to do in the second decade of their research. The foremost objective is to extend the limits of human judgment. We are particularly concerned with extending the limits of human judgment in the complex circumstances in which social policy is formulated. The reason for that is straightforward: Social, political, economic, and physical disasters of large scale appear to be imminent, and all of these problems require the exercise of human judgment. Estimates of the time remaining for human judgment to form effective social policies to cope with these problems range from a decade to a quarter- or perhaps a half-century. Social judgment theorists firmly believe that *all* students of human judgment should engage in research that will help provide better social policies and thereby increase our chances for a decent life on earth.

## ACKNOWLEDGMENTS

Preparation of this chapter was facilitated by National Institute of Mental Health Grant 1647-36. Although all four authors contributed substantially to the chapter, Hammond was mainly responsible for the material on theory and method, Stewart on quantitative method, Brehmer on interpersonal conflict and interpersonal learning, and Steinmann on the application of Social Judgment Theory to formulation of social policy.

## REFERENCES

Adelman, L., Stewart, T. R., & Hammond, K. R. A case history of the application of social judgment theory to policy formulation. *Policy Sciences*, 1975, *6*, 137–159.

Anderson, N. H. Integration theory and attitude change. *Psychological Review*, 1971, *78*, 171–206.

Balke, W. M., Hammond, K. R., & Meyer, G. D. An alternative approach to labor-management negotiations. *Administrative Science Quarterly*, 1973, *18*, 311–327.

Brady, D., & Rappoport, L. Policy-capturing in the field: The nuclear safeguards problem. *Organizational Behavior and Human Performance*, 1973, *9*(2), 253–266.

Brehmer, B. *The roles of policy differences and inconsistency in policy conflict*. (Umeå Psychological Reports No. 18) Umeå, Sweden: University of Umeå, 1969.

Brehmer, B. The effects of communication and feedback on cognitive conflict. *Scandinavian Journal of Psychology*, 1971, *12*, 205–216. (a)

Brehmer, B. Subjects' ability to use functional rules. *Psychonomic Science*, 1971, *24*, 259–260. (b)

Brehmer, B. Policy conflict as a function of policy differences and policy complexity. *Scandinavian Journal of Psychology*, 1972, *13*, 208–221.

Brehmer, B. Effects of cue validity on interpersonal learning of inference tasks with linear and nonlinear cues. *American Journal of Psychology*, 1973, *86*, 29–48. (a)

Brehmer, B. Effects of task predictability and cue validity on interpersonal learning of inference tasks including both linear and nonlinear cues. *Organizational Behavior and Human Performance*, 1973, *10*, 24–46. (b)

Brehmer, B. Policy conflict and policy change as a function of task characteristics: 2. The effects of task predictability. *Scandinavian Journal of Psychology*, 1973, *14*, 220–227. (c)

Brehmer, B. Effect of cue intercorrelations on interpersonal learning of probabilistic inference tasks. *Organizational Behavior and Human Performance*, 1974, *12*, 397–412. (a)

Brehmer, B. Effects of task predictability and cue validity on interpersonal learning of linear inference tasks. *Organizational Behavior and Human Performance*, 1974, *12*, 17–29. (b)

Brehmer, B. Policy conflict and policy change as a function of task characteristics: 3. The effects of the distribution of the validities of the cues in the conflict task. *Scandinavian Journal of Psychology*, 1974, *15*, 135–138. (c)

Brehmer, B.  Policy conflict, policy consistency, and interpersonal understanding. *Scandinavian Journal of Psychology*,
1974, *15*, 273-276.  (d)

Brehmer, B.  Policy conflict and policy change as a function of
task characteristics:  4.  The effects of cue intercorrelations. *Scandinavian Journal of Psychology*, 1975, *16*, 85-96.

Brehmer, B., Azuma, H., Hammond, K. R., Kostron, L., & Varonos,
D. D.  A cross-national comparison of cognitive conflict.
*Journal of Cross-Cultural Psychology*, 1970, *1*, 5-20.

Brehmer, B., & Garpebring, S.  Social pressure and policy
change in the "lens model" interpersonal conflict paradigm.
*Scandinavian Journal of Psychology*, 1974, *15*, 191-196.

Brehmer, B., & Hammond, K. R.  Cognitive sources of interpersonal conflict:  Analysis of interactions between linear
and nonlinear cognitive systems. *Organizational Behavior
and Human Performance*, 1973, *10*, 290-313.

Brehmer, B., & Kostron, L.  Policy conflict and policy change
as a function of task characteristics:  1.  The effects of
cue validity and function form. *Scandinavian Journal of
Psychology*, 1973, *14*, 44-55.

Brunswik, E.  Organismic achievement and environmental probability. *Psychological Review*, 1943, *50*, 255-272.

Brunswik, E.  The conceptual framework of psychology.  In
*International Encyclopedia of Unified Science*.  (Vol. 1,
No. 10)  Chicago:  University of Chicago Press, 1952.

Brunswik, E. *Perception and the representative design of
psychological experiments*.  (2nd ed.)  Berkeley:  University
of California Press, 1956.

Brunswik, E.  Scope and aspects of the cognitive problem.  In
H. Gruber, R. Jessor, and K. Hammond (Eds.), *Cognition:
The Colorado symposium*.  Cambridge, Mass.:  Harvard Uni-
versity Press, 1957.

Castellan, N. J., Jr.  The analysis of multiple criteria in
multiple-cue judgment tasks. *Organizational Behavior and
Human Performance*, 1972, *8*, 242-261.

Castellan, N. J., Jr.  Comments on the "lens model" equation
and the analysis of multiple-cue judgment tasks. *Psychometrika*, 1973, *38*, 87-100.

Darlington, R. B.  Multiple regression in psychological research and practice. *Psychological Bulletin*, 1968, *69*,
161-182.

Dawes, R. M., & Corrigan, B.  Linear models in decision making.
*Psychological Bulletin*, 1974, *81*, 95-106.

Draper, N., & Smith, H. *Applied regression analysis*.  New
York:  Wiley, 1966.

Earle, T. C.   Interpersonal learning.   In L. Rappoport and
  D. Summers (Eds.), *Human judgment and social interaction.*
  New York:  Holt, Rinehart, & Winston, 1973.
Edwards, W.   Conservatism in human information processing.   In
  B. Kleinmuntz (Ed.), *Formal representation of human judgment.*
  New York:  Wiley, 1968.
Einhorn, H. J.   The use of nonlinear, noncompensatory models
  in decision making.   *Psychological Bulletin*, 1970, *73*,
  221-230.
Flack, J. E., & Summers, D. A.   Computer aided conflict reso-
  lution in water resource planning:  An illustration.   *Water
  Resources Research*, 1971, *7*, 1410-1414.
Gillis, J. S.   Effects of chlorpromazine and thiothixene on
  acute schizophrenic patients.   In K. R. Hammond and C. R. B.
  Joyce (Eds.), *Psychoactive drugs and social judgment:
  Theory and research.*  New York:  Wiley, 1975.
Gillis, J. S., Gritz, E. R., & Stewart, T. R.   New procedures:
  Interactive computer graphics terminals enhance cognitive
  control.   In K. R. Hammond and C. R. B. Joyce (Eds.),
  *Psychoactive drugs and social judgment:  Theory and research.*
  New York:  Wiley, 1975.
Goldberg, L. R.   Five models of clinical judgment:  An empiri-
  cal comparison between linear and nonlinear representations
  of the human inference process.   *Organizational Behavior
  and Human Performance*, 1971, *6*, 458-479.
Gritz, E. R.   Effects of methylphenidate on mildly depressed
  hospitalized adults.   In K. R. Hammond and C. R. B. Joyce
  (Eds.), *Psychoactive drugs and social judgment:  Theory and
  research.*  New York:  Wiley, 1975.
Hammond, K. R.   Probabilistic functioning and the clinical
  method.   *Psychological Review*, 1955, *62*, 255-262.
Hammond, K. R.   New directions in research on conflict resolu-
  tion.   *Journal of Social Issues*, 1965, *21*, 44-66.
Hammond, K. R.   Probabilistic functionalism:  Egon Brunswik's
  integration of the history, theory, and method of psychology.
  In K. R. Hammond (Ed.), *The psychology of Egon Brunswik.*
  New York:  Holt, Rinehart, & Winston, 1966.
Hammond, K. R.   Computer graphics as an aid to learning.
  *Science*, 1971, *172*, 903-908.
Hammond, K. R.   Inductive knowing.   In J. R. Royce and W. N.
  Rozeboom (Eds.), *The psychology of knowing.*  London:
  Gordon & Breach, 1972.
Hammond, K. R., & Brehmer, B.   Quasi-rationality and distrust:
  Implications for international conflict.   In L. Rappoport
  and D. Summers (Eds.), *Human judgment and social interaction.*
  New York:  Holt, Rinehart, & Winston, 1973.

Hammond, K. R., Hursch, C., & Todd, F. J.   Analyzing the components of clinical inference. *Psychological Review*, 1964, *71*, 438–456.

Hammond, K. R., Kern, F., Crow, W., Githens, J., Groesbeck, B., Gyr, J., & Saunders, L.   *Teaching comprehensive medical care: A psychological study of a change in medical education.*   Cambridge, Mass.:   Harvard University Press, 1959.

Hammond, K. R., & Stewart, T. R.   *The interaction between design and discovery in the study of human judgment.*   (Program of Research on Human Judgment and Social Interaction Report No. 152)   Boulder:   Institute of Behavioral Science, University of Colorado, 1974.

Hammond, K. R., & Summers, D. A.   Cognitive control. *Psychological Review*, 1972, *79*, 58–67.

Hammond, K. R., Summers, D. A., & Deane, D. H.   Negative effects of outcome feedback in multiple-cue probability learning. *Organizational Behavior and Human Performance*, 1973, *9*, 30–34.

Helenius, M.   Socially induced cognitive conflict:   A study of disagreement over child rearing policies.   In L. Rappoport and D. Summers (Eds.), *Human judgment and social interaction*.   New York:   Holt, Rinehart, & Winston, 1973.

Hoffman, P. J.   The paramorphic representation of clinical judgment. *Psychological Bulletin*, 1960, *47*, 116–131.

Hursch, C., Hammond, K. R., & Hursch, J.   Some methodological considerations in multiple-cue probability studies. *Psychological Review*, 1964, *71*, 42–60.

Jenkins, J. J.   Remember that old theory of memory? Well, forget it! *American Psychologist*, 1974, *29*, 785–795.

Kelley, H. H.   The processes of causal attribution. *American Psychologist*, 1973, *28*, 107–128.

Lindell, M. K.   *Differential effects of cognitive and outcome feedback in improving judgmental accuracy.*   (Program of Research on Human Judgment and Social Interaction Report No. 178)   Boulder:   Institute of Behavioral Science, University of Colorado, 1974.

Mumpower, J. L., & Hammond, K. R.   Entangled task-dimensions: An impediment to interpersonal learning. *Organizational Behavior and Human Performance*, 1974, *11*, 377–389.

Naylor, J. C., & Wherry, R. J., Sr.   The use of simulated stimuli and the "JAN" technique to capture and cluster the policies of raters. *Educational and Psychological Measurement*, 1965, *25*, 969–986.

Newton, J. R.   Judgment and feedback in a quasi-clinical situation. *Journal of Personality and Social Psychology*, 1965, *1*, 336–342.

Rappoport, L.   Cognitive conflict as a function of socially-induced cognitive differences.  *Journal of Conflict Resolution*, 1969, *13*, 143–148.

Rappoport, L., & Summers, D. A. (Eds.).  *Human judgment and social interaction*.  New York:  Holt, Rinehart, & Winston, 1973.

Slovic, P., & Lichtenstein, S.   Comparison of Bayesian and regression approaches to the study of information processing in judgment.  In L. Rappoport & D. A. Summers (Eds.), *Human judgment and social interaction*.  New York:  Holt, Rinehart, & Winston, 1973.

Smith, T. H.   *A method for improving human judgment*.  Unpublished doctoral dissertation, University of Colorado, 1973.

Steinmann, D. O.   *The effects of cognitive feedback and task complexity in multiple-cue probability learning*.  (Program of Research on Human Judgment and Social Interaction Report No. 175)  Boulder:  Institute of Behavioral Science, University of Colorado, 1974.

Steinmann, D. O., Smith, T. H., Jurdem, L., & Hammond, K. R. *Application and evaluation of Social Judgment Theory in policy formulation:  An example*.  (Program of Research on Human Judgment and Social Interaction Report No. 174) Boulder:  Institute of Behavioral Science, University of Colorado, 1975.

Steinmann, D. O., & Stewart, T. R.   *Measuring the relative importance of community goals*.  (Program of Research on Human Judgment and Social Interaction Report No. 156) Boulder:  Institute of Behavioral Science, University of Colorado, 1973.

Stenson, H. H.   The lens model with unknown cue structure. *Psychological Review*, 1974, *81*, 257–264.

Stewart, T. R.   *Components of correlations and extensions of the lens model equation*.  (Program of Research on Human Judgment and Social Interaction Report No. 146)  Boulder: Institute of Behavioral Science, University of Colorado, 1974.

Stewart, T. R., & Carter, J.   *POLICY:  An interactive computer program for externalizing, executing, and refining judgmental policy*.  (Program of Research on Human Judgment and Social Interaction Report No. 159)  Boulder:  Institute of Behavioral Science, University of Colorado, 1973.

Stewart, T. R., & Gelberd, L.   *Capturing judgment policy:  A new approach for citizen participation in planning*.  (Program of Research on Human Judgment and Social Interaction Report No. 151)  Boulder:  Institute of Behavioral Science, University of Colorado, 1972.

Stewart, T. R., Joyce, C. R. B., & Lindell, M. K. The application of judgment theory to clinical trials. In K. R. Hammond and C. R. B. Joyce (Eds.), *Psychoactive drugs and social judgment: Theory and research.* New York: Wiley, 1975.

Stewart, T. R., West, R. E., Hammond, K. R., & Kreith, F. Improving human judgment in technology assessment. *Technology Assessment*, 1975, *3*, in press.

Todd, F. J., & Hammond, K. R. Differential feedback in multiple-cue probability learning tasks. *Behavioral Science*, 1965, *10*, 429–435.

Tolman, E. C. Cognitive maps in rats and men. *Psychological Review*, 1948, *55*, 189–208.

Tolman, E., & Brunswik, E. The organism and the causal texture of the environment. *Psychological Review*, 1935, *42*, 43–77.

Tucker, L. R. A suggested alternative formulation in the development by Hursch, Hammond, & Hursch and Hammond, Hursch, & Todd. *Psychological Review*, 1964, *71*, 528–530.

Tversky, A., & Kahneman, D. Judgment under uncertainty: Heuristics and biases. *Science*, 1974, *185*, 1124–1131.

Weichselbaum, H. New concepts: Effects of methadone maintenance on cognitive control. In K. R. Hammond and C. R. B. Joyce (Eds.), *Psychoactive drugs and social judgment: Theory and research.* New York: Wiley, 1975.

Wherry, R. J., & Naylor, J. C. Comparison of two approaches-- JAN and PROF--for capturing rater strategies. *Educational and Psychological Measurement*, 1966, *26*, 267–286.

Winer, B. J. *Statistical principles in experimental design.* (2nd ed.) New York: McGraw-Hill, 1971.

Zachariadis, N., & Varonos, D. Effects of methylphenidate and barbiturate on normal subjects. In K. R. Hammond and C. R. B. Joyce (Eds.), *Psychoactive drugs and social judgment: Theory and research.* New York: Wiley, 1975.

# AUTHOR INDEX

## A

Abelson, R. P., 230, *267*
Adelman, L., 305, *307*
Ajzen, I., 232, *267*
Alker, H. A., 162, *164*
Altrocchi, J., 144, 154, 162, *164, 169, 170*
Anderson, J. R., 41, 42, 57, *59, 60*
Anderson, N. H., 110, 111, 112, 113, 116, 118, 119, 123, 124, 129, 130, 133, 134, *134, 135, 136,* 140, 141, 142, 143, 144, 146, 150, 151, 152, 156, 159, 162, *164, 168, 169,* 175, *197,* 212, 213, 214, 214, 218, *225, 227,* 230, 231, 252, *267,* 273, 292, *307*
Aronson, E., 151, *170,* 214, *225*
Armstrong, G. W., *198*
Asch, S. E., 142, 153, 162, *164,* 212, *225*
Atkins, A., 149, *165*
Atkinson, R. C., 46, *59*
Azuma, H., 298, *308*

## B

Baldwin, P. M., 148, *165, 197*
Balke, W. M., 305, *307*
Banks, W. P., 46, *59*

Beach, L. R., 232, *268*
Bem, D. J., 162, *165,* 202, *225*
Berglund, B., 130, *135*
Berglund, V., 130, *135*
Bernoulli, D., 64, *83*
Bezembinder, T. G., 132, *135*
Bieri, J., 149, *165*
Birnbaum, M. H., 119, 123, *135,* 231, *267*
Bjork, R. A., 41, 57, *60*
Blevans, S. A., 216, *226*
Block, R. A., 42, *59*
Boucher, J., 153, *165*
Bowen, J. N., 66, *84*
Bower, G. H., 178, *199*
Brady, D., 30ʳ, *307*
Brandstadter, J., 155, *166*
Bransford, J. D., 41, 53, 55, 56, *59*
Brehm, J. W., 215, 216, *225, 226*
Brehmer, B., 294, 295, 296, 297, 298, 299, 300, 301, 302, 303, *307, 308, 309*
Briar, S., 149, *265*
Broadbent, D. E., 43, 44, 46, *59*
Brockway, J., 42, *59*
Brooks, D. H., 42, *60*
Bruner, J. S., 146, *165*
Brunswick, E., 272, 273, 274, 276, 287, 294, 305, *308, 312*
Burwen, L.W., 162, *165*
Byrne, D., 140, *165,* 251, *267*

# C

Campbell, D. T., 128, 129, *135,* 221, 226
Campbell, L. S., 162, *165*
Carroll, J. D., 147, *165,* 213, *226, 228*
Carter, J., 294, *311*
Carterette, E. C., 133, *135*
Castellan, N. J., Jr., 288, 289, *308*
Chammah, A. M., 90, *107*
Chaplin, W., 97, *106*
Chapman, J. P., 263, *267*
Chapman, L. J., 263, *267*
Chmielewski, D., 42, *59*
Cofer, C. N., 42, 55, *59*
Cohen, B. D., 174, *198*
Coombs, C. H., 66, 68, 69, 72, 78, 80, *83, 84,* 116, 121, 122, 132, *135*
Corrigan, B., 20, *36,* 150, *165,* 280, *308*
Costantini, A. F., 150, 159, *167*
Craik, F. I. M., 56, *59*
Crane, K. A. 216, *226*
Crockett, W. H., 149, 154, *165, 169*
Cronbach, L. J., 146, 147, 153, 162, *165, 166,* 176, 177, *197, 198*
Crow, W., 287, *310*
Crumbaugh, C. M., 94, *106*

# D

Dalkey, N. C., 26, *36*
Darlington, R. B., 286, *308*
Davidson, D., 132, *135*
Dawes, R. M., 20, *36,* 97, 98, *106,* 116, 121, *135,* 142, 150, *165, 169,* 280, *308*
DeCharms, R., 152, *167*
Delay, J., 97, *106*
DeSoto, C. B., 188, *197*
Deutsch, M., 216, *226*
Draper, N., 279, 280, *308*
Dustin, D. S., 148, *165, 197*

# E

Earle, T. C., 302, *309*
Edwards, A. L., 154, *165*
Edwards, W., 2, 4, 5, 10, 13, 17, *36,* 129, 131, 132, *135,* 175, *198,* 230, 232, *268,* 292, *309*
Ehrlich, h. J., 150, *165*
Einhorn, H. J., 151, *165,* 283, *309*
Ellis, H. C., 57, 58, *59*
Evans, G. W., *94,* 106
Ewens, W. J., 150, *167*

# F

Fallot, R. D., 141, *166*
Fama, E. F., 65, *84*
Feather, N. T., 149, *166*
Felipe, A. I., 146, *166*
Festinger, L., 202, 205, 215, 216, 219, *226*
Fishbein, M., 155, *167,* 175, 189, *198,* 230, *268*
Fiske, D. W., 221, *226*
Fitts, P. M., 189, *198*
Flack, J. E., 305, *309*
Franks, J. J., 41, 53, 56, *59*
Frick, F., 265, *268*
Friedman, M., 64, 66, *84*
Friedman, M. P., 133, *135*
Frolich, N., 103, *106*
Fryback, D., 10, *36*

# G

Gage, N. L., 153, 162, *166,* 176, *198*
Gardiner, P. C., 24, *36*
Garpebring, S., 300, *308*
Garskof, B. E., 155, *166*
Gelbard, L., 305, *311*
George J., 49, 50, *60*

Gerard, H. B., 216, *226*, 251, *268*
Gibbs, G., 50, *60*
Gillis, J. S., 292, 300, 303, *309*
Githen, J., 287, *310*
Gleason, T. C., 175, *198*
Gleason, T. C., 142, *169*
Gleser, G. C., 177, *197*
Goehring, D. J., 105, *106*
Goldberg, L., 230, 232, 248, 249, *269*
Goldberg, L. R., 150, *166, 283, *309*
Golledge, R. G., 65, *84*
Gollins, E. S., 147, 149, *166*
Goode, F. M., 132, *135*
Goodman, B. C., 10, *36*
Gravetter, F., 217, *226*
Griffitt, W. B., 152, *166*
Gritz, E. R., 292, 303, *309*
Groesbeck, B., 287, *310*
Gross, C. F., 162, *166*
Grzelak, J., 91, *106*
Gullikson, H., 129, *135*
Guttentag, M., 2, 4, 5, *36*
Gyr, J., 287, *310*

**H**

Halverson, C. F., 147, *166*
Hamburger, H., 88, 89, 90, 93, 96, 97, *106*
Hamilton, D. L., 141, 147, 162, *166*
Hammond, K. R, 272, 274, 278, 286, 287, 288, 291, 292, 293, 294, 295, 296, 297, 298, 301, 303, 305, 306, *307, 308, 309, 310, 311, 312*
Hardin, G., 97, 100, *106*
Harvey, O. J., 147, 149, *167, 171*
Hays, W. L., 10, *36*
Heider, F., 230, 231, *268*
Helenius, M., 196, *310*
Hendrick, C., 150, 159, *167*
Henninger, M., 248, *268*
Hicks, J. M., 128, 129, *135*
Hintzman, D. L., 42, *59*

Hinkle, R., 236, *268*
Hoffman, P. J., 150, 151, 152, *167, 171,* 284, *310*
Holt, L. E., 249, *269*
Howes, D. H., 48, *59*
Huang, L. C., 66, 68, 69, 72, 78, *84*
Huffman, L. J., 162, *166*
Hulin, W. S., 185, *198*
Hunt, D. E., 147, 149, *167*
Hunt, R. R., 57, 58, *59*
Hunter, R., 175, 189, *198*
Hursch, C., 286, 287, *310*
Hursch, J., 287, *310*
Hyde, T. S., 42, *59*

**I**

Ingleby, J. D., 47, 48, 49, 50, *59, 60*
Inskeep, N. R., 42, *59*

**J**

Jackson, P., 148, *167*
Jacobson, A., 159, *164*
Janis, I. L., 215, 217, *226,* 265, *268*
Jenkins, J. J., 42, *59,* 305, *310*
Johnson, D. M., 255, 268
Johnson, H. H., 149, 150, *171*
Johnson, M. K., 55, *59*
Johnson, M. P., 150, *167*
Jones, E. E., 140, 152, 154, *167,* 251, *268*
Jones, F. N., 222, *226*
Jones, L. V., 129, *136*
Jöreskog, K. G., 221, *226*
Joyce, C. R. B., 305, *312*
Juola, J. F., 46, *59*
Jurdem, L., 305, *311*

**K**

Kahneman, D., 187, 188, *198,* 293, *312*

Kanouse, D. E., 140, *167*
Kaplan, K. J., 155, *167*
Kaplan, M. F., 110, 140, 141, 142, 148
    148, 149, 151, 152, 153, 154,
    155, 156, 157, 158, 159, 160,
    161, 162, *167, 168,* 231, *268,*
Kaplan, R. J., 12, *36*
Kates, S. L., 154, *168*
Katz, D., 185, *198*
Keeney, R. L., 13, 20, *36*
Kelley, H. H., 91, *106,* 140, 152,
    *167, 168,* 292, *310*
Kelly, J. S., 149, 150, *168*
Kern, F., 287, *310*
Kinsbourne, M., 49, 50, *60*
Kintsch, W., 42, 48, 50, *60*
Kirsner, K., 42, 51, *60*
Kolers, P. A., 42, *60*
Koltuv, B.B., 157, *169*
Kostrun, L., 298, 300, 301, *308*
Krantz, D. H., 80, *84*
Krauss, R. M., 174, *198,* 216, *226*
Kreith, F., 305, *312*
Kuusinen, J., 146, *169*


**L**


Lampel, A. K., 151, *169*
Lantz, D., 174, *198*
Leaman, R., 149, *165*
Lee, W., 65, *84,* 130, *135*
Leon, M., 133, *135,* 151, *169*
Levin, I. P., 159, *169*
Lichtenstein, S., 112, 116, 122, 123,
    132, 133, *135, 136,* 175, *198,*
    218, *227* 232, *268,* 280, 283,
    *311*
Lindell, M. K., 288, 294, 305, *310*
Linder, D. E., 216, *226*
Lindman, H., 10, *36*
Lindvall, T., 130, *135*
Lipsey, C., 150, *165*
Lloyd, W. F., 97, *106*
Lockhart, R. S., 46, 56, *60*

Lockhead, G. R., 217, *226*
Lord, F. M., 221, *226, 227*
Lowenthal, K., 50, *60*
Luce, R. D., 46, *60,* 65, *84,* 218, *227*
Luria, A., 41, *60*


**M**


Major, G., 152, *168*
Malcolm, T., 216, *226*
Maney, J., 55, *61*
Manis, M., 142, *169,* 174, 175, 179,
    191, 196, *198*
McClelland, G. H., 80, *84*
McClelland, L., 142, *170*
McClintock, C. G., 94, *106*
McGuire, W. J., 202, 206, 220, 224,
    *227,* 230, 232, 246, 248, 265,
    268
McLeod, M. A., 154, *164*
Mann, L., 215, 217, *226*
Markowitz, H., 64, *84*
Marks, L. E., 51, *60*
Marschak, J. 64, *84*
Matcom, A. J., 147, 154, *169*
Mayo, C. W., 149, *169*
Meidinger, T., 154, *165*
Messick, D. M., 94, 100, 102, 103,
    104, *106*
Meyer, D. E., 66, 72, *84*
Meyer, G. D., 305, *307*
Miller, A. G., 151, *169*
Miller, G. A., 51, *60*
Miller, H., 149, *165*
Miller, L. W., 12, *36*
Miller, M. H., 65, *84*
Mischel, W., 162, *169*
Morgenstern, O., 64, 66, *85*
Mumpower, J. L., 303, *310*
Murdoch, P., 220, *227*
Murdock, B. B., 46. *60*
Mussen, P., 154, *170*

## N

Nagy, G., 117, 118, *136*
Naylor, J. C., 289, *310, 312*
Neisser, U., 41, *60*
Nelson, C., 141, *170*
Nelson, D. L., 42, *60*
Newcomb, T., 153, *169*
Newton, J. R., 293, *310*
Nidorf, L. J., 149, *169*
Nisbett, R. E., 140, *167*
Norman, W. T., 146, *169*
Novick, M. R., 221, *227*

## O

Oden, G. C., 124, 130, *136*, 151, *169*
Olsen, M., 103, 104, *106*
Olshan, K., 141, 146, *170*
Oppenheimer, J. A., 103, *106*
Osgood, C. E., 141, 153, *165, 169*, 177, *198*, 252, *268*
Ostrom, T. M., 220, *227*

## P

Palmer, J., 154, *169*
Passini, F. T., 146, *169*
Payne, J. W., 122, 132, 133, *136*
Peabody, D., 141, 146, *169*
Pederson, D. M., 147, *170*
Peterson, C. R., 248, *268*
Pettigrew, T. F., 150, *170*
Pfanzagl, J. A., 80, *85*
Phelps, R., 117, 126, 128, *136*
Phillips, L. D., 10, *36, 37*
Pollatsek, A., 66, *85*
Posner, M. I., 189, *198*
Pruitt, D. G., 94, *107*

## R

Raiffa, H., 10, 13, 16, 17, *37*, 65, *84*
Rapoport, Amnon, 105, *107*, 131, 132, *136*
Rapoport, Anatol, 90, *107*
Rappoport, L., 196, 198, 305, *307, 311*
Reder, L. M., 41, 57, *60*
Rice, L. E., 149, 150, *168*
Richey, M. H., 142, *170*
Rorer, L. G., 150, *167*
Rosen, N. A., 248, *268*
Rosenau, N., 216, *226*
Rosenberg, M. J., 230, *267*
Rosenberg, S., 141, 146, 147, *170*, 174, *198*
Rosenthal, R. A., 154, *170*
Rushton, G., 65, *84*

## S

Saunders, L., 287, *310*
Savage, L. J., 10, *36*, 64, 66, *84*
Schelling, T. S., 88, 89, 90, 91, 104, *107*
Schlaifer, R., 10, *37*
Schlosberg, H., *198*
Schmidt, C. F., 158, 159, *170*
Schneider, D. J., 146, 147, *170*, 251, *268*
Schroder, H. M., 147, 149, *167*
Schulman, A. I., 49, *60*
Schwartz, S., 42, 47, 48, 49, 53, 55, 56, *60, 61*
Scodel, A., 154, *170*
Sedlak, A., 141, 146, 147, *170*
Segall, H., 151, *170*
Sells, S. B., 256, *269*
Shanteau, J., 111, 112, 113, 114, 115,

116, 117, 118, 119, 120, 121,
123, 124, 125, 126, 127, 128,
129, 130, 133, *135, 136,* 140,
218, *227*

Shapiro, D., 147, *170*

Shapiro, E. G., 155, *166*

Sharpe, W. F., 65, *85*

Sherman, R., 147, *170*

Shimkunas, A. M., 142, *170*

Shrauger, S., 144, 154, 162, *164, 170*

Siegel, S., 132, *135*

Slamecka, N. J., 42, 52, *61*

Slovic, P., 112, 116, 122, 123, 132, 133
133, *135, 136,* 150, *167,* 175,
*198,* 218, *227,* 232, *268,* 280,
283, *311*

Smith, H., 279, 280, *308*

Smith, T. H., 286, 305, *311*

Snapper, K., 2, *36*

Solomon, R. L., 48, *59*

Starr, C., 65, *85*

Stefflre, V., 174, *198*

Steiner, I. D., 147, 149, 150, *171*

Steinmann, D. O., 292, 305, *311*

Stenson, H. H., 277, *311*

Stevens, S. S., 213, 222, *227*

Stewart, T. R., 288, 289, 291, 292,
294, 305, 306, *307, 309, 310,
311, 312*

Suci, G. I., 141, *169,* 177, *198*

Summers, D. A., 278, 288, 292, 294,
298, 305, *309, 310*

Suppes, P., 132, *135*

Svensson, L. T., 130, *135*

Swets, J. A., 44, 46, *61*


T


Taguiri, R., 146, 147, 162, *165, 170,
171,* 176, *198*

Tannenbaum, P. H., 141, *169,* 252, *268*

Tanner, W. P., 44, 46, *61*

Tesser, A., 150, *171*

Thomson, D. M., 42, 57, *61*

Thorndike, E. L., 141, 146, 153, *171*

Thurstone, L. L., 129, *136,* 202, 207,
*227*

Tintner, G., 64, *85*

Todd, F. J., 293, *312*

Tolman, E. C., 272, 273, 294, *312*

Torgerson, D., 27, *37*

Trabasso, T., 178, *199*

Tripodi, T., 149, *165*

Trope, Y., 232, *268*

Tucker, L. R., 287, 288, *312*

Tukey, J., 218, *227*

Tulving, E., 40, 42, 57, *61*

Tversky, A., 66, 80, *84,* 116, 120,
121, 122, 129, 131, 132, *135,
137,* 187, 188, *198,* 219, *227,*
293, *312*


U


Upshaw, H. S., 202, 207, 214, 217,
220, 222, *227, 228*


V


Valins, S., 140, *167*

Van Rooijen, L., 174, 179, 187, 191,
196, *198, 199*

Varonos, D. D., 298, 303, *308, 312*

Veitch, R., 152, *166*

Vivekananthan, P., 141, *170*

Von Neumann, J., 64, 66, *85*


W


Wallsten, T. S., 131, 132, *136*

Walster, E., 216, *228*

Ware, R., 149, *171*

Warr, P., 148, *167*

Watts, W. A., 249, *269*

Weichselbaum, H., 292, *312*

Weiner, B., 140, *167*
Weinheimer, S., 174, *198*
West, R. E., 305, *312*
Wherry, R. J., Sr., 289, *310, 312*
Wiggins, N. L., 151, 152, *171*
Winer, B. J., 280, *312*
Wish, M., 213, *226, 228*
Witherspoon, K. D., 42, 53, 55, 56, 61
Woodworth, R. S., 256, *269*

Wortman, C. B., 216, *226*
Wyer, R. S., 142, *171*, 220, *228,* 230
231, 232, 233, 234, 235, 236,
238, 244, 245, 247, 248, 249,
251, 252, 253, 254, *268, 269*

**Z**

Zachariadis, N., 303, *312*

# SUBJECT INDEX

## A

Attitudes, 201-225, 233-236, 253
  affective component of, 234
  changes in beliefs and, 253
  cognitive dissonance, and, 202
  communication of *see* Communi-
    cation of attitudes
  evaluative component of, 234-236
  functions of, 204
  judgment, and, 201-225
  measurement of, 202, 207
Attitude change, 205-207, 224
  alternatives to, 205-206
  social comparison and, 224
  sources of, 224
Attitude formation, 204, 207-219
  choice of alternatives, 214-219
    predecisional and postdecisional
      judgment behavior, 214-217
    preference criterion model, 217-
      219
  definition and appraisal of alterna-
    tives, 208-214
  social pressures and, 204
Authoritarianism, 56

## B

Balance theory, 231, 251
Beliefs, 233-234, 253

## C

Causal ambiguity, 272-273, 275-276,
  294
Cognitive complexity, 149
Cognitive dissonance, 215
Cognitive maps, 273, 294
Cognitive organization and social
  inference, 229-267
Commodity bundles, 129-130
Commons dilemma, 97-101
  definition and conditions of, 98
  graphing of, 99-100
  size of N, 100
Communication of attitudes, 202,
  204-205, 219-223
  congeneric tests, 221-223
  determinants of, 205, 219-220
    social comparison, 205, 219
    normative demands, 220
  information content effects,
    220-221
  response effects, 220-221
Configurality and information integration, 143, 150-152
Conflict theory, 215
Congeneric tests, 221-223
  equivalence judgments, 223
Conjoint measurement, 121-122, 218
Consistency and cognitive control,
  278-280, 292
Context effects, 143, 214

**D**

Decision analysis, 8-12, *see also*
    Multiattribute-utility analysis
Decision model of memory recognition
    tasks, 35-48, 56, *see also* Levels
    of analysis framework
    familiarity and, 35-44
    semantic processing and, 35-48, 56
Descriptive meaning, 141
Dimension of value, 13-14, 16-19, *see*
    *also* Simple multiattribute-rating
    technique
    outcome location measures on, 14,
    17-19
    upperbounds, 20
Dispositional tendencies, differences
    in, 149, 152-156, 159-162,
    *see also under* Information
    integration theory
    global dispositions, 153-156, 162
    inconsistent information, effects of,
    149, 159-160
    information variables and disposi-
    tional effects, 149, 159-161
    cognitive complexity, and, 149
    relative weighting of, 161
    source of information and, 159, 161
    transient situational states, 152-153

**E**

Elimination-by-aspect model, 219
Empathy, *see* Predictive accuracy
Episodic memory, 40-47, 49-51,
    53, 56
    definition of, 40-41
    encoding of, 42
    filtering, and, 44, 46, 49
    semantic features of, 42-43
    trace of, 41-43, 50, 53, 56
    word order, and, 53
Evaluative meaning, 151

**Expected utility**, 64-80, *see also*
    Portfolio theory, risky decisions,
    and, 65-80

**F**

Filtering, 44, 46, 49, 51
Functional measurement, 111, 116,
    120-122, 146, 213, 218

**H**

Halo effects, 141, 153

**I**

Impression formation, 140-163,
    212-213, 250-254, *see also*
    Information integration theory
    and Initial impression
    probability model of syllogistic
    inference, and, 150-254
    social evaluation, 150-154
Individual differences, 118-123, 143-
    156, 162-163, *see also* disposi-
    tional tendencies, differences in
    cognitive styles of integrating infor-
    mation, in, 149-150
    cognitive complexity and incon-
    sistency of information, 109
    differential weighting tendencies,
    and, 150-152
    order effects, 149-150
    implicit personality theories, in, 144,
    146-148
    individual subject analyses, 118-123
    information valuation, in, 144-146
    processing strategies in risky decision
    making, in, 120
Information integration theory, 110-
    114, 117-134, 141-163, 175,

213-214, *see also* Configurality
and information integration;
Individual differences; Scale
value; and Stimulus weighting
adding model, 111, 113, 122-131,
133-134
averaging model, 124, 142-143, 148-
151, 156-157, 159, 161
dispositional effects, and, 156-157,
159, 161
combination rules in, 111, 113, 122-
131, 133-134, 142-143, 148-151,
156-157, 159, 161
multiplying model, 110-114, 117-
125, 130-134
operations of, 111
redundancy, and, 158
Initial impression, 142-144, 150, 157-
158, 163, *see also* Dispositional
tendencies, differences in
amount of information, and, 157-
158
extreme judgments, and, 150
Interactive computer graphics, 285-
287, 293-295
cognitive feedback, 293-295
hierarchical judgment models, 286
multimethod analysis, 286-287
subject control, 285-286
Interpersonal conflict, 22-24, 295-302,
*see also* Social dilemmas and
Values, conflicts of
inconsistency, 297-298, 300
behavioral validation, and, 300
lens model, and, 296-298
negative consequences of good
intentions, 298-299
Research paradigm, 295-296
sources of, 297-298
task adaptation, and, 300
task characteristics and, 300-302
consistency, 300
cue intercorrelations, 301-302
ecological validation of cues, 301
task-function forms, 301

**L**

Lens model, 274-275, 287-289
equation, 287
principle of parallel concepts,
274-275

**M**

Memory recognition tasks, 40-58, *see
also* Decision model of memory
recognition task
bias in, 46-47, 53, 55
episodic memory, and, *see* Episodic
memory
filtering, and strategies in, 44-46,
49, 51
input modality, and, 50-51
learning and testing context, and,
57-58
levels of analysis framework, 56
pigeonholing, and strategies in,
43-44, 46
rare words, and, 48-50, 57-58
filtering of episodic information,
and, 49
semantic memory, and, *see* semantic
memory
sensitivity in, 46-47, 53, 55
syntactical relationships, 42
word frequency, and, 42, 47-50, 57
word strings, and, 51-56
complexity of, 53-55
nonsense vs. meaningful, 51-52
syntactic structure of, 53
Messick's union game, 100-104
definition and conditions of, 100-
102
expected-value maximizers, and,
102-103
size of N, and, 103
Multiattribute-utility analysis, 13-35,
*see also* Simple multiattribute

rating technique (SMART)
Multidimensional scaling procedures, 213
Multidimensionality of stimuli, 141
Multiple regression approach, 132-133, 278, 283, 288
  risky decisions, and, 132-133
  social judgment theory (SJT), and, 278, 283, 288
Multitrait-multimethod matrix, 221


O


Order effects, 149-150


P


Pigeonholing, 43-44, 46
Portfolio theory, 66-83
  assumptions of, 66, 71-72, 80-81
  qualitative tests of, 67-69, 74-79
  theorems and proofs of, 80-83
Predictive accuracy, 176-177
Preference criterion model, 217-219
Prisoners' dilemma, 88-90, 93-94, 96-97, 99, 102, 104
  separable type, 93-94, 99, 102
  simultaneous type, 96-97, 99, 102
Probability model of syllogistic inference, 237, 243-267
  belief and opinion change, and, 249-250
  cognitive organization and, 246-267
  nonlogical factors in, 255-265
    principles of, 255-266
    test of, 260-265
  social evaluation and impression formation, 250-254


R


Redundancy, see under Referential

communication and Information integration
Referential communication, 174-197
  communication accuracy, 174-196
    additive model with overload postulate, 196
    intended referent, 174
    recipient's inference, 174
    research in, 174-175, 177-196
    quantity of information and, 189-196
  conceptual definition of, 178-179
  confidence in response, 187
  decoding performance, and, 183-188
  forgetting, and, 181-183
  redundancy, and, 177-187
    measurement of, 177-178
    subjective uncertainty, 187
Response-scale linearity, 125-126
Risky decision making, 66-80, 110-134, see also Expected utility and risky decisions
  adding model in, see under Information integration theory
  individual differences in processing strategies in, 120
  information integration theory and, 110-134
  measurement of risky decisions, 73-80
  multiplying model in, see under Information integration theory
  portfolio theory and, 66-80
  subadditivity in, 126-134


S


Scale effects, 213-214
Scale values, 140-143, 145-146, 148-152, 157, 163
Semantic memory, 50-58
  decision criterion, and, 46
  definition of, 40-41
  encoding in, 41-43

episodic features of, 42-43
   physical aspects of, 42-43
interference with, 47-48, 53
nonsense vs. meaningful sentences,
   and, 51-52
response bias of, 43, 46-47, 53, 55
Signal detection theory, 44, 46, 57
Sign-significate (S-S) theory, 273
Similarity and interpersonal attraction,
   251
Simple multiattribute rating technique
   (SMART), 14-35
benefits-to-cost ratio and decisions,
   19
case study of, 24-33
environmental correlations, 21-22
independence properties, 20-21
multiplying model, 20
special cases of, 19
weighted average model, 14
Social dilemmas, 88-105, *see also*
   Specific games
graphing of, 91-97, 99, 104
repetition of, 105
size of N, and, 100, 103
varying payoff structure in, 104-105
Social judgment theory (SJT), 275-
   305, *see also* Lens model
analysis of relations between cognitive systems, 287-290
   cluster analysis, 289-290
   lens model equation, 287-289
double-system case, 293-295
N-system case, 304-305
objectives of, 276, 283-284
pictorial display of systems, *see*
   Interactive computer graphics
regression analysis approach, and,
   278, 280-283

research, and, 290-305
single-system case, 292-293
surface-depth distinction, 275
triple-system case, 295-304, *see also*
   Interpersonal conflict
zone of ambiguity, 275-276
Stimulus-response (S-R) theory, 273
Stimulus weighting, 142-143, 145,
   148-152, 161, 163, *see also*
   Configurality and information
   integration and Context effects
context effects and, 143
relative weighting rule, 142-143,
   149-151, 161
Subjective expected utility (SEU)
   theory, 66
Subjective probability models of social
   inference, 234-267
averaging model, 240
Bayesian model, 236-237, 242-243
multiplying model, 236-242

**T**

Test-theory model, 221, 223

**U**

Utilities, 14, 17, 18, 19

**V**

Values, conflicts of, 1-36, 295-302,
   *see also* Multiattribute-utility
   analysis existing evaluation
   techniques, 4-8